Knowledge Production, Area Studies and Global Cooperation

Whereas Area Studies and cross-border cooperation research conventionally demarcates groups of people by geographical boundaries, individuals might in fact feel more connected by shared values and principles than by conventional spatial dimensions. *Knowledge Production, Area Studies and Global Cooperation* asks what norms and principles lead to the creation of knowledge about cross-border cooperation and connection. It studies why theories, methods, and concepts originate in one place rather than another, how they travel, and what position the scholar adopts while doing research, particularly 'in the field'.

Taking case studies from Asia, the Middle East and North Africa, the book links the production of alternative epistemologies to the notion of global cooperation and reassesses the ways in which the concept of connectedness can be applied at the translocal and individual rather than the formal international and collective level.

Knowledge Production, Area Studies and Global Cooperation provides an innovative and critical approach towards established means of producing knowledge about different areas of the world, demonstrating that an understanding of pluri-local connectivity should be integrated into the production of knowledge about different areas of the world and the behavioural dimension of global cooperation. By shifting the view from the collective to the individual and from the formal to often invisible patterns of connectedness, this book provides an important fresh perspective which will be of interest to scholars and students of Area Studies, Politics, International Relations and Development Studies.

Claudia Derichs is Professor of Comparative Politics and International Development Studies at Philipps University Marburg, Germany, and a senior associate fellow at the Käte Hamburger Kolleg/Centre for Global Cooperation Research in Duisburg, Germany. Her research interests are Muslim societies and political transition in Southeast Asia and the Middle East, as well as gender and development studies in Asia and the Middle East. She has published various books and articles on Malaysia, Indonesia, Japan and the Arab world, and is an advisor to several academic and political institutions, journals and think tanks. Prior to her studies of Japanese and Arabic, she worked as a journalist.

Routledge Global Cooperation Series

This series develops innovative approaches to understanding, explaining and answering one of the most pressing questions of our time – how can cooperation in a culturally diverse world of nine billion people succeed?

We are rapidly approaching our planet's limits, with trends such as advancing climate change and the destruction of biological diversity jeopardising our natural life-support systems. Accelerated globalisation processes lead to an ever-growing interconnectedness of markets, states, societies, and individuals. Many of today's problems cannot be solved by nation states alone. Intensified cooperation at the local, national, international, and global level is needed to tackle current and looming global crises.

Series Editors:
Tobias Debiel, Claus Leggewie, and Dirk Messner are co-directors of the Käte Hamburger Kolleg/Centre for Global Cooperation Research, University of Duisburg-Essen, Germany. Their research areas are, among others, global governance, climate change, peacebuilding, and cultural diversity of global citizenship. The three co-directors are, at the same time, based in their home institutions, which participate in the Centre, namely the German Development Institute/Deutsches Institut für Entwicklungspolitik (DIE, Messner) in Bonn, the Institute for Development and Peace (INEF, Debiel) in Duisburg and the Institute for Advanced Study in the Humanities (KWI, Leggewie) in Essen.

Titles:
Global Cooperation and the Human Factor in International Relations
Edited by Dirk Messner and Silke Weinlich

Peacebuilding in Crisis
Rethinking paradigms and practices of transnational cooperation
Edited by Tobias Debiel, Thomas Held and Ulrich Schneckener

Humanitarianism and Challenges of Global Cooperation
Edited by Volker M. Heins, Kai Koddenbrock and Christine Unrau

Gifts of Cooperation, Mauss and Pragmatism
Frank Adloff

Democratization and Memories of Violence
Ethnic minority rights movements in Mexico, Turkey, and El Salvador
Mneesha Gellman

Knowledge Production, Area Studies and Global Cooperation
Claudia Derichs

Knowledge Production, Area Studies and Global Cooperation

Claudia Derichs

SPONSORED BY THE

First published 2017 by Routledge

2 Park Square, Milton Park, Abingdon, Oxfordshire OX14 4RN
52 Vanderbilt Avenue, New York, NY 10017

Routledge is an imprint of the Taylor & Francis Group, an informa business

First issued in paperback 2018

British Library Cataloguing-in-Publication Data
A catalogue record for this book is available from the British Library

Library of Congress Cataloguing-in-Publication Data
A catalogue record for this book has been requested

ISBN: 978-1-138-18874-7 (hbk)
ISBN: 978-0-367-17266-4 (pbk)

DOI: 10.4324/9781315642123

Typeset in Bembo
by Out of House Publishing

This work and its open access publication has been supported by the Federal Ministry of Education and Research (BMBF) in the context of its funding of the Käte Hamburger Kolleg/Centre for Global Cooperation Research at the University of Duisburg-Essen (grant number 01UK1810).

Contents

Preface vii
Notes on the text x
Abbreviations and acronyms xii

1. Introduction: Knowledge production, Area Studies, and global cooperation 1

PART I
Alternative epistemologies 31

2. The Islamisation of Knowledge 33
3. Review: spill-over and diffusion 63
4. Empirical case studies: Islamic economy and Islamic feminism 96

PART II
Areas and pluri-locality 125

5. At home away from home (emotional geographies) 127
6. Tunnel vision in Area Studies 150
7. Connectivity and cooperation: concluding thoughts 173

Index 192

Preface

I would have loved to quote here the inspiring second verse of The Rolling Stones' song 'Something Happened to Me Yesterday' (Jagger/Richards, 1967, track 12 on the album 'Between The Buttons' London Music PS499), but had to refrain from doing so for copyright reasons. (Please go to www.rollingstones.com/release/between-the-buttons and scroll down to track 12.)

In the present study, I have spread out the trajectory of projects of an Islamisation of knowledge (with both a capital and a lower-case 'K') and the global movement of Islamic resurgence, in which the Islamisation of knowledge was embedded. I have chosen this example from the Muslim world since the emotional geographies in faith-based worlds are those that, throughout the years of research, challenged me most in trying to understand what I see instead of analysing it with pre-defined concepts in mind. Trying to understand means making sense of the bits and pieces of diverse worldviews that I have got to know – worldviews that were sometimes utterly different from what I had ever come across in my own socialisation, and sometimes entirely compatible with what I would imagine for myself as a 'good life'. I met with various types of rationalities and ways of learning in different parts of the world, which connected people across huge geographical distances. I took this as an empirical indicator for the existence of socio-cognitive geographies that had thus far escaped my attention. Moreover, those geographies did not match with the scales and units I had internalised during my times as a student of Area Studies in Germany. There was so much 'Mecca' in Kuala Lumpur and so much 'Singapore' in the United Arab Emirates that I wondered why Southeast Asia and the Persian Gulf states did not form a unit for Area Studies research. Why had I learned so much about the 'Asian miracle', newly industrialising economies and 'tiger states', but not about Islamic student movements with all their transnational and transregional connections in the neighbouring countries and the Middle East? This type of (geographical) affiliation really struck me. However, what I considered extraordinarily interesting areas to explore were rejected by those whom scholars in the academic business are dependent upon, i.e. funding agencies. One of my postdoc proposals in the 1990s dealt with the issue of Islamisation and political transition from a gender perspective, taking case studies from the Middle East and Southeast Asia into account. Although my academic record approves of the relevant language and disciplinary skills to study these two regions, my proposal was rejected by the adjudicating committee because it was considered impossible and gratuitous to combine two such 'different' regions in one research project. In retrospect, the failure of the proposal was an enlightening moment for my future research orientation – because the reason for its rejection made clear how the segmentation of the globe into areal units of study was lagging behind the empirical reality in the regions that had caught my interest.

It took several years until transregional approaches were gradually pushed and promoted in the German research landscape. Initiatives from above – recommendations from the German Council of Science and Humanities (*Wissenschaftsrat*) in the mid-2000s to strengthen Area Studies in larger research networks – motivated funding agencies and scholars to engage in a critical stock-taking of Area Studies and to produce a vision for the future direction of this field of knowledge production. As discussed in some chapters of this book, the Area Studies debate is ongoing; much has changed with regard to cross-regional Area Studies research, but it is change at a low pace. Knowledge production in Area Studies is still a rather path-dependent enterprise.

The present study is a piece of cross-regional area research if I stick to the conventional nomenclature of departments and units in Area Studies. At the same time, it questions the appropriateness of the label 'cross-' or 'transregional', since this designation implies a prior demarcation of territorial units which count as regions (or areas). Informed by concepts such as belonging, emotional geographies, trans- and pluri-local connectivity etc., it attempts to look at lived realities and shared concerns as potential presuppositions for interpersonal cooperation.

My thanks for making this book possible go to so many people that I am incapable of listing them individually. The study is a project based on several decades of academic engagement and fieldwork in different parts of the world, which means that any attempt to do justice to all who deserve to be thanked is likely to fail miserably. I am well aware of the positionality that comes alongside my gleaning and gathering up research during these years. I will most probably not live up to the expectations of those who inspired me, provoked my thinking and helped me understand their point of view – now that I am tapping from the information that they have shared with me. Nonetheless, I have made an honest effort not to explain things by using precast theories, methods, and approaches, but to convey the idea that there is a lot 'out there' to see, learn and understand. I am deeply grateful to those whom I had a chance to meet and get to know in and outside the 'field'. I hope that my endeavour may inspire others to walk along avenues of unconceptualised knowledge and immerse themselves in socio-cognitive spaces that do not conform to the units of conventional Area Studies.

In my immediate academic environment of the last 24 months, working on the manuscript was largely facilitated by the Käte Hamburger Kolleg/Centre for Global Cooperation Research of the University of Duisburg-Essen, whose fellowship grant allowed me to 'think freely'. This book proposal was one of the results of the fellowship, and since its acceptance by the publisher, a great team of editing experts in Germany and the UK made working on the manuscript a pleasant experience. Particular thanks go to those who formatted and proofread the text. My home University of Marburg granted me a sabbatical to finish the final chapters of the book; I am grateful for the faculty's trust in my ability to use this time productively. My university team and colleagues covered my back many times and absolved me from various obligations. Last but not least, I am grateful to my husband who uncomplainingly accepted that I surrender the bulk of our family time to reading and writing. I know I have been quite a grumpy partner at times.

Notes on the text

This book's main language is English, but I use a number of Japanese characters as well as Arabic and Malaysian/Indonesian terms. A note on transcription and transliteration of these terms should thus be made to avoid confusion. The transliteration of Japanese syllables follows the Hepburn system of transliteration. Japanese names are listed in the bibliography like European names, i.e. family name followed by given name. Malaysian and Indonesian names are quoted either in the local style (the given name is the name listed first), or in the European sequence (the given name listed second) if this is the established style of quoting the respective person in the literature. The Indonesian tradition is not bound to family name and given name; sometimes there is only one given name (e.g. in the case of the former president of the country, Suharto). Malaysians prefer to abbreviate long names by using only the first letters, hence an 'A.B.' or 'J.S.' behind the given name does not indicate that the person's name is not known, but is adopted with respect to local tradition. Many Indonesian and Malaysian names vary in their spelling in Latin letters, especially when the transliteration is one from Arabic. The Arabic honorific سيد, for instance, can be spelt Sayed, Seyyed, Syed – numerous versions exist. I have attempted to choose the most conventional version as observed in the literature.

The Arabic letter *'ayin* (ع) is indicated by ' (e.g. in *sharî'a*) and so is a *hamza* (ء) (e.g. in Qur'ân); long vowels are indicated by a circumflex accent (^) above the letter. Emphatic consonants have not been made recognisable. In many cases, I provide the original Arabic writing for clarification. In the Malaysian or Indonesian transcription of Arabic terms, the end character ة or *tâ' marbûta* is usually represented by the letters *ah*. In some other transcriptions, the version *at* is used (in particular when the ة is preceded by a long vowel). I have tried to be consistent, but not ultimately strict in the transcription and transliteration of Arabic terms. This is due, among other reasons, to different transliteration systems between and within Arabic, English, German and Southeast Asian academia, and to the fact that popular transliterations differ from scholarly ones (e.g. spelling the letter و with a *u* or a *w* – *tauhîd* or *tawhîd*). In the case of *u* or *w*, I have opted for the *u*, except when citing directly from literature where the *w* is used. The same goes for the letter ش, which is usually spelled *sh* in Western transliterations (e.g. *sharî'a*), but *sy* in Southeast Asia (*syari'ah*). Moreover, many names and terms appear in a simplified spelling in the mass media, which sometimes makes it difficult to trace back the original letters or characters. I have avoided resorting to such spellings. On balance, I have tried to be consistent and provide a reader-friendly way of spelling, transcription and transliteration. Arabists will have a lot to criticise, but I have opted to negotiate the potential expectations of a diverse readership.

Abbreviations and acronyms

ABIM	Angkatan Belia Islam Se-Malaysia [Muslim Youth Movement of Malaysia]
AKP	Adalet ve Kalkınma Partisi [Justice and Development Party]
ASEAN	Association of Southeast Asian Nations
CEDAW	Convention on the Elimination of All Forms of Discrimination against Women
DAC	Development Assistance Committee
DDII	Dewan Dakwah Islamiyah Indonesia [Indonesian Council for Islamic Propagation]
ESQ	Emotional and spiritual quotient
FIS	Front Islamique du Salut [Islamic Salvation Front]
HMI	Himpunan Mahasiswa Islam [Muslim Students Association (of Indonesia)]
IAIN	Institut Agama Islam Negeri [State Institute of Islamic Religion]
IAIS	International Institute for Advanced Islamic Studies
IC	Islamic College
ICAS	Islamic College for Advanced Studies
ICC	Islamic Cultural Centre
ICMI	Ikatan Cendekiawan Muslim Indonesia [Association of Muslim Scholars of Indonesia]
ICT	Information and Communication Technology
IIFSO	International Islamic Federation of Student Organizations
IIIT	International Institute of Islamic Thought
IIUM	International Islamic University Malaysia
INSISTS	Institute for the Study of Islamic Thought and Civilization

IoK	Islamisation of Knowledge
IR	International Relations
IS	Islamic State
ISTAC	Institute for the Study of Islamic Thought and Civilization
LDMI	Lembaga Dakwah Mahasiswa Islam [Islamic Education and Propagation]
LIPIA	Lembaga Ilmu Penggetahuan Islam dan Arab [Islamic and Arabic College]
MENA	Middle East and North Africa
MSA	Muslim Students' Association
MUI	Majlis Ulama Indonesia [Indonesian Council of Ulama]
NAM	Non-Aligned Movement
NEP	National Economic Policy
NGO	Non-governmental organisation
NU	Nahdlatul Ulama [Awakening of Ulama]
OECD	Organisation of Economic Cooperation and Development
OIC	Organisation of Islamic Cooperation
PAN	Partai Amanat Nasional [National Mandate Party]
PAS	Parti Islam Se-Malaysia [Islamic Party of Malaysia]
PB LDMI	Pengurus Besar Lembaga Dakwah Mahasiswa Islam [Central Board of Islamic Education and Propagation]
PDI-P	Partai Demokrasi Indonesia Perjuangan [Indonesian Democratic Party of Struggle]
PDR	People's Democratic Republic
PKB	Partai Kebangkitan Bangsa [National Awakening Party]
PKI	Partai Kommunis Indonesia [Indonesian Communist Party]
PKS	Partai Keadilan Sejahtera [Prosperous Justice Party]
PMI	Persatuan Mahasiswa Islam [Muslim Student Society (of Malaysia)]
PPP	Partai Persatuan Pembangunan [United Development Party]
PR	People's Republic
SH	Seyyed Hossein (Nasr)

SIS	Sisters in Islam
SN	Syed Naguib (Al-Attas)
TAN	Transnational Advocacy Network
UIN	Universitas Islam Negeri [State Islamic University]
UMNO	United Malays National Organisation
UN	United Nations
UN ECOSOC	United Nations Economic and Social Council
UUCA	University and University Colleges Act
WLUML	Women Living Under Muslim Laws

1 Introduction

Knowledge production, Area Studies, and global cooperation

This chapter discusses the three key terms of the book. It introduces the line of thought that is further expanded and empirically grounded in the subsequent chapter.

The key terms in the title of this volume are three compound words that seem to be commonly understood and in general use: knowledge production, Area Studies and global cooperation. While they are commonly known and elaborated upon, they are rarely studied in relation to each other or with a focus on their mutual relationship. Directing my gaze at what particular kinds of knowledge production lead to particular views of global cooperation, I argue that the area where knowledge is generated and spread has a role to play for our view of actors' cooperation on a global scale. Theories 'from the South' (Comaroff and Comaroff 2012), for instance, have not become consumed as thoroughly and frequently among scholars around the world as theories from the Northern part of the globe have. But let us first attend to an exercise that usually precedes the study of mutual relationships between words and concepts: A solid treatise would require providing clear definitions, distinctions from similar terms and concepts, and maybe include a reflection on synonyms and conceptual fields. Clarifying what is meant by knowledge (and its production), areas (and their study) and (global) cooperation would thus form the first steps of the overall attempt to connect them to each other. In what follows, I am certainly not living up to the expectations going along with the provision of clear-cut definitions. Rather than offering something succinct and precise, I strive to raise awareness for the dependence of any definition not just on time and place, but on language as the very medium through which meaning is conveyed. Words and terms are patient carriers of the meanings they ought to transmit. But what exactly they transmit varies across space and time, across speakers and listeners.

The problem of defining

Synonyms in one language may not be considered as such in another tongue. And even if they were, it is not guaranteed that people associate the same thing with the very term they use. Scholarship, science and learning, for instance, are

DOI: 10.4324/9781315642123-1

frequently associated with the term knowledge, even used synonymously, but they do not connote the same. One of the first tasks before immersing into the waters of reflection and interpretation is to raise awareness for the boundedness of words and terms we are so much 'at ease' with in everyday academic life. Definitions deserve their due merit, they help holding authors and presenters accountable towards readers and audiences and they provide orientation. But they are also a means to narrow down the semantic scope. The exercise of defining may become reconsidered through the attempt of translation, because translating a term or concept requires clarity about its meaning. However, translations may also become defying tasks. I take knowledge and its potential synonyms as a case in point. Translating the term from Japanese into English language (and vice versa) illustrates the difficulty of conveying an exact or 'original' meaning. The common Japanese translation of knowledge is 知識 (*chishiki*). It consists of two characters, each of them hosting a meaning of its own. The character 知 (*chi*) is commonly understood to signify the intellect (intellectual competence), whereas the character 識 (*shiki*) refers to discriminating, knowing, or writing. The composite *chishiki* is also translated as scholarship, but when scholarship bears the connotation of 'bookishness' and literary ability, the character combination for 'scholarly vigor/power' and achievement, 学力 (*gakuryoku*) would rather be the matching compound. The semantic difference of the characters used is obvious and immediately visible; translators are expected to carefully choose the most appropriate ones – a task which becomes imperative when English language texts use knowledge and scholarship interchangeably. It gets even more difficult (but also more interesting) when the conceptual basis of a term is different or even absent at all in the target language. This has been the case with words like society, nation, religion and others – words exported from one part of the world to another (cf. Nawa 2016). Citizens of the Japanese island prefecture Okinawa related to me that the local Ryukyu languages did not have a word for 'peace' in pre-modern times; peace had always been there, relations to neighbouring regions were fine and there was thus no need to coin a term for this 'normal' state of affairs.[1] Only when the Ryukyu islands became occupied by Japanese clans and formerly friendly relations to neighbouring regions turned sour, 'peace' became a notion to refer to. Adding to the complexity is the change of meaning of words and concepts over time. 'Family', for instance, came to replace the 'household' as the reference for a common unit of social organisation in modern societies. This change in language indicates the conceptual change that took place. House, household and kinship are nowadays notions associated with a societal organisation characterised as 'traditional' or pre-modern, whereas family signifies something more modern, something disentangled from kinship-based societies and hence representing the emergence of territorially based societies in which, eventually, the individual gained priority as a subject of rights. When we turn to the Japanese translation of family, this conceptual disentanglement is rather latent and not as obvious: the term 家族 (*kazoku*) which is the common translation today for family is composed of the character for house (家 *ka*) and tribe/people (族 *zoku*). The same character for house (家) read as *ie* was the dominant unit of social organisation in pre-modern Japan. Thinking of family as a social unit detached from the concept of house seems thus to be quite an alien idea in Japanese, although today's Japan would not be considered a kinship- or household-based society. I come back to the example of kinship and family in the discussion of disciplines as an ordering principle of knowledge production.

In Arabic, to raise another example, the translation of conceptual terms such as 'gender' is a contested task and a challenging endeavour (Kamal 2008: 262–64). While the pragmatic version of using the Anglicism and converting the letters (i.e. writing the Arabic consonant letters جندر (*jndr*) and omitting the vowels as commonly done when they are short) is a frequent one, it is not always preferred. *J(e)nd(e)r* has the smack of a Western concept and may, as such, be missing cultural 'authenticity'. Knowledge, family, gender and other 'commonly understood' terms reveal their contextual embeddedness once they migrate into different contexts and are made comprehensible through translation. Definitions only help as long as the experiential commensurability of the underlying ideas and concepts is given.

I am raising these examples since they nurture my everyday business as a scholar of Asian and Middle Eastern societies and a social scientist who is expected to deliver findings (in fact knowledge) serving to understand 'the world' writ large. It is the daily encounter with 'translations' of presumably universally known terms and concepts that has caught my constant attention for fallacies coming along with the exercise of producing knowledge on areas and connections between people around the globe (i.e. cooperation). Most of my reflections on global cooperation draw from knowledge accumulated in world regions different from the one I grew up in; the natural question to ask is how can I be confident in having translated empirical reality 'properly' into research findings which are then shared by an ever-expanding scientific community? It is not necessary to mention that 'proper' findings in the social sciences are neither achievable nor can they be decreed because they are always constructed to a certain extent and based on subjective interpretations. As feminists, for example, have learned, gender equality means different things to different people. As obvious as this realisation is, it does not prevent me from reflecting thoroughly on the key terms of this volume. The only thing it does is to urge an understanding based on awareness of the subjectivity and, at times, the definitional hegemony in social science research. The exercise of translating necessitates due attention to the context wherein ideas and concepts are embedded, but it also has its limits as I have demonstrated. I have therefore opted to make as transparent as possible the mental avenue I walked when trying to comprehend the terms 'knowledge production', 'Area Studies' and 'global cooperation'.

The subsequent sections of this chapter address the semantics of knowledge and its production; the comprehension of regions and areas in social science; and global cooperation with a focus on actors' connectedness across localities, nations, and regions. The chapter discusses concrete aspects of international relations and cooperation and builds the bridge to the next chapter on alternative epistemologies. A question to be tackled throughout the book is what the study of global cooperation may gain from the inclusion of alternative epistemologies and, eventually, the behavioural dimensions of translocal, transnational and transregional connectedness that are nurtured in epistemic settings other than the dominant 'Western' or 'Northern'. Depending on the literature consulted, the West, the (global) North, Northern-American or European are the preferred terms to refer to the part of the world where most of the hegemonic knowledge that pervades institutions of learning around the globe has been generated. I leave the different cardinal directions uncommented and use the West (and adjectives Western and non-Western) as my own term of choice. I do so in the most neutral way possible, i.e. neither implying a 'West versus X' relationship nor ignoring the fact that cardinal directions such as the West have emerged from a particular worldview. The West is a fuzzy but tenaciously utilised denominator, one which has become settled in academia.

Knowledge

Knowledge is a household term, yet it is rarely digested in the myriads of contexts in which it is used. Searching for a handy explanation of what knowledge is about, I came across a textbook by Kristof van Asshe and Anna-Katharina Hornidge on rural development. According to these authors (2015: 22), knowledge is:

> [a]nything that helps us to understand the world and ourselves in it, anything that gives insight and the insight itself. [...] All other distinctions between sorts of knowledge, between expertise and local knowledge, between disciplines, between experts and laymen, are contingent, can be drawn in different ways, and the way you do that has implications for your perspective on development.

I subscribe to both writers' simply held explanation which links knowledge to understanding and insight. In an attempt to structure the conceptual field of knowledge – contingent as it were on my own subjective perspective – I find it useful to distinguish between three ways of approaching knowledge as a topic of social scientific as well as Area Studies research. These approaches also relate to the three key terms of the title. The first is to apply an historical perspective and get an idea of the epistemic concepts that knowledge in general and science – 'as a collection of different forms of expert knowledge' (van Asshe and Hornidge 2015: 19) – in particular were based on in different world regions. I examine this with reference to East Asia. The second is a critical appraisal of how acquisition and dissemination of knowledge of our times have become organised in institutions of learning and research. Disciplines and areas as globally utilised ordering principles are discussed as cases in point. In the third, I attend to the dependence of knowledge production on political environments and politically informed world views. This issue harks back to the critical discussion of knowledge organisation in the preceding section, but it also inverts the perspective from local to global and looks at politically motivated constraints of knowledge production *in* different regions and nation-states (or areas, as it were).

Recent endeavours to compile a global history of knowledge appear to aim at decentring the diffusion of knowledge (cf. Goh 2011). The perceived unidirectional flow from a Western centre to non-Western peripheries is seen as problematic and means to confront the hegemonic power, style of knowing and epistemological imperatives of knowledge deriving from one part of the world surface in articulations of distinctive regional epistemologies.[2] The hitherto uncommon aspect of bringing in regional epistemologies is the impetus to counter a perceived hegemony. Why the Western style of knowledge assumed a hegemonic or even imperative role becomes apparent through a glance at the study of knowledge and science during the preceding decades. In the past, regional knowledge systems have well been part of scholarly attention, as for example in comparative studies such as the 'comparative history of science' (Pyenson 2002: 1–33). On the one hand, comparing the genesis and development of science historically has been a scarce and relatively young activity. Lewis Pyenson (2002: 7) has attributed the beginnings of a '[s]ophisticated, comparative history of science' in the 1950s to the work of merely four scholars: Edward Shils, Ludwig Fritz Haber, Joseph Ben-David, and Derek J. de Solla Price'. On the other hand, Western scholars did not rid themselves of normative predispositions – despite the honest appreciation of non-Western science systems. A case in point is the work of Joseph Needham, a scholar whose name shows up, apart from the four mentioned, in almost any treatise of comparative historiographies of knowledge. Needham's studies of science and medicine in East and West from the 1950s into the 1970s are frequently cited.[3] He compared China to Europe, but also the Arabic world to China and Europe – especially in the realm of medicine. He praised what China was able to achieve in the Middle Ages – much more than Europe – and points to the entanglements, interplays, and 'marriages' of ideas in Chinese, Greek and Arabic alchemy (cf. Pyenson 2002: 11). Needham's appreciation of Asian and Arabic science notwithstanding, he and most of his contemporaries were still convinced that a 'scientific revolution' had not taken place in the non-European world, whereas it had taken place in sixteenth- to eighteenth-century Europe. Hence, in retrospect, the 'Why Not' question came up, as Yung Sik Kim (2014b) calls it, i.e. the frequent question why China and others did not experience a scientific revolution. Underlying this question, Kim reasons, was 'the assumption that there is a universal development pattern of the growth of scientific knowledge' (Kim 2014a: 107). To cure this misleading assumption, Kim (2014a: 116) suggests a de-narrowing of perspectives:

> Of course, the modern perspective cannot be eliminated from our attempt to understand traditional Chinese science. A minimal amount of basic modern vocabulary and concepts are needed to expound to others what

> we have understood. What is to be avoided in the choice of subjects for our investigation into Chinese science, however, is the preponderant, if not exclusive, emphasis, on those concepts and aspects that were significant in the development of modern science in the West.

His criticism targets the apparently unquestioned setting of norms and priorities in comparative history without pondering about the particularity and context-dependence of these norms. The consequence of such criticism does not mean to claim that 'there was indeed something like a scientific revolution in China, we just missed discerning it'. Rather than claiming the existence of something by twisting and stretching the facts of technical development in sixteenth- and seventeenth-century China, the task may be 'to understand the nature, place, role and impact of these technical branches in traditional Chinese culture' (Kim 2014a: 117). As the author unfolds, technical 'progress' was neither absent in China nor was it ignored:

> Of course, there did exist traditions of technical natural knowledge in traditional China. But most often they consisted simply of technical knowledge used for practical purposes, such as calendars, healing, divination, manufacturing or warfare; they were not pursued with a theoretical or 'intellectual' interest.
>
> (Kim 2014a: 110f)

The classification of knowledge in traditional China – distinguishing, for instance, between 'the rule behind everything' (理 *li*) and 'the substance of things' (気 *qi*)[4] – relegated technical knowledge to a lower rank than it enjoyed in medieval Western Europe. Moreover, the radical transformation of Western science which brought about the scientific revolution 'was a very complex and historical phenomenon uniquely rooted in Western culture'. A universal pattern of knowledge growth is, from this point of view, a mistaken belief. Kim's observation and approach are akin to Timothy Mitchell's (2002a: 19–119) critical assessment of naïvely held 'principles true in every country'. Mitchell's recall of this expression of a British colonial administrator in Egypt points to a similar assumption of universality as Kim exposes the case for development patterns and the growth of knowledge. Mitchell's (2002a: 13f) core concern is 'the question of how one can relate what happens in one place to what we call the global forces of modernity, of science and technology, and of the expansion of capitalism'. His empirical example, the making of the economy in nineteenth- and twentieth- century Egypt, serves to disclose the uni-directionalism of social theory. 'The possibility of social science', he claims, 'is based upon taking certain historical practices of the West as the template for a universal knowledge' (Mitchell 2002: 7). The logic of, for instance, a law of property was based on the unquestioned conviction that universal rules of modern systems of law would eradicate the shortcomings of 'native' systems like those in Egypt – arbitrary rules and ad hoc law-making or what was perceived as unstable '*qadi* justice' by Max Weber. But this logic, this principle, was simply not true for every country; it was not universal. Again, the consequence of criticising the belief in universal rules, laws and principles for the good of mankind is not to rest in the defence of arbitrary judgments. Rather, it is about equating the absence of certain rules or laws with irrationality, backwardness, or lack of order and systemic stability. Understanding, if we transfer Kim's reasoning to Mitchell's observation, 'the nature, place, role and impact' of the concept of property in Egyptian society of the time, would lead to a re-think of the dictum of 'principles true in every country' (which is what Mitchell's study eventually does).

The list of examples for concepts and conceptions allegedly meeting a globally uniform understanding and acceptance, presuming a global 'we', could be continued. I want to raise only one more, the choice of which prompts me to shift the view from historic to post-war (1945-) times. In his reflections on religion, politics, and communities in an age of global terrorism, Scott Thomas (2007: 57f) provokingly states that 'we tend to forget that the Cold War was only cold if you happened to live in Europe or North America – it got rather hot in Vietnam, Central America, or Southern Africa'. The striking issue behind this remark is that it may indeed be questioned who 'has the power to name the present era' (Thomas 2007: 60) (or the preceding era, for that matter)? The power to not only name eras but also to have a whole branch of a scholarly discipline, such as international relations (IR),[5] subscribe to a Cold War worldview of bi-polarisation and theorise the relations between states accordingly, is no doubt impressive. Huge numbers of studies have been conducted in the spirit of a bi-polar world order as seen from the Western vantage point of the Cold War, many of them published or utilised for policy counselling. The conceptual basis for theorising 'relations' was the nation-state. However, the repercussions of ordering and structuring the world into scaled units designated as nation-states and regions (e.g. the Middle East, Latin America, Eastern Europe, Central Asia. Southern Africa or Southeast Asia) are conspicuous. This view of how the world is structured is also manifested in the overall organisation of knowledge generation, learning, and knowledge dissemination: Area Studies programmes in Japanese Studies, Chinese Studies, Southeast Asian Studies or Middle East Studies have adopted the language that reflects how the world has become structured (politically) by accepting these area names for their study programmes. Why else would today's students study Southeast Asia? Had they lived in colonial times, they would presumably have studied Indochinese Studies or Javanese Studies, but certainly not Southeast Asian Studies: this subject did not exist – for obvious political reasons. I address this topic in the following discussion of areas and disciplines as ordering principles in the social and other sciences. It is important for a critical reflection of knowledge, as the above examples have shown, to acknowledge that assumptions of universal principles and developments in human interaction have frequently led to the foreclosure of alternative perspectives.

Area Studies and disciplines

Area Studies suffer from various epistemic borderlines which have been drawn and have grown during decades of constructing a 'world order' that is ultimately defined by political power structures.[6] The question of what constitutes an 'area' or a 'region' is timely and contested. Moreover, epistemic borderlines have been constructed by a hegemonic way of identifying academic disciplines. The separation between Area Studies and disciplines and the knowledge produced within their frameworks, too, is related to global epistemic power relations. As Van Asshe and Hornidge (2015: 25) put it, '[w]hat is recognized as knowledge and as useful knowledge is shaped in a history of shifting power relations, and those power relations partly spring from access to, use of, privileging of, certain types of understanding of self and environment'. This also suggests asking how Area Studies and disciplines came about as ordering principles in science and academia.

The designation 'Area Studies' sounds innocent. Its latent pitfalls surface when we disassemble the compound into its elements: What constitutes an area and what is the concept behind the scholarly activity called the study of one or more area(s), hence *Area Studies*? In terms of a conventional understanding of Area Studies with a view on the European science landscape, we can follow Birgit Schäbler's (2007: 12) description. She conceives of the concept of Area Studies as the:

> scholarly research on a world region/world civilisation, i.e. on a territory that is defined both geographically and epistemically. Another generally accepted definition of what constitutes area studies is that researchers learn the languages of their respective world region, have spent longer periods of fieldwork there, and have thoroughly reflected upon the local history, different local viewpoints, material and interpretations according to their disciplinary or interdisciplinary approaches in order to understand non-European societies, cultures/civilisations, literatures and histories from within the region.

Two terms merit attention here, namely 'world region' and 'non-European'. While Area Studies mostly take whole regions or even continents into their view (Latin America, Africa, East Asia, Eastern Europe, Middle East etc.), they are simultaneously concentrated on one particular country – Chinese Studies, Japanese Studies etc. – or on a sub-region, such as Southeast Asia. What counts as an area is thus not precisely scaled. Moreover, the designation of a particular geographic territory as an area is subject to political developments and the world order at a certain time in history. Before World War II and decolonisation, nobody would have studied, for instance, Southeast Asian Studies in Europe. The colonial powers had allocated their names of choice to the territory of today's Southeast Asia depending on what area they controlled (e.g. 'Indochina' for French-occupied Myanmar, Laos, and Vietnam, or the Dutch East Indies for today's Indonesia). Since international power relations and academic demarcations between different Area Studies are almost inseparably connected to each other, Southeast Asian Studies are a comparatively recent label for this field of research. Area Studies are, as Schäbler (2007: 15) puts it, 'indubitably a child of the Cold War' and have frequently been subjected to the task of getting to know the enemy. I have already pointed out that the very term Cold War implies the perspective from a particular part of the world. Ruth Benedict's (1967) wartime study of Japan for the US Office of War Information, *The Chrysanthemum and the Sword. Patterns of Japanese Culture*, is an illustrative product showing how anthropological works were meant to inform politics. The Japanese represented 'the most alien enemy' the USA had hitherto fought against (Benedict 1967: 1). Benedict was assigned to study Japan in 1944 and to 'spell out what the Japanese were like' (Benedict 1967: 3). Her findings demanded an understanding of cultural diversity and the tolerance of difference. The 'ideology of tolerance' that informed Benedict's research, Christopher Shannon (1995: 662) writes, 'grew out of the understanding of cultural relativism that rose to prominence in anthropological circles during the first half of the twentieth century'. Scrutinising the idea of tolerance, Shannon (1995: 662) states that it requires consensus over a single, universal standard of 'freedom as self-determination and autonomy from nonconsensual social relations'. This, however, is not unproblematic:

> [A]s an anthropologist, she [= Benedict; C.D.] worked primarily on non-Western culture not organized around this conception of freedom. For all of its 'tolerance' of diversity, Benedict's anthropology set the acceptance of freedom-as-autonomy as the price of inclusion in a world made safe for differences and excluded all who would not submit to this single standard.
> (Shannon 1995: 662)

The above mentioned assumption of a 'principle true in every country' surfaces again in the consensus over 'freedom as self-determination'. Timothy Mitchell (2002b: 29) formulates similar thoughts relating to the link between Cold War Area Studies and the knowledge production project of social sciences:

> The genealogy of area studies must be understood in relation to the wider structure of academic knowledge and the struggles not [only] of the Cold War but of science – and social science in particular – as a twentieth-century political product.

However, Area Studies should not be understood as mere delivery service institutions for political decision makers. Rather than notoriously complying with official politics, we find Area Studies representatives as critical observers who articulate well-grounded arguments against the dynamics that are at work in *Realpolitik* (Schäbler 2007: 15f).[7]

The second term that merits attention in Schäbler's definition is 'non-European'. Indeed it is a rather strange, phenomenon that, at least in Europe, the concept of Area Studies is usually applied to regions outside (Western) Europe. It is only recently that Comparative Area Studies scholars articulate the need to include Europe – or the West in its extension – into the concept of Area Studies. It is obvious that the long-time perception of Area Studies as non-European/non-Western studies has shaped the status of Areas Studies vis-à-vis the so-called systematic disciplines. Results arrived at during research *outside* this region were recognised if they matched the theoretical assumption developed *in* Europe/the West. Mitchell (2002b: 8) succinctly points this out by stating that Area Studies contributed to the Western social sciences in two ways: on the one hand, 'area studies would cleanse social theory of its provincialism' and on the other hand, '[a]rea studies would serve as a testing ground for the universalization of the social sciences'. Or in Zawawi Ibrahim and NoorShah's (2012: 166) words, the periphery, i.e. the target areas of Area Studies scholarship:

> has been reduced to the position of receiver and consumer of theoretical knowledge, rather than its initiator or producer. At most, the periphery remains a laboratory of rich empirical data for Western social scientists to investigate and utilize at will when undertaking research, and ultimately to create new theories or engage in current theoretical discourses pertaining to the periphery.

The latter 'function' of areas in particular has informed social science research for a long time. Spin-offs of classical modernisation theory based on empirical reality in the West are but one example of the testing of their universal validity in other parts of the world. 'The history of social science in Europe', states Habibul Haque Khondker (2012: 62), 'reveals that social science is an outgrowth of modernity; it is a product of the Enlightenment and it embraced the notions of progress and modernization'. The missing compatibility of modernity-based theoretical assumptions of the 'centre' with the empirical reality in the 'periphery' gradually led to a self-critical questioning in the West if the 'travel of concepts' across the globe could be conducted so easily (if at all).[8]

The results of putting the application of theories and methods of Western origin to non-Western contexts under scrutiny brought about novel and well-known approaches such as Shmuel N. Eisenstadt's (2000: 1–29) *Multiple Modernities*. While these studies had a clearly refining effect on social science thinking, the fact remained that the reasoning behind such approaches was still embedded in Western epistemic logic, standards and semantic contexts. Not surprisingly, this prompted ideas departing from 'theory production in the West and theory application in the rest' of the world. Sebastian Conrad and Shalini Randeria's (2002) *Entangled Modernities* are emblematic of this trend. Jean and John Comaroff's (2012) *Theory from the South*, too, was a paradigmatic work in this regard. It invites the reader to imagine that the theories explaining how the world functions, i.e. the production of universal knowledge, came from the African continent (instead of Europe/the West/the global North). The logic of Comaroff and Comaroff is different from that of an elder study with a similar title – *Southern Theory* by Raewyn Connell (2007: ix) – which denounces the formula of 'data gathering and application in the colony' and 'theorizing in the metropole'. What this whole strand of scholars has in common, though, is an appreciating stance towards explaining the production of knowledge and world views from regions that have hitherto hardly been recognised as originators of (universal) theories and methods, but 'reduced to the position of receiver and consumer of theoretical knowledge' (Zawani and NoorShah 2012: 166). Why has the gap between perceived producers and receivers of theoretical knowledge been so persistent over time? What is questionable about areas and disciplines in the way they have become demarcated in today's institutions of learning? I reflect on these questions with a focus on assumptions that feed into the perception of an incline between West and non-West – or 'centre' and 'periphery', to use Zawawi and NoorShah's wording – in the generation and initiation of theory and methodology.

When we turn back to Yung Sik Kim and science in traditional China for a moment, we find the author wondering about the hegemonic power of structuring science into disciplines. Regardless of Kim's deep respect for the comparative studies of historian Joseph Needham, he nonetheless notices that Needham 'uses the names of modern scientific disciplines to classify various areas of Chinese traditional knowledge' among them astronomy, meteorology, geography, geology, mineralogy, physics, and the like. 'This classification' Kim (2014: 108) continues, was not consistent with what he found in China, but rather 'consistent with Needham's outlook' of the time because:

> although he fully realizes that such subjects as biology or physics did not exist in traditional China as separate, autonomous areas of knowledge, they are, for him, the ultimate forms into which Chinese science would have had to develop in its march towards a 'universal' science.
>
> (Kim 2014a: 108)

The underlying assumption of a universal pattern of knowledge development thus seduced Needham to squeeze what he found in China into the disciplinary compartments of his own academic scheme. The comparison of the history of science which Needham pursued was hence embedded in a landscape of units called disciplines, and of geographical areas which reflected the political world order of the particular period in history. Not too much has changed since the 1950s in regard to the designation of areas and disciplines, I would argue. As a matter of fact, Islamic Studies have for decades focused almost exclusively on the Middle East as their empirical reference region. A systematic inclusion of other parts of the world with Muslim-majority populations into the field is a comparatively young development – probably spurred by the political identification of non-Arab hotspots of 'Islamic terrorism'. But cross-disciplinary collaboration between, for instance, Islamic Studies and Southeast Asian Studies has yet to become intensified, as has the study of relations across (non-Western) regions. The turn towards 'Middle East Asia', as John Calabrese promotes it in bringing scholars on the Middle East and Asia together, is a rare example of such an endeavour.[9] The almost blind eye in Western social science and Area Studies towards the increasing connection and cooperation between Muslim Southeast Asians and Muslim Middle Easterners, as an empirically salient case in point, will be discussed in Chapters 5 and 6. A conceptual watershed for Area Studies that has to be mentioned with regard to the ups and downs of this field of knowledge production in the West is the post-1990 development. The connection between the change taking place in Area Studies and the world political change due to the end of the Cold War does not need particular emphasis. According to Katja Mielke and Anna Katharina Hornidge (2014: 6), Area Studies as practiced before 1990 had become anachronistic:

> In the new circumstances they proved to be problematic heuristic devices for the study of objects/actors in motions, global flows and cultural processes without being delimited by previous established boundaries in academia and physical/assumed cultural boundaries or political borders 'out there'.

Subsequently, scholars geared up to put their finger on the major cause for the perceived anachronism. This was, among others, found in an area concept that had been too much occupied by looking at geographically bound areas. Departing from this approach and taking process-geographies into account would better enable researchers 'to capture flows and motions of ideas, ideologies, discourses, people, goods, images, messages, technologies, techniques' (Mielke and Hornidge 2014: 6). Particularly groundbreaking proposals in this direction were presented by Arjun Appadurai (2010) ('new Area Studies architecture') and Willem van Schendel (2002) ('jumping scale'). Van Schendel presented a spectacular study of a region he called *Zomia* – one that had never been acknowledged as an area in the post-war set-up of (geopolitically influenced) Area Studies.

Disciplines, and post-1945 social science disciplines in particular, have deepened their methodological and theoretical repertoire over time. In the realm of methodology, the invention and refinement of data-processing software notwithstanding, quantitative and qualitative research methods alike have become the mission and vocation of many academicians. For a couple of decades, this prevented scholars from fostering inter- and transdisciplinary collaboration, seeking instead the refinement of a certain discipline-based methods. Intra-disciplinary competition for 'the better method' was frequent. When the demand for more interdisciplinary projects intensified in the 1980s, the situation had already entered a stage in which tunnel vision was hard to change. Research proposals for project funding handed in by two or more scholars from different disciplines were often declined by the adjudicating committees of the funding agency because the respective (discipline-based) reviewers found something missing based on their particular point of view. This often concerned the methods of data gathering and data interpretation. To some, the project in question seemed to be glossing over important facts; to others, it seemed to get lost in too much detail and micro-level analysis. Area Studies proposals in particular suffered because of their (allegedly) theory-distant approach. Consequently, truly inter and transdisciplinary approaches struggled to take off in the discipline-orientated structure of knowing; the pushing of disciplinary borders was slow to progress.

Apart from these trends in the landscape of discipline-orientated knowledge production, the governance of the machinery of learning and scholarship in national as well as in world politics played a role of its own. Hardly noticed in those parts of the world where the knowledge was generated, this acquired a more or less hegemonic status on the global scale, the parts of the world 'receiving' this knowledge tended to – willingly or unwillingly – comply with ideologically bound imperatives of knowledge production. Goh Beng Lan (2012: 80) looks at this situation examined through the diffusion of theories in postcolonial Southeast Asia:

> The unspoken politics of theory at the time, supposedly speaking on behalf of some universal and objective standard, determined which scholarship could be regarded as theory and which relegated to more subjective and parochial forms of knowledge.

The acceptance of theory from outside the region was at odds with ethno-cultural identities and their relationships with socio-economic structures on the nation-state level in postcolonial Southeast Asia. The ideological divisions that characterised the social sciences in the West during Cold War times were not confined to debates there, but travelled to 'the periphery', where the empirical contexts were far from similar to 'the centre'. As Goh (2012: 86) finds:

> Nevertheless, even as local scholarship began to take on ideological divisions, the heavily secularist grounds upon which political ideologies were fought out in US social scientific frameworks proved to be constraining when applied to Southeast Asian contexts. If there is one thing that the Cold War made clear it is that ideological discourses in Southeast Asian contexts were often inseparable from ethno-religious dogmas and were never fought over in secular terms alone.

The Cold War in Southeast Asia was rather hot, as Scott Thomas' previously mentioned remark succinctly depicts. Accordingly, local scholars became not only divided along ideological lines (communist versus capitalist bloc) but, as Goh's (2012: 86) quote emphasises, were drawn into politicised ethnic classifications. 'Communists were often associated with particular ethnic groups, such as the Chinese in the cases of Malaysia and Indonesia [...].' Collective ethnic segmentation overlapped with religiously informed discrimination. The Indonesian massacre against communists in 1965 targeted Indonesian Chinese who were not only perceived as political enemies but 'also became an anti-atheist pogrom' (Goh 2012: 87). Social science theories imported from the West would neither picture these developments nor could they provide answers to the domestic and transnational turbulences in the region. Hence:

> For some who had pursued graduate studies overseas their encounters with the rigidity of contemporary theoretical and disciplinary divides were often eye-openers, marking the beginning of a critical distance from Western theories and disciplinary politics.
>
> (Goh 2012: 87)

The rigidity of disciplinary divides affected the Western sciences, too, albeit in another guise. I refer to the terms 'family' and 'kinship' mentioned at the beginning of this chapter to illustrate the phenomenon. The binary classification of kinship and family has been paramount for the 'division of labour' in anthropological, political science and sociological research. While Anthropology became responsible for research in kinship and 'political organisation without states', Political Science explored state politics and Sociology examined the family relations in the states and societies of the West. The question how the process of developing a terminological and epistemological distinction between kinship and family took place at the beginning of the nineteenth century has yet to be answered. Remarkable for our inquiry into the delineation of world regions and the division of disciplines, however, is the perception that emerged from leaving kinship research to anthropology and state/family research to the social sciences. The epistemological shift consigned to oblivion a centuries-old understanding of Western politics in terms of dynasties, succession, and alliances. History, which until then had mainly been written as extended genealogy, now projected the logic of kinless states onto the Western past and the 'others' who still had to rid themselves of kin-based state structures and social organisation. This representation not only made social commentators often overlook central features of their own society (in which kinship played a vital role), but promoted the later hegemonic narrative of a decline of kinship in Europe with modernisation and the role of the nuclear family for Western economic success and political dominance. Kinship became associated with regions of tribal or clan allegiance, which anthropologists would analyse. Modern states and societies, researched in the social sciences, were not subjected to analysis with the conceptual tool of kinship. Regardless of the emerging trend of 'new' kinship research on Euro-America and other parts of the world, a thorough review of the epistemic history of kinship within the disciplines is as lacking as a review of the disciplinary split between the sociology of the family and the anthropology of kinship.[10] The equation of kinship with traditional and family with modern social organisation (and kinless state order in extension of this organisation) is thus directly reflected in the disciplinary division of anthropology, sociology and political science. Moreover, the narratives nurturing this distinction facilitated an indexing of areas according to their achievements in overcoming social and political organisational features that purportedly had no role in the modernised West. What others have called centre and periphery is mirrored in the perception of Area Studies as studies of non-Western regions and in the configuration and subject matters of the disciplines.

The inadequacies of Western theories compared to empirical realities at home or in other parts of the world have today become relatively strong push factors for a re-thinking of the rigidity of disciplinary divides. In the field of international relations research (IR), the demand for a 'Global IR', as Amitav Acharya articulated it, is nonetheless a comparatively recent one.[11] An integrated research approach with input from Area Studies, history, anthropology, cultural studies and others would produce more appropriate tools and perspectives than the hitherto dominant analysis of, for example, East Asia's security situation (China, Japan, the Koreas, Taiwan) allows. East Asia's relative stability in view of security issues is a surprising fact for Western IR theorists. Despite territorial disputes (e.g the South China Sea and others), varying stages of development, ethnic and cultural diversity, high defence expenditures, different orientations and alliances in foreign policy and frequent exposure to natural disasters, the region has presented a remarkably stable security record throughout the last few decades (the Korean War from 1950–1953 being the last major intra-regional event). Although competition between avowed IR schools such as realism, liberalism and constructivism is a daily business in the discipline, localised knowledge in Asian IR theory building is an under-researched and conceptually under-developed topic. Local perspectives on international relations have hardly made any inroads into mainstream theory building in the West. I return to the issue of local IR perspectives in the subsequent paragraphs, introducing Middle Eastern and Islamic viewpoints of international relations.

The local brings us back to the question of the importance of contextualisation for the generation of knowledge on areas different from the 'centre'. 'Context', say Van Asshe and Hornidge (2015: 39), 'comes from linguistics, where it refers to those things outside the text that influence the interpretation of texts'. Context mapping, be it in linguistics or other sciences, 'is always a matter of selection and interpretation'. The observer, the scientist, 'always relies on interpretations of context to get an understanding' of the object of his or her examination. Attention to context 'points to the need for self-awareness, for reflexivity' and '[…] can be useful to structure the analysis, to guide the thinking' (Van Asshe and Hornidge 2015: 39f). Any formation of theory, invention and application of methodology ideally incorporates this reflexivity into the practice of knowledge production. If it works out, it is an issue in itself. I argue, however, that in the research on international relations and global cooperation, self-awareness of a scholar's positionality and reflexivity in thinking are not completely free from underlying world views and hegemonic narratives which miss out on grasping the context of the situation elsewhere – just as the term Cold War missed recognising the 'hot' context of the war in Southeast Asia. I discuss this theme in view of both non-Western IR perspectives and development cooperation. These never acquired a prominent position in Western theoretical reflection, yet determined developments in other parts of the world to a considerable extent. Before I attend to some concrete examples, I reflect on the problematic nature of politically regulated and orchestrated knowledge production.

Knowledge production, international relations and global cooperation

Knowledge production is a power-related process. The nation-state as an ordering principle in world politics is as strong a player as powerful regional blocs such as (Western) Europe, North America or the West. One of the most obvious issues of politically constrained knowledge production on the nation-state level is history writing. History schoolbooks in Japan, Korea, and China for instance, are filled with contrary information on historical events – numbers killed in massacres, the designation of war heroes or war criminals, acceptance of war crimes like forced prostitution, and many more.[12] Admitting the fact of a human rights violation or a war crime is less a moral issue for regimes and governments than, ultimately, a strategic and economic one. Japan's avowal of forced prostitution during World War II entailed explicit financial consequences. When the governments of Japan and South Korea agreed to an end of the so-called 'comfort women' issue in December 2015, Japan agreed to pay one billion Yen (US$ 8.3 million) in redress.[13] An official admission of genocide in Namibia by the German army between 1904 and 1908 took more than 100 years but was not accompanied by any payment, despite several attempts to mobilise support for compensation for the Nama and Herero communities.[14] The Turkish admission of Armenian genocide is another case in point, and dozens more could be added. Thorough studies of all cases exist, but have little effect on the official narrative that determines political action. If research 'non-compliant' with the official narrative is published at all, it is usually less eye-catching than other studies of the same topic.[15] Apart from the legal aspects that may engender economic consequences, the fuzzy concept of the 'national interest' often impedes the emergence of 'critical' knowledge. A striking example is Japan's suppression of research and analytical results underlining the dangers of electricity generated by nuclear power plants. Even after the country's triple catastrophe in March 2011 (earthquake, tsunami and nuclear meltdown) the expertise of scientists critical of the process hardly made it into mainstream information media. During fieldwork in Japan in 2014, many of my interlocutors had experiences of oppression to share, among them labour union activists who had been struggling to inform workers about the danger of direct exposure to radioactivity in the contaminated area around the Fukushima nuclear power plant. The kind of knowledge unions wanted to convey obviously met with disapproval from employers who enjoyed political backing for their own 'security policies'. Medical scientists analysing the consequences of radioactive contamination for humans – e.g. susceptibility to certain types of cancer –advertised their research findings via flyers distributed at public gatherings rather than through officially endorsed information campaigns. These examples touch on the difficulties of dissemination and publication of knowledge. Another aspect to think about is the constraint of the initial generation and production of knowledge. Before I move to this latter dimension, it is important to stress that there is no automatic causal relation between a political regime type and the conditions for gathering and spreading knowledge. A democratic system does not, by default, guarantee the free pursuit of knowledge (as the Japanese example of nuclear power research illustrates). Similarly, guided or bound knowledge production is not causally affiliated with the developmental status of a state. Developing countries may at times have greater chances to achieve expertise in specialised fields of knowledge through development cooperation, domestic or foreign funding and access to congenial research infrastructure via scholarships and stipends.

National interest, represented in what governments and ruling regimes declare and identify as such, and international relations form a reciprocal conjunction. In the early days of Southeast Asian post-colonialism, Indonesia and Malaysia competed to build up stable and resilient nations. The task was challenging for both countries in view of their ethnic, religious, linguistic, and cultural diversity.[16] In addition to managing plurality in various guises, Indonesia had to cope with the task of reconstruction. Many parts of the country were devastated as a result of warfare not only against the Dutch (the colonial power in today's Indonesia from 1800–1942 and from 1945–49) but also against the Japanese (who occupied Indonesia between 1942 and 1945). The population was mentally and physically weakened. The 'resurgence of epidemic and endemic diseases' was likely, writes Vivek Neelakanatan (2015: 4), leading President Sukarno to declare that 'independence had ushered a new period of development in all fields, including health. As the key problem of health was economic, Indonesians should focus their efforts on economic development'. The decision to concentrate on economic development affected the overall organisation of knowledge production, which turned into an activity almost co-opted by state agendas. Urged on by the government, institutions of higher learning, think tanks and other research entities focused on applied science rather than generating theoretical knowledge. A member of a government-sponsored think tank who recalled the monitoring effects of states and regimes over local scholarship in the early decades of Indonesian independence, recalled that he had 'to juxtapose the demands of being a "good citizen" [...] on the one hand, and being a good researcher who is critical of the "objectivity" of scholarship, on the other' (Fadjar Thufail, paraphrased in Goh 2011: 25). 'Such constraints' Goh Beng Lan (2011: 25) states, 'demand ingenuity on the part of researchers to carve strategies which can tailor research projects to meet state requirements without sacrificing theoretical rigour'.

The situation illustrated here for Indonesia is similar in other countries, too. To a certain extent, the global theory slope from 'centre' to 'periphery' can be explained by countries' intense pursuit of applied rather than theoretical knowledge production – and research in service to 'the nation'. This appropriation of knowledge-generating institutions has most presumably facilitated the acquisition of a hegemonic position of theories developed in the global 'centre' and tested in the 'periphery'.

Knowledge production geared towards serving 'the nation' and national interest is a double-edged sword. As Maznah Mohamad and Soak Koon Wong (2001: 39) relate:

> There is a clash between the inexorable and inevitable universalisation of worldviews instilled within civil society and the manufactured and reconstituted national identity and culture that leaders are determined to promote in order to avoid their own displacement.

In other words, a 'manufactured national identity' may avert the displacement of incumbent leaders or regimes. North Korea's *ju'che* (主体) ideology may spring to mind immediately as an extreme version of 'manufacturing' identity. In post-revolutionary Iran as well as in Saudi Arabia and Pakistan, the religion of Islam has a central position in the narrative of the genesis and identity of the nation. But there are also more subtle approaches, such as the post-1969 Malaysian government's efforts to educate the 'new Malay' (*Melayu Baru*) – an idiom for a complex melange of national-cultural and ethnic-religious identity markers expected to further economic progress among ethnic Malays.[17] In post-war Japan, a whole scientific genre became devoted to the notion of Japanese uniqueness. *Nihonjinron* (日本人論) was the term for this discourse which purported to analyse Japan's cultural essentialism (cf. Befu 2001). Proving this uniqueness and distinctiveness included psychological studies such as Doi Takeo's (1973) famous treatise on *The Anatomy of Dependence*. In Western social sciences, where social conflict and power relations flourished as topics of scholarly debate (fuelled by the effects of '1968'), *Nihonjinron* engendered particular interest. The 1970s and 1980s were the decades of rapid economic growth in Japan; relating this quite spectacular economic rise of a non-Western country to its cultural features was tempting not just for the social sciences. This aspect then hints at the nexus between IR and Social Science Theory, and eventually the production of knowledge with regard to theories of IR. Moving to more recent developments, I raise the debate about 'Chinese IR' as an example.

The rise of non-Western powers, emerging powers, regional powers or whatever label is applied, has led (Western) IR theorists to concentrate on examining the changed world order since the 1990s. The bipolar order of the Cold War was superseded by a short period of perceived unipolarity in the 1990s, until 'polycentric', 'interpolar' and 'multimodal' became catchy adjectives for describing the current world order (cf. Derichs 2014). Having more centres of power on the global turf, IR theory building had to adjust accordingly and look at how the 'newly emerging powers' perceived world affairs. Are there alternative concepts of world order? Or is theory building in non-Western parts of the world characterised by a 'localising' of Western theories? China's IR scholarship, in particular, attracted the Western scientific community, presumably fuelled by the country's intensified engagement on the African continent. Accounts of China's research landscape today mostly conclude with the inference that its IR scholarship is extremely diverse and complex.[18] On the one hand, it would be exaggerated to speak of a distinctively Chinese IR or any centralised, uniform IR discourse; on the other hand, there are some salient features that point to a particular if not subjective Chinese assessment of world affairs. The normative commitments then suggest a preoccupation with strengthening China's international status, thereby supporting the national interest. China's role as a responsible power wishing to democratise international organisations and create harmonious relationships feeds into the analytical predilections for arriving at theoretical understandings that conform to unequivocal viewpoints on global politics. Some observers are tempted to detect therein a 'key distinction from Western IR theory, where the explanation and understanding of any school is expected to conform to a particular understanding of objectivity and scientific method' (Kavalski 2015: 39). I would like to differ and suggest asking whose 'scientific method' we are referring to. Coming back to the underlying need for self-awareness and reflexivity pointed out before may serve to put the dominance of Western IR theory, its categories and scales into perspective. The postcolonial period in Southeast Asia and the Middle East provides a suitable example to support this argument.

The above criticism of the Cold War is immediately understandable from a Southeast Asian perspective. Reflexivity in one's own attempt to take context into consideration, however, also applies a multitude of perspectives rather than sticking to a selected few. Doing so in the case of the term Cold War discloses that the period name is dominated by the Western worldview underpinning it. But once the term enjoyed acceptance as a signifier of confrontation between super powers, it was then applied to confrontations in other parts of the world (albeit confrontations that are less commonly known and debated). This is true for the Arab-Islamic region, where in the late 1950s Egypt and Saudi Arabia fought out a Cold War in competition over their respective regional power position. Gamal Abdel Nasser's idea of Pan-Arabism stood against Saudi Arabia's model of regional hegemony on the basis of Wahhabism (cf. Seale 1987 [1965]: 56f; see also Derichs 2014). In terms of state and system, Egypt represented the socialist republican and Saudi Arabia the conservative monarchical model. Malcolm Kerr (1965) sees this power struggle constellation as valid until the mid-1960s; in later decades the regional actor map was extended to include Islamist forces who had established themselves as players in the power game. The outreach of this Arabic Cold War has lasted until the present day, although Egypt and Saudi Arabia ended their rivalry in the late 1960s. The Wahhabi branch of Islam is prominent throughout Muslim communities around the world, brought about to a large extent by charities and development assistance from the Gulf states (which I touch upon below). With the collapse of the 1967 war, the ideological and cultural consensus of the Arab republics also collapsed. Arab nationalism, socialism, and populism ushered in a vacuum which eventually facilitated the 'return' to Islam and Islamism as more credible than the failed regimes of the immediate past. During the 1970s, the rhetoric of Islam became even more strident and a wave of Islamic resurgence swept the Muslim world, preliminarily crowned by the Iranian revolution in 1979.

How did non-European Muslim-majority states perceive of international relations during these decades? The trans- and international connection between Muslim states – symbolised through the establishment of the Organisation of Islamic Conference in 1969 – merits attention because it did not figure as prominently on the UN level as, for instance, other institutionalised formats like the Non-Aligned Movement (NAM). For many Muslim states a 'third world' identity went hand-in-hand with an Islamic identity. Foreign policy decisions and perspectives of Muslim-majority states were frequently driven by developments in fellow Muslim states and by a clear distancing from others. Pakistan's 'strategic depth' doctrine vis-à-vis Afghanistan was meant to meet the Indian threat, and was nurtured by the view that 'Pakistan did not have to compete with India within the Islamic bloc, whereas in the Third World movement, India remained a formidable force' (Tikekar 2005: 17). In terms of foreign policy, Pakistan's turn towards the Arab world reflected the country's emphasis on Islamic links across borders, whereas domestically, the state-led Islamisation has also been interpreted as a strategy of a weak regime seeking to garner legitimacy. Following Vali Nasr's (2001) observation, Islamisation as a strategy for national political stability, security and regime legitimacy was a hallmark of the time. But not all Muslim-majority states adopted the strategy. In contrast to state-led Islamisation, the narrowing of the sphere for politically inclined expressions of Islam in public became a core policy in Indonesia. From 1984 onward, Indonesia's New Order regime (i.e. the rule of Suharto from 1965–1998) decreed that 'no organization was allowed to have Islam as its ideological foundation, and security forces violently confronted civilian Muslim groups' (Formichi 2014). These groups then looked at movements outside Indonesia; they were deeply inspired by groups in other Muslim countries such as the Muslim Brotherhood in Egypt. After the fall of Suharto (1998) and the widening of the public sphere for religiously inclined political actors, Turkey's Justice and Development Party (AKP) became 'a source of inspiration' in Indonesia (Hadiz 2014). The Muslim Brotherhood lost some of its appeal, due to its political performance and forced toppling of President Muhammad Mursi (a Brotherhood member) in Egypt (2013). Nonetheless, Islamically based political movements among state leaders as well as in civil society were well received across the Muslim world. Where Islamic activism was repressed, as in Indonesia, student activists in the 1980s 'were semi-clandestinely organized within groupings that adopted the structures as well as methods of recruitment and political socialization that had been tried out particularly in Egypt' (Hadiz 2014). The 1970s had paved the way for trans-border connection and mutual learning. As Vedi Hadiz (2014) stresses:

> It should be recalled that the Muslim Brotherhood was already a growing global influence by this time [the 1970s; C.D.] and had numerous 'branches' all over the world. Moreover, in places like Saudi Arabia in particular, where

> many Indonesians went to study, what had already taken place was a melding of Wahhabi doctrinal rigidity and Muslim Brotherhood organizational discipline and capacity introduced by the latter's substantial diaspora.

It remains to summarise here that transnational and transregional patterns of Muslim inspiration and cooperation took place after the end of World War II, but were widely ignored by theorists of Western IR. This is even more surprising since the intellectual (fore-)fathers of activist organisations in the Muslim world were not unknown among Western scholars. Jamal ad-Din al-Afghani or Fazlur Rahman were respected names and could well be subsumed under the label of 'IR thinkers' in the modern sense (cf. Hassan 2007: 175–79). Less well known were thinkers like Burhanuddin, whose theory of colonialism only inspired a limited number of students and followers; yet they represented a clearly local or non-Western view (cf. Aljunied 2012). Overall, institutions of higher learning played a significant role in the establishment of cross-border contacts and mobilisation in the Muslim world. I will elaborate more broadly on contemporary patterns of translocal, -national and -regional Islam in the coming chapters.

Islamic resurgence across the Muslim world made Islam more directly relevant to the crises that confront states and regimes since the 1970s. State-led Islamisation as a strategy to cope with the loss of regime legitimacy on the one hand, and cross-border inspiration among Islamic civil society organisations on the other were the most visible inputs that enhanced an Islamic identity as part of the multiple identities of individuals. As the decades went by, technological progress enabled an unprecedented physical and mental mobility all around the globe. In the field of knowing and learning, 'new Islamist intellectuals' surfaced and spread their thoughts (Mandaville 2001: 176). Peter Mandaville (2007: 176f), who analysed the developments in transnational Muslim politics during the 1990s and early 2000s, states:

> Neither mosque nor state is to be trusted as a source of authentic Islam, and this allows us to understand the popularity of cassette-based sermons and pamphlets on Islam which originate from outside these institutions. The new Islam hence exists in spaces which institutionalized forms of politics cannot reach. […] The new Islamist intellectual thus represents an interstitial political identity, one which inhabits the gaps between institutional forms.

Mandaville (2007: 177) sees the 'hybridity of the new Islamist project' as a phenomenon deserving of more attention than it actually got in the wake of the end of the bipolar world order. Certainly, his reminder has not lost importance since his book was published in 2001. On the contrary, the Islamist project grew, part of it transmuting into gruesome ideological currents, the Islamic State (IS) being one of them. Beyond those currents which fall under the category of Islamist, catch global media attention and gain political mileage in parts of the world's conflict zones, the feeling of 'having something to share' across Muslim communities all over the world has become increasingly visible. Rather than fading within a landscape that is, at least under the monitors of Western media, dominated by information that sells, the hybridity of what may be called the 'new Muslim project' has constantly evolved. It is important not to gloss over this, but to distinguish between Muslims and Islamists. Whereas Islamists – who are no doubt Muslims by belief – pursue an explicitly politico-ideological project, non-Islamist Muslims to whom I devote the subsequent chapters employ the opportunities that communication, mobility and 'globalisation from below' offers, but do not seek any hegemony or power. Before I expand my argument that *their* connectivity merits deeper consideration in the study of global cooperation, I end this section with a brief glance at Islamic transregional development assistance as a final example of cooperation and connectivity that is seldom integrated into the mainstream aid discourse.

The global terrain of development cooperation is primarily recognised as a collective project of the Organisation for Economic Cooperation and Development (OECD) countries. Within the OECD cloud, the Development Assistance Committee (DAC) manages the flow of development aid on the basis of multilateral collaboration. Post-war development theory and development policy alike were the brainchilds of agenda setters in DAC, the World Bank and the International Monetary Fund, seeking global standards for what counted as 'underdeveloped' and 'developed' countries – third world and first world. The ongoing evolution of revised theories and instruments of international development assistance deriving from theoretical reasoning notwithstanding, development aid beyond the OECD was rarely problematised as a topic of 'aid discourses' before the emergence of so-called 'new donors' in the early 2000s.[19] Even less attention has been paid to Islamic visions of development which were discussed in affiliated circles as early as the 1980s and entailed clear policy goals.[20] In a rough characterisation, Islamic development concepts emphasise the spiritual and moral equally (if not more than) the material aspects of development. The goal is welfare for life on earth as well as in the hereafter; the ethical component development theory is the main focus. Some authors categorise the Islamic vision of development as 'countermodernist in tone' and add it to 'the list of those other critiques of developmentalism such as liberation theory and feminist ecology' (Alatas 1995: 93f). I am not going to reflect on this further, since it is more relevant for our discussion here to devote a glimpse to actual Islamic development cooperation and donors from, for instance, the rich monarchies of the Persian Gulf region.

Typical patterns of transregional efforts to 'Islamise aid' (Petersen 2012: 126–155) show up in the massive presence of charitable organisations from the Gulf, relief missions or the sponsorship of schools and other educational institutions. Indonesian scholar Hilman Latief (2014: 5) observes a 'particular pattern of Muslim social activism' in his country and traces this back to a 'cultural propinquity between international charities and domestic civil society organizations' which led 'to an open reception from domestic organizations to transregional aid agencies'. Due to the moral commitment of the 'secular' aid apparatus in the OECD – delivering aid and performing development cooperation regardless of religious beliefs and confessions – Islamic charitable and philanthropic organisations as well as educational institutions escaped the 'donor spotting' radar; mainstream research in development studies, too, paid little attention to Islamic organisations (see Petersen 2012: 136). The trajectory of inter- and transnational Islamic NGOs and their standing at the UN in general is still-emerging field for development studies (see Petersen 2010). The number of Islamic aid organisations is not high compared to 'secular' ones, but within the group of 'religious' NGOs alone, a huge variety of orientations surfaces. Marie Juul Petersen in a study of international religious NGOs with consultative status at the UN's ECOSOC (Economic and Social Council) in 2010 counted only 320 religious NGOs out of a total of 3,183 (Petersen 2010).[21] Among those 300 plus, the majority were Christian (58%), followed by Muslim NGOs (16.3%); all other world religion-affiliated or spiritual organisations ranked below the 10 per cent mark (Petersen 2010). Numbers of NGOs, however, are not a central indicator for Islamic development activities. On the one hand, the figures vary according to international political circumstances. In the period after 9/11, for instance, many Islamic NGOs were discouraged from continuing their activities, having become suspect of affiliations to Al-Qaida. Others were encouraged to be active as bridge builders using dialogue and pre-empting misunderstandings (Petersen 2012: 131). On the other hand, it is government-sponsored rather than non-governmental actors who engage as faith-based organisations in international aid (cf. Latief 2014). While most of the former have their home base in the MENA region, the latter – international Islamic NGOs in particular – operate from Europe and North America. Their commitment to religious values and principles in their daily work is as diverse as the spectrum of organisations. Petersen's (2012) analysis of the British-based NGO Islamic Relief and the NGO International Islamic Relief Organization based in Saudi Arabia is a case in point. Her study reveals that Islamic Relief's work and language is shaped by the non-religious mainstream development and humanitarian aid discourse, whereas the International Islamic Relief Organization uses the language of religion and 'promotes an understanding of Islam as pervasive and relevant to all spheres of human life, influencing all aspects of aid provision' (Petersen 2012: 140, 145). The term 'Islamic' is not really indicative of the extent to which developmental work is faith based.

For the purpose of studying religious aid work in general and Islamic aid work in particular, it is worth bearing in mind that the landscape of charitable organisations and NGOs such as the two with 'Islamic Relief' in their name is highly diversified. Organisations may not be strong in numbers but are active in dozens of countries around the world; exert their own portion of influence on the perception of development and ideas of 'the good life'. The segment that they occupy in global development cooperation is different from that of the so-called new donors. The International Islamic Relief Organization, for example, has been a donor since 1979 and was well established before the expansion of the discourse surrounding emerging powers and new donors. The influence of Islamic developmental work is hard to measure in statistical data, yet it is tangible in language and physical identity markers of all kinds among those who are part of or affected in whatever form by Islamic charitable work (emergency relief, infrastructure support, spiritual assistance etc). The point to be made – and to be expanded in the following chapters – is that global cooperation has dimensions that oftentimes escape the structural frameworks established by big players in the international arena (such as OECD, the World Bank, the International Monetary Fund or private foundations such as the Bill and Melinda Gates Foundation in the realm of development cooperation). As a consequence, these dimensions do not form an integral part of the general knowledge produced around aid and development. The connectivity between individuals and communities that they engender are highlighted when they become suspicious – as in the case of many transnational Islamic NGOs after 9/11. I assume that the neglect of knowledge generation about trans- and international Islamic cooperation on the far side of conflict, terror, war and extremism occurs to a large extent because of less- or even unknown communicational codes and concepts. Quoting Petersen (2012: 146) one more time:

> Islam shapes the language of the organisation [i.e. International Islamic Relief Organization; C.D.] and the provision of aid is explained and legitimated with reference to Muslim traditions and concepts such as zakat, sadaqa and hadiths rather than the Millenium Development Goals, the Universal Rights Declaration or the Human Development Report.

Mission (دعوة *da'wah*), worship (عبادة *'ibâda*), spiritual counselling (ارشاد الروحي *irshâd ar-rûhî*), education (تربية *tarbiya*) and donations (صدقة *sadaqa*) are familiar terms and concepts in 'Islamised' developmental conversation; although they may match 'secular' values and concepts in several regards, they rarely appear in the glossary of international development cooperation. The entry of an alternative repertoire of terms and concepts deriving from Arabic or Qur'anic language respectively is one of the signifiers of an Islamisation of knowledge that has taken place over time in many parts of the globe. The following chapter will discuss this development in more detail.

This chapter has explored the relation between knowledge – its production and dissemination – and politics. It has exemplified how knowledge as a topical term in different cultural and regional settings is framed by political world views and is arranged accordingly. Knowledge arranged into disciplines as ordering principles and the empirical world arranged into areas has assumed a globally hegemonic status. This makes it difficult to expand the view beyond the scales, boundaries and container categories that have become dominant in research and theory-building. International relations and development cooperation have been discussed as particular fields of study in which alternative views and concepts are hardly visible. Islamic views and concepts have been raised as cases in point. Connectedness and cooperation based on language and concepts that trace back to Islamic sources have evolved over decades in the shadow of mainstream discourses which dominate with their particular lexicons. The area of this kind of connectedness and cooperation cuts across the conventionally researched world regions; the understanding of having something to share (as Muslims) produces new geographies that have hitherto not been captured by conventional Area Studies approaches. My argument is that the development that has taken place is embedded in a process generally called 'Islamisation'. I consider one specific dimension of such Islamisation, namely the epistemic project of an Islamisation of knowledge, an important precursor for the formation of the new geographies which are best described as emotional geographies (Davidson, Bondi and Smith 2007; Anderson and Smith 2001) based on faith and feelings of belonging. In the following chapter, the project of an Islamisation of knowledge is introduced with a focus on its evolution through the writings of four selected scholars.

Notes

1 Fieldwork in Okinawa, March 2014.
2 See Goh (2012). Goh discusses a distinctive Southeast Asian epistemology.
3 See, for example, Needham (1965, 1969, 1970).
4 This is valid for most of the famous currents of Neo-Confucian thought, but should be treated as a rough and fairly basic description.
5 The classification of IR as a branch of the discipline of political science is by no means definite. Fellow scholars may well consider IR a discipline in its own right. I have chosen to apply the classification I was socialised with in Germany.
6 Parts of this subchapter are taken from Claudia Derichs, 'Shifting Epistemologies in Area Studies: From Space to Scale', *Middle East: Topics and Arguments* 4 (2015) 29–36.
7 The author mentions the Vietnam War, the Cuba crisis of 1962 and the Post-9/11 politics as particular cases in point.
8 See also Mandaville (2001: 85–90) on travelling theories.
9 Information on Calabrese's Middle East Asia Project is available at: www.mei.edu/map-project/about (accessed 10 September 2015). For an account of transregional relations see Ehteshami and Miyagi (2015).
10 This research topic has been picked up by a group of anthropologists, historians and social scientists, myself among them. Our studies aim at a critical analysis of the conceptual tools of our disciplines and the re-tracing of the 'division of labour' between them.
11 Acharya raised this demand at the 2015 Annual Convention of the International Studies Association (ISA); his idea is the creation of a universal IR research that integrates and is enhanced by area studies expertise.
12 For the history book controversy in Japan see Nozaki (2002), with a focus on forced prostitution see Tawara (1997).
13 The one billion fund does not apply to Philippine, Dutch and women from other nations who had been forced into prostitution. See Kim and Park (2015).
14 In July 2016, the official confirmation of genocide came from the German government. As yet, this has not triggered legal consequences in terms of reparations payments.
15 Exceptions confirm the rule: Some studies become famous and received huge funding, such as publications from a research project on the direct involvement of German Foreign Ministry officials in the Holocaust.

16 For Malaysia, see Derichs (2004).
17 See Embong (2002) and Chong (2005).
18 For this and the subsequent appraisal see, representative for others, Binhong (2013); Noesselt (2010).
19 Conventionally, four decades of OECD-centred theoretical reflection on development assistance and policy are identified (1961–70; 1971–80; 1981–90; 1991–2000); after the turn of the century, 'new donors' such as China emerged as influential non-OECD actors.
20 For a summary of vision and policy goals see Alatas (1995: 93f).
21 The author's criteria for designating an international NGO as religious are based on organisational self-understanding: 'NGOs that describe and understand themselves as religious, referring in their name, activities, mission statements or elsewhere to religious traditions, values and ideas' (Petersen 2010).

References

Alatas, Syed Farid, 'The Sacralization of the Social Sciences: A Critique of an Emerging Theme in Academic Discourse', *Archives de sciences sociales des religions* 40 (1995) 91: 89–111.

Aljunied, Syed Muhd Khairudin, 'Theorising Colonialism in the Malay World', in Zawawi Ibrahim (ed.), *Social Science and Knowledge in a Globalizing World*. Petaling Jaya: Strategic Information and Research Development Centre, 2012: 201–16.

Anderson, Kay and Susan J. Smith, 'Editorial: Emotional Geographies', *Transactions of the Institute of British Geographers* 26 (2001) 1: 7–10.

Appadurai, Arjun, 'How Histories make Geographies', *Transcultural Studies* 1 (2010). Available at: https://journals.ub.uni-heidelberg.de/index.php/transcultural/article/view/6129 (accessed 8 September 2015).

Befu, Harumi, *Hegemony of Homogeneity: An Anthropological Analysis of 'Nihonjinron'*. Melbourne: Trans Pacific Press, 2001.

Benedict, Ruth, *The Chrysanthmum and the Sword. Patterns of Japanese Culture.* Cleveland: Meridian Books, 1967.

Binhong, Shao, *China and the World: Balance, Imbalance, Rebalance.* Leiden/Boston: Brill, 2013.

Chong, Terence, 'The Construction of the Malaysian Malay Middle Class: The Histories, Intricacies and Futures of the Melayu Baru', *Social Identities. Journal for the Study of Race, Nation, and Culture* 1 (2005) 6: 537–87.

Comaroff, Jean and John Comaroff, *Theory from the South. Or, How Europe is Evolving toward Africa.* Boulder, CO: Paradigm Publishers, 2012.

Conell, Raewyn, *Southern Theory. The Global Dynamics of Knowledge in Social Science*, Sydney: Allen and Unwin, 2007.

Conrad, Sebastian and Shalini Randeria, *Jenseits des Eurozentrismus. Postkoloniale Perspektiven in den Geschichts- und Kulturwissenschaften* [Beyond Eurocentrism. Postcolonial Perspectives in History and Cultural Studies]. Frankfurt am Main: Campus, 2002.

Davidson, Joyce, Liz Bondi and Mick Smith (eds), *Emotional Geographies.* Aldershot: Ashgate, 2007.

Derichs, Claudia, *Nationenbildung in Malaysia als strategisches Staatshandeln* [Nation-Building in Malaysia as Strategic State Activity]. Hamburg: OAG, 2004.

Derichs, Claudia, 'Asiatische Zeitenwende? – Von der bipolaren zur polyzentrischen Weltordnung' [Asian Sea Change? – From Bipolar to Polycentric World Order], in

Franziska Müller et al. (eds), *Entwicklungstheorien* [Development Theories]. Baden-Baden: Nomos, 2014: 41–66.

Derichs, Claudia, 'Shifting Epistemologies in Area Studies: From Space to Scale', *Middle East: Topics and Arguments* 4 (2015): 29–36. Available at: http://dx.doi.org/10.17192/meta.2015.4.2981 (accessed 29 January 2015).

Doi, Takeo, *The Anatomy of Dependence.* Tokyo: Kodansha International, 1973.

Ehteshami, Anoushiravan and Yukiko Miyagi (eds), *The Emerging Middle East-East Asia Nexus.* London & New York: Routledge, 2015.

Eisenstadt, Shmuel Noah, 'Multiple Modernities', *Daedalus* 129 (2000) 1: 1–29.

Embong, Abdul Rahman, *State-led Modernization and the New Middle Class in Malaysia.* New York: Palgrave, 2002.

Formichi, Chiara, 'Contemporary Patterns in Transregional Islam: Indonesia's Shi'a', *Middle East Institute series*, October 2014. Available at: www.mei.edu/content/map/contemporary-patterns-transregional-islam-indonesia%E2%80%99s-shi%E2%80%98 (accessed 3 August 2015).

Goh, Beng Lan (ed.), *Decentring and Diversifying Southeast Asian Studies*, Singapore: Institute of Southeast Asian Studies, 2011.

Goh, Beng Lan, 'Southeast Asian Perspectives on Disciplines and Afterlives of Area Studies in a Global Age', in Zawawi Ibrahim (ed.), *Social Science and Knowledge in a Globalizing World.* Petaling Jaya: Strategic Information and Research Development Centre, 2012: 79–102.

Hadiz, Vedi, 'Islamic Politics in Indonesia: Domestic Challenges, Cross-National Inspirations', *Middle East Institute series*, November 2014. Available at: www.mei.edu/content/map/islamic-politics-indonesia-domestic-challenges-cross-national-inspirations (accessed 29 January 2015).

Hassan, Riffat, 'Religion, Ethics and Violence: Developing a New Muslim Discourse', in Berma Klein Goldewijk (ed.), *Religion, IR and Development Cooperation.* Wageningen: Wageningen Academic, 2007: 161–85.

Kamal, Hala, 'Translating Women and Gender. The Experience of Translating the *Encyclopedia of Women and Islamic Cultures* into Arabic', *Women's Studies Quarterly* 36 (2008) 3: 254–68.

Kavalski, Emilian, 'Quo Vadis China?', *IIAS The Newsletter* 71 (2015): 38–39.

Kerr, Malcom, *The Arab Cold War.* Oxford: Oxford University Press, 1965.

Khondker, Habibul Haque, 'Rethinking Social Science in Asia in an Age of Globalisation', in Zawawi Ibrahim (ed.), *Social Science and Knowledge in a Globalizing World.* Petaling Jaya: Strategic Information and Research Development Centre, 2012: 62–77.

Kim, Jack and Ju-Min Park, 'South Korea, Japan agree to irreversibly end "comfort women" row', *Reuters World*, 28 December 2015. Available at: www.reuters.com/article/us-japan-southkorea-comfortwomen-idUSKBN0UB0EC20151229 (accessed 22 February 2016).

Kim, Yung Sik, *Questioning Science in East Asian Contexts.* Leiden: Brill, 2014a.

Kim, Yung Sik, 'The "Why Not" Question of Chinese Science: The Scientific Revolution and Traditional Chinese Science', in Yung Sik Kim, *Questioning Science in East Asian Contexts.* Leiden: Brill, 2014b: 189–204.

Klein Godewijk, Berma (ed.), *Religion, International Relations, and Development Cooperation.* Wageningen: Wageningen Academic, 2007.

Latief, Hilman, 'Gulf Charitable Organizations in Southeast Asia', *Middle East Asia Project Bulletin*, 24 December 2014. Available at: www.mei.edu/content/map/gulf-charitable-organizations-southeast-asia (accessed 30 March 2015).

Mandaville, Peter, *Transnational Muslim Politics. Reimagining the Umma.* New York: Routledge, 2001.

Meyer, Harald (ed.), *Begriffsgeschichten aus den Ostasienwissenschaften* [Conceptual Histories from East Asian Studies]. München: iudicium, 2014.

Mielke, Katja and Anna Katharina Hornidge, 'Crossroads Studies: From Spatial Containers to Interactions in Differentiated Spatialities', *Crossroads Asia Working Paper Series* 15 (2014).

Mitchell, Timothy, *Rule of Experts. Egypt, Techno-Politics, Modernity.* Berkeley, CA: University of California Press, 2002a.

Mitchell, Timothy, 'The Middle East in the Past and Future of Social Science', in David L. Szanton (ed.), *The Politics of Knowledge: Area Studies and the Disciplines.* Berkeley: University of California Press, 2002b: 1–32. Available at: https://escholarship.org/uc/item/59n2d2n1 (accessed 13 March 2015).

Mohamad, Maznah and Soak Koon Wong, 'Malaysian culture, politics and identity: a reappraisal', in Maznah Mohamad and Soak Koon Wong (eds), *Risking Malaysia. Culture, Politics and Identity.* Bangi: Penerbit Universiti Kebansaan Malaysia, 2001: 23–41.

Nasr, Vali, *Islamic Leviathan. Islam and the Making of State Power,* Oxford: Oxford University Press, 2001.

Nawa, Katsuo, 'Triangulating the Nation-state through Translation: Some Reflections on "Nation", "Ethnicity", "Religion", and "Language" in Modern Japan, Germany, and Nepal', *Internationales Asienforum/International Quarterly on Asian Studies* 1–2 (2016): 11–31.

Needham, Joseph, *Time and Eastern Man.* London: Royal Anthropological Institute, 1965.

Needham, Joseph, *The Grand Titration: Science and Society in East and West.* London: Allen & Unwin, 1969.

Needham, Joseph, *Clarks and Craftsmen in China and the West.* Cambridge: Cambridge University Press, 1970.

Neelakantan, Vivek, 'Disease Eradication and National Reconstruction', *IIAS The Newsletter* 71 (2015): 4–5.

Noesselt, Nele, *Alternative Weltordnungsmodelle? IB-Diskurse in China* [Alternative Models of World Order? IR Discourses in China]. Wiesbaden: Springer VS, 2010.

Nozaki, Yoshiko, 'Japanese Politics and the History Textbook Controversy, 1982–2001', *International Journal of Educational Research* 37 (2002) 6: 603–22.

Petersen, Marie Juul, 'International Religious NGOS at the United Nations', *Journal of Humanitarian Assistance* (2010). Available at: https://sites.tufts.edu/jha/archives/847 (accessed 29 February 2016).

Petersen, Marie Juul, 'Islamizing Aid: Transnational Muslim NGOs after 9/11', *Voluntas. International Journal of Voluntary and Nonprofit Organizations* 23 (2012) 1: 126–55.

Pyenson, Lewis, 'Comparative History of Science', *History of Science* 40 (2002): 1–33.

Schäbler, Birgit, 'Das Studium der Weltregionen (Area Studies) zwischen Fachdisziplinen und der Öffnung zum Globalen: Eine wissenschaftliche Annäherung' [The Study of World Regions Between Disciplines and Opening to the Global: A Scholarly Approximation], in Birgit Schäbler (ed.), *Area Studies und die Welt. Weltregionen und Globalgeschichte* [Area Studies and the World. World Regions and Global History]. Vienna: Mandelbaum, 2007, 11–44.

Seale, Patrick, *The Struggle for Syria: A Study in Post-War Arab Politics, 1945–1958.* New Haven, CT: Yale University Press, 1987 [1965].

Shannon, Christopher, 'A World Made Safe for Differences: Ruth Benedict's *The Chrysanthmum and the Sword*', *American Quarterly* 47 (1995) 4: 659–80.

Shao, Binhong, *China and the World: Balance, Imbalance, Rebalance.* Leiden/Boston: Brill, 2013.

Tawara, Yoshifumi, '*'慰安婦' 問題と教科書攻撃. ドキュメント*'*['Ianfu' mondai to kyôkasho kôgeki. Dokyumento; The Issue of 'Comfort Women' and Attacks on Textbooks. A Document]*. Tokyo: Kobunken, 1997.

Thomas, Scott M., 'How Shall We Then Live? Rethinking Religion, Politics and Communities in an Age of Terrorism', in Berma Klein Goldewijk (ed.), *Religion, International Relations, and Development Cooperation.* Wageningen: Wageningen Academic, 2007: 57–78.

Tikekar, Maneesha, 'Islamizing a Muslim Nation: Politics of Identity, Legitimacy and Security in Pakistan', *International Centre for Ethnic Studies (ICES) Lecture/Discussion series*, Colombo, December 2005.

Van Asshe, Kristof and Anna-Katharina Hornidge, *Rural Development. Knowledge and Expertise in Governance.* Wageningen: Wageningen Academic, 2015.

Van Schendel, Willem, 'Geographies of Knowing. Geographies of Ignorance. Jumping Scale in Southeast Asia, *Environment and Planning D: Society and Space* 20 (2002): 647–68.

Zawawi Ibrahim (ed.), *Social Science and Knowledge in a Globalizing World*, Petaling Jaya: Strategic Information and Research Development Centre, 2012.

Zawawi Ibrahim and NoorShah M.S., 'Indigenising Knowledge and Social Science Discourses in the Periphery: Decolonising Malayness and Malay Underdevelopment', in Zawawi Ibrahim (ed.), *Social Science and Knowledge in a Globalizing World.* Petaling Jaya: Strategic Information and Research Development Centre, 2012: 165–200.

Part I

Alternative epistemologies

2 The Islamisation of Knowledge

This chapter introduces the epistemic project of an Islamisation of Knowledge (IoK), which started in the 1970s and is ongoing today. The IoK project serves as a case in point for an attempt to introduce an alternative way of knowledge production to an audience that had been predominantly socialised with scientific approaches developed in and emanating from non-Islamic parts of the (scholarly) world. The chapter embeds the IoK project historically and relates it to knowledge production and alternative epistemologies on a broader basis. As the capital 'K' suggests, the IoK project is a unique phenomenon of limited outreach. It is not to be equated with attempts to bestow all existing knowledge with a faith-based approach to understanding. I therefore distinguish between the capital and the small letter k. The heuristic merit of discussing the IoK project lies in the fact that it sparked huge waves of criticism as well as approval, inveigling various contemporaneous scholars to position themselves on the scale from pro to con. Geographically, Malaysia and Indonesia are at the centre of inspection.

The first part of the chapter introduces the epistemic project of an Islamisation of Knowledge (IoK), sometimes also termed Islamisation of Science, which started in the 1970s. The IoK project serves as an illustrative case for an attempt to submit an alternative – i.e. Islamic – approach to knowledge. The thoughts and visions of three protagonists of the project: Syed Muhammad Naguib Al-Attas, Isma'il Raji Al-Faruqi, and Seyyed Hossein Nasr are described. Another influential scholar introduced briefly is Fazlur Rahman. He is not associated directly with IoK or Science, but has provided intellectual inspiration for a whole range of prominent scholars in Malaysia and Indonesia by taking a clear stance vis-à-vis the role of Islam in the field of knowledge and education. On balance, Indonesia has been less affected by the ideas of IoK than Malaysia.

The IoK project was introduced to an intellectual audience that had been predominantly socialised with scientific approaches developed in and emanating from non-Islamic/Western parts of the (scholarly) world. Those who introduced IoK, however, were trained both in their indigenous (religious), local traditions and in Western science. The second part of the chapter embeds the IoK project historically and relates it to knowledge production and alternative epistemologies on a broader basis. As explained in the previous chapter, I do

DOI: 10.4324/9781315642123-3

not wish to follow up on the noble mission of defining the terms knowledge and science. The purpose of the present study is much more modest. I look at how the arrangement of knowledge in scientific disciplines and the forms of its retrieval (e.g. via Area Studies) may become fields for debate and re-thinking, particularly in the social sciences.

The IoK project suggests that the exercise of knowledge production itself, represented in science, has become polycentric – despite a still-hegemonic power of knowledge and styles of learning deriving from the West. A critique of the hegemonic power of Western science – social science being a particular case in point – surfaced in the course of a strong feeling in the global South that conventional development theory was undergoing a massive crisis, 'having reached an impasse', as Syed Farid Alatas[1] formulates. He continues: 'This state of affairs has brought forth various reactions from scholars in the Third World, including the call to the indigenization of the social sciences' (Alatas 1995: 90). The idea of indigenising encompassed the creation of a body of knowledge based on the historical experiences and cultural practices of local communities in non-Western parts of the world; it went far beyond 'testing' Western theories and methods elsewhere and adding specificities to them according to the local circumstances. It is important to mention, however, that indigenisation was not necessarily meant to reject Western science altogether – as certain currents of an Islamisation of knowledge indeed demanded. The unease felt outside the West emanated from an all-too-insouciantly held belief that the scientific theories developed there could be applied universally.

The fact that Western science had been accepted as universal and had not been questioned, was picked up by the Malaysian sociologist Syed Hussein Alatas in his writings on the 'mental captivity' or the 'captive mind', i.e. a state of mind dependent on what others had produced, conceptualised, and also institutionalised (Alatas 1972, 1974). The captive mind, in Hussein Alatas' view, is passive in the sense that it does not raise original problems and is rather imitative and uncritical than creative and sceptical. 'This', says Farid Alatas (1995: 90), 'is manifested in the areas of problem selection, choice of research methods, as well as the suggestion of solutions and policies'. There were also a lot of self-applied myths going along with the image of the captive mind – which inspired Syed Hussein Alatas later (1977) to speak of the 'myth of the lazy native'. That natives are by definition 'lazy' and that this opinion is probably a great myth, was carved in his treatise with a critical hint at the dominant development theory of the time (Alatas 1977). Myth and displaced perspectives notwithstanding, passiveness of the captive mind was apparent, as it 'also manifested at the metatheoretical and epistemological levels as well as at the levels of theory and substantive work' (Alatas 1995: 90). It is here where the IoK and science can be located: it seeks to provide an alternative comprehension of knowledge by looking from a different epistemological vantage point.

The IoK project can be regarded as a specific attempt at an indigenisation of the social sciences, although it also claims validity for the natural sciences and other fields. However, sharp judgements are fairly impossible since fine lines of distinction between indigenisation, Islamisation, de-colonisation, de-Westernisation and other forms of -isation are, in fact, hard to draw. Browsing through the biographies of proponents of one or the other -isation and the respective literature in an Islamic context, it becomes apparent that classifications have often been made on the basis of subjective impressions and have been driven to a large extent by individual authors' biographical circumstances and conditions for research. An example for the sometimes peculiar conflation of biographies is the relationship of two prominent scholars whose understandings of an Islamisation of knowledge differ to a considerable extent, but who were friends for decades. One is a scholar of South Asian origin Fazlur Rahman (1919–88), the other is a Southeast Asian scholar Syed Muhammad Naguib Al-Attas' (born 1931). Rahman's writings and papers in Urdu have been archived in the Fazlur Rahman Collection at Institute of Islamic Thought and Civilization (ISTAC) – a core institute of IoK in Malaysia founded by the Al-Attas. In a description of ISTAC, Mona Abaza (1999: 201f) writes that 'in 1996, the institute comprised 19 members of the Academic Staff, Iranian and Turkish national academics who studied at McGill (Canada) and Chicago (USA) Universities under the supervision of the late scholar Fazlur Rahman'. While these facts suggest that Al-Attas was particularly fond of Fazlur Rahman's intellectual qualities, descriptions of the two scholars' positioning towards IoK reveal that they were often far from agreement on each other's ideas. Syed Farid Alatas, for instance, has pointed out in an analysis of three promoters of an Islamisation of knowledge, among them Al-Attas, that Fazlur Rahman did not comply with an Islamisation of knowledge as proposed by scholars such as Al-Attas. Elaborating on the relationship between Islam and the social sciences, Alatas (1995: 99) stresses that Rahman 'conceive[s] of this relationship in terms radically different from the proponents of Islamization of knowledge'. Fazlur Rahman (1988) published critical perspectives on the IoK project, thereby communicating his own view of what an Islamisation of knowledge should entail if understood properly. There was little common ground between Al-Attas and Rahman with regard to the IoK project – irrespective of their perceived friendship.

Ideological contestations, combined with particular political leanings and connections, pervade the whole period of the establishment of institutes for the implementation of IoK and the dissemination of the project's ideas into the broader public. Abaza (1999: 201), for instance, underscored in her article that Al-Attas was always quick to point out that his thought project had nothing to do with the IoK project as performed by the International Islamic University Malaysia (IIUM) – of which, ironically, his ISTAC was initially a part.[2] At IIUM, the explicit rejection of certain approaches of IoK may also be related to the enmity between Al-Attas and his 'rival' Isma'il Raji Al-Faruqi[3] (discussed in more detail below), as well as to the personal animosity between Al-Attas and his brother Syed Hussein Alatas (Farid Altas' father), who ranked as the leading Malaysian sociologist.[4] Since Al-Faruqi (1921–86) is still highly respected at IIUM, it can be assumed that personal as well as political connections of individual scholars have played an important role in the implementation of an Islamisation of knowledge.

I will not immerse myself too deeply into the biographical conditionalities of the local, national, as well as trans- and international controversies around IoK. What I have chosen to reflect on is the IoK/Islamisation of Science approach of three authors who have become particularly influential in Malaysia and Indonesia: Syed Naguib (SN) Al-Attas, Isma'il Al-Faruqi, and Seyyed Hossein (SH) Nasr (born 1933). Al-Attas did most of his work on IoK while living in Malaysia, whereas Al-Faruqi and SH Nasr exerted their influence on students and followers in Southeast Asia from outside, either through their writing or through the academic guidance of students from the region. Al-Faruqi made considerable discursive inroads in Malaysia through the publications of his International Institute of Islamic Thought (IIIT). This was based in the USA but had a branch in Petaling Jaya near the Malaysian capital Kuala Lumpur. I came across IIIT publications from the USA in Kuala Lumpur bookstores even in the late 1990s, when the IoK had already peaked. The legacy of Al-Faruqi's approach to IoK in Southeast Asia can be traced, most notably in the curricular and organisational set-up of the International Islamic University Malaysia. Overall, however, intellectual influence is hard to measure; the researcher is bound to rely on qualitative rather than quantitative indicators. One qualitative method is to trace personal connections and networks. This is what I have chosen to do here – I am aware of the shortcomings of such an approach, but it gives merit to the cumulative strength of putting fragments of evidence together.

Islamisation of Knowledge with a capital 'K'

The Islamisation of Knowledge (IoK) emerged, as Mohammad Nejatullah Siddiqi puts it, as an 'offshoot' of Islamic revival, regeneration, renewal, and reform movements in various parts of the world (Siddiqi 2011: 16; see also Abaza 1994: 151–55). In the early to mid-twentieth century, influential Muslim leaders in Egypt (Hasan Al-Bannâ, 1906–49; Sayyid Qutb, 1906–66), India/Pakistan (Abu al-Â'lâ Maudûdî, 1903–79) or Indonesia (Mohammad Natsir, 1908–93) had attracted a huge following among both locals and foreigners. They themselves stood in a tradition of – albeit not always in full agreement with – prominent Muslim reformers of the past, such as Jamâl ad-Dîn Al-Afghânî (1839–97), Muhammad 'Abduh (1849–1905), Rashîd Ridâ (1865–1935) or Muhammad Iqbâl (1877–1938). Al-Bannâ founded the Muslim Brotherhood, Maudûdî's theocratic thoughts became formative for the movement Jamâ'at Al-Islâmi (JI), and Mohammad Natsir, who was also Indonesia's prime minister from 1950 to 1951, left his imprint on many scholars who rejected the constitutional separation of church/religion and state. The revivalist intellectuals of the time aimed to restore Islam's and Muslims' moral strength and power – particularly in view of the loss of status that colonial, secular and Kemalist currents had caused to Islam as a world religion. In post-World War II and post-colonial times, their thoughts continued to exert influence among scholars of Islam. Coupled with concurrent critiques of Western models of development and science as embodied, for instance, in the above-mentioned indigenisation of the social sciences, the revivalist approach fell on fertile ground. Consequently, restoring an Islamic order was not an exclusively political task, but was also targeted at basic institutions of human learning and value internalisation – at *tarbiyya* (تربية) in the classical sense of 'education'. 'Understandably', writes Siddiqi, 'the educational agenda presented to Muslims [by the 'post-colonial' intellectuals; C.D.] was prefaced by a strong criticism of Western systems' (Siddiqi 2011: 17). Technology and the natural sciences as its base was conceptualised as serving the revival of Islam and framed in the idea of an epistemological unity between reason and faith (Siddiqi 2011: 17).

One of the first publications carrying the paradigmatic phrase of an Islamisation of Knowledge in its title was Isma'il Raji Al-Faruqi's booklet *Islamization of Knowledge: General Principles and Work Plan* (Al-Faruqi 1982). Al-Faruqi (1921–86) was a scholar of Islam and comparative religions, and a scholar-activist who sought to put his ideas into practice. Trained at US and Canadian universities, he co-founded the International Institute of Islamic Thought (IIIT) in Herndon, Virginia. Together with his wife Lamya, the Al-Faruqis became inspiring minds for a whole generation of young Muslims who subscribed to the idea of an Islamisation not only of knowledge but of all dimensions of life, including politics and economics. However, Malaysian scholar Syed Naguib Al-Attas, who had begun working on knowledge, education and Islam in the 1970s, accused Isma'il Al-Faruqi of having appropriated his ideas of an Islamisation of Knowledge (capital 'K'). Al-Attas (1993: xii, fn 4) had used the phrase in a keynote address to the World Conference on Muslim Education held in Mecca in 1977. He had then made his thoughts known to Al-Faruqi and left him with a book manuscript, expecting it to be published in the USA with Al-Faruqi's help. As nothing had happened and he has never seen his manuscript again, Al-Attas concluded that Al-Faruqi 'was betraying the trust I had put in him concerning the authorship of the seminal ideas contained in the book' (Al-Attas 1993: xii, fn 4). Trying to prevent intellectual theft, Al-Attas had his opus published in Kuala Lumpur in 1978 (under the title *Islam and Secularism*, discussed below). His anger about Al-Faruqi's behaviour is nonetheless explicitly articulated the preface to the second printing of *Islam and Secularism*:

> There is no doubt that this book [i.e. the one he had handed over] and the book elaborating on the concept of education and Islâm have been appropriated by al-Faruqi for the convening of the seminar at Islamabad, to which I was obviously not welcomed and after which his *Islamization of Knowledge*, printed in Maryland, U.S.A. in 1982, appeared.
>
> (Al-Attas 1993: xii, fn 4)

Al-Faruqi had presented at the same conference in Mecca and talked about an Islamisation of social sciences (Alatas 1995: 95). Neither motion was entirely innovative, though, since the Iranian scholar Seyyed Hossein Nasr had published his philosophical reflections on an Islamisation of Science in 1975.

The *political* motivation of the movements that emanated from the intellectual mentors around Al-Faruqi, Al-Attas and others became epitomised in a provocative question of the time: Did Muslims want to be the subjects of history or merely its objects? (Siddiqi 2011: 17f). The phrase was appealing to activists, especially to the Muslim youth. The *epistemic* endeavour underlying the plan of an Islamisation of knowledge was more complex and involved 'subjects' not just as activists but first and foremost as thinkers. The term 'scholar-activist' matches this combination well. The epistemic project encompassed, among others, the establishment of an Islamic University, which was seen as the necessary physical site where key concepts 'pertaining to the nature and purpose of knowledge from the Islamic viewpoint' formed the basis an Islamic system of education (Al-Attas 1993: 160). Such a university was set up in Malaysia in 1983 by the Malaysian government (i.e. the IIUM), its establishment relying upon intensive lobbying by Al-Faruqi and leaders of the Islamic Youth Movement ABIM (Angkatan Belia Islam Malaysia). Al-Attas distanced himself from this IIUM initiative and founded his own institute, the ISTAC, in 1987 – having secured the necessary political backing. His intended distinction from IIUM went so far as claiming autonomy for ISTAC, which had initially been attached to the Islamic University. ISTAC was granted this autonomy in 1991 (until 2002), again due to political support for the project. In the following section, I summarise Al-Attas' ideas in the pursuit of an IoK and why he considered it, in this frame of thought, important to contrapose Islam and secularism. After that, I continue with a brief description of Al-Faruqi's conception of IoK and proceed to Seyyed Hossein Nasr, whose vision of a *scientia sacra* (sacred science) influenced both Al-Attas and Al-Faruqi and received strong attention from, among others, renowned Indonesian Muslim scholars such as Nurcholish Majid and Komaruddin Hidayat. Fazlur Rahman is then introduced in a separate section.

Naguib Al-Attas: Islam and secularism

The key concepts for an Islamic system of education in Al-Attas' sense are: religion (دين *dîn*), man (انسان *insân*), knowledge (علم و معرفة *'ilm* and *ma'rifah*), wisdom (حكمة *hikmah*), justice (عدل *'adl*), right action (عمل كأدب *'amal* as *adab*) and university (كلية جامعة *kulliyyah-jâmi'ah*) (Al-Attas 1993: 160). These are juxtaposed to the key concepts identified as concepts of Western knowledge, in fact of Western culture and civilisation; which are:

> Reliance upon the powers of human reason alone to guide man through life; adherence to the validity of the dualistic vision of reality and truth; affirmation of the reality of the evanescent-aspect of existence projecting a secular worldview; espousal of the doctrine of humanism; emulation of the allegedly universal reality of drama and tragedy in the spiritual, or

> transcendental, or inner life of man, making drama and tragedy real and dominant elements in human nature and existence.
>
> (Al-Attas 1993: 137)

According to Al-Attas, these key concepts are moulding 'the Western concept of knowledge and the direction of its purpose, the formulation of its content and the systematization of its dissemination' (Al-Attas 1993: 137). They have to be isolated from the body of knowledge in order to arrive at an Islamised knowledge which is not infused 'with the character and personality of Western culture and civilization' (Al-Attas 1993: 162).

Syed Naguib Al-Attas is seen as the one who elevated the Islamisation of knowledge from a work plan to an epistemic project – Islamisation of Knowledge. His publication *Islam and Secularism* from 1978, which advanced to becoming a core reference for the IoK project, is a compilation of writings and public lectures conducted between 1974 and 1977 (Al-Attas 1993: Author's note to the first edition).

Knowledge in Al-Attas conception derives from God:

> Since we have said that all knowledge comes from God and is interpreted by the soul through its spiritual and physical faculties, it follows that the most suitable epistemological definition would be that knowledge, with reference to God as being its origin, is the arrival (husûl) in the soul of the meaning (ma'nâ) of a thing or an object of knowledge; and that with reference to the soul as being its interpreter, knowledge is the arrival (wusûl) of the soul at the meaning of a thing or an object of knowledge.
>
> (Al-Attas 1993: 163)

Knowledge for Al-Attas is transcendental and ordered, in fact it is hierarchical. It is an attempt to formulate a conception of science that does not negate but rather appreciates the spiritual dimension of science. 'Secular' knowledge in this view is based on this-worldly humanism and the physical cosmos of 'rationality'; it has produced a desacralisation of science constructed along the lines of a monolithic and 'universal' science. Al-Attas attacks Western or secular materialism, wrapping his criticism in an intellectual concern for ultimate moral and ethical norms. Abaza categorises Al-Attas' approach to an Islamisation of knowledge as a 'de-Westernization of knowledge' and points to his habit of writing in English as a wayto convey his thoughts to a Western audience in particular, and to demonstrate that ISTAC is an alternative institution to Western knowledge institutions (Abaza 1999: 211).

In the context of knowledge acquisition, Al-Attas lends particular devotion to 'intuition'. His recognition of intuition is succinctly captured in his ISTAC publication *The Intuition of Existence*:

> The metaphysical vision of the world and the ultimate reality envisaged in Islam is quite different from that projected by the statements and general

> conclusions of modern philosophy and science. We maintain that all knowledge of reality and of truth, and the projection of a true vision of the ultimate nature of things is originally derived through the medium of intuition. The intuition that we mean cannot simply be reduced to that which operates solely at the physical level of discursive reason based upon sense-experience, for since we affirm in man the possession of physical as well as intelligential or spiritual powers and faculties which refer back to the spiritual entity, sometimes called intellect, or heart, or soul, or self, it follows that man's rational, imaginary and empirical existence must involve both the physical and spiritual levels.
>
> (Al-Attas 1990: 1)

Intuition is a medium with both a physical and, more importantly, a spiritual dimension; it is those two together which enable man to arrive at knowledge. The intellect is a spiritual entity, which Al-Attas renders as a synonym to heart, self or soul. In SH Nasr's thoughts, to which we attend below, the intellect (*intellectus)* is an important concept; it is similarly conceptualised. For both Nasr and Al-Attas, Islamic knowledge or science is an alternative mode of viewing reality which includes metaphysical control over the process of knowing and reasoning. 'Syed Muhammad Naguib al-Attas' philosophy and methodology of education', relates Muhammad Khalid Masud (2005: 373), 'aims at an Islamization of the mind, body and soul'. Leaving the soul aside is secular; hence secularism is to reject in an Islamised framework of education. What exactly this means is best described by looking at Al-Attas' conception of secular as opposed to Islamic knowledge.

Islam and secularism

As Masud points out, discourses on secularism in the Western world are different from those in the Muslim word:

> A critical study of discourses on secularism in Muslim countries cannot be modelled on the Western experience because religion and religious values have different political and cultural trajectories in the Muslim experience.
>
> (Masud 2005: 381)

Against the backdrop of this factual condition, the discourse on secularism is highly contested and has been discussed by various Muslim thinkers and Islamic scholars (علماء *'ulamâ'*). According to Masud, the cardinal fault which brings the religion of Islam and secularism into direct opposition, however, was the ideologisation of both. Since he describes this observation succinctly, it merits quoting his inference at length:

> Secularism has been constructed and deconstructed in the Muslim world in response to diverse experiences. A focus on the deconstruction

> of secularism as an ideology in Islamic political thought in modern times was the result of several factors, including failure of modernist and secular regimes, threat of communism during the Cold War and recent threat of Western hegemony. Islam was constructed as an ideology in the sense that it was presented as a natural, historical and eternal system. Its construction as an ideology protected it from other ideologies because an ideology must be exclusive to all others. This strategy was useful against the threat of Communism. The same strategy has been used against the threat of secularism. Secularism was part of Communist ideology; hence, its refutation was also strategized by constructing it as an ideology. Once a threat is ideologized, it is easy to project it as a counter religion to Islam.
>
> (Masud 2005: 381)

Al-Attas is seen by Masud as having ideologised secularism and Islam to an extent that allows him to contrapose them in terms of their actualisation. For Al-Attas, both Islam and secularism are absolute in the sense that they 'project a closed worldview and an absolute set of values in line with an ultimate historical purpose that has a final significance for men' (Masud 2005: 374). As in the conception of knowledge introduced above – all knowledge comes from God and the reliance on human reason is misleading – the mundane life is also governed by divine authority. No political power or organisation can claim legitimacy when it does not obey and comply with divine law. In this regard, secularism is un-Islamic because it does not recognise the authority of God, and therefore has to be rejected by all means. Relating this extreme refutation of any compatibility between Islam and secularism to the realm of education, an Islamised mind in Al-Attas' line of thinking is one that believes in a God-given order behind everything. In short, worldly life in any regard and every dimension is theologised. It is the rejection of divine authority and spiritual/metaphysical power that renders secular institutions of education dysfunctional and inacceptable for the pursuit of Islamised knowledge. According to Farid Alatas, Al-Attas considers the 'Islamization of knowledge [...] a liberation of knowledge from interpretations based on secular ideology' (Alatas 1995: 96). The comprehensiveness of Islam extends to all spheres of life including politics and economic activity. I will discuss how this belief system siplls over into politics and economics in the next chapter.

Muhammad Khalid Masud (2005: 376, 382) typologises representatives of the above line of thought as Islamists who also deny the compatibility of Islam and modernity. Among the representatives of the other 'camp', i.e. those who do not see secularism and modernity as totally opposed to Islam, he lists Muhammad Iqbâl and Fazlur Rahman. Again, it is interesting to note that although Al-Attas' and Rahman's thinking is rated as differing in very fundamental ways, a special relationship between them prevailed as seen in Al-Attas' hosting of the Fazlur Rahman Collection and his admission of quite a group of students of the latter at ISTAC.

Isma'il Al-Faruqi: The tauhîdic worldview

Isma'il Al-Faruqi had a slightly different vision of the paradigm of knowledge in Islam and its role in Islamic education. His overarching aim was to integrate the existing dominant body of knowledge into the corpus of Islamic legacy, or, in other words, to integrate 'acquired' and 'revealed' knowledge. This proposition entailed a recasting and streamlining of all disciplines, including economics, engineering, the natural science disciplines, medicine, law, architecture, mathematics, information technology and the like. By recasting and streamlining, Al-Faruqi meant to bring these disciplines in line with Islamic principles, for instance those practiced in Islamic banking rejecting interest and usury. Al-Faruqi strove to implement his vision of the Islamisation of Knowledge in the International Institute of Islamic Thought and Civilization (IIIT), which he founded in 1981 in Virginia, USA.

The core term of Al-Faruqi's version of IoK is *tauhîd* (توحيد unity, also spelled *tawhid*). With regard to education, Al-Faruqi demands that each discipline be 'remolded to incorporate the relevance of Islam along a triple axis that constitutes the concept of *tawhid* (unity of God), that is, the unity of knowledge, the unity of life, and the unity of history' (Alatas 1995: 96). It is clear from his concept that the understanding of unity extends to the realm of creation and truth; there is only one truth and only one creator. Human beings live to serve this unity, which means that the 'process of the Islamization of knowledge requires the subjugation of the theory, method, principles and goals of knowledge' to this unity to make man understand his *raison d'être* accordingly (Alatas 1995: 97). Any power operative in nature beside God is to be eliminated (Ebrahim 2012). In his book *Al Tawhid. Its Implication for Thought and Life* from 1982, Al-Faruqi describes the centrality of the unity of God and elevates the concept to man's normative guideline:

> God as normativeness means that He is the Being Who commands. His movements, thoughts, and deeds are all realities beyond doubt; but every one of these, insofar as man conceives of it, is for him a value, an ought-to-be, even when, in the case where it is already realized, no ought-to-do flows from it. Besides being metaphysical, God's ultimacy is not, for the Muslim, isolable from or emphasizable at the cost of the axiological. Were we to allow the Muslim here to use the category of "the value of knowledge," he would say the value of the metaphysical is that it may exercise its imperativeness, its moving appeal or normativeness.
>
> (Al-Faruqi 1982: 2)

Al-Faruqi fills this normativeness with five principles: duality (God and non-God; creator and creature); ideationality (ideational relationship between creator and creature or rather the two orders of reality emanating from it); teleology (teleological, purposive nature of the cosmos); capacity of man (for moral action) and malleability (i.e. transformability) of nature; responsibility and judgement (moral obligation of man requires responsibility; judgement as the consummation of responsibility). These five principles constitute the core of *tauhîd*, the quintessence of Islam, and the core of all revelations that came from heaven (Al-Faruqi 1992: 9–15). 'Naturally, all Islamic culture is built upon them, and together they form the core of *al-tawhid*, knowledge, personal and social ethics, esthetics and Muslim life, and action throughout history' (Al-Faruqi 1992: 15). Man has the moral obligation to serve this unity (*tauhîd*) and this view should not only be internalised by the individual but also applied to all dimensions of education and learning.

For the lay person, Al-Faruqi's stress of normativeness does not seem to be too far apart from the normative framework of Al-Attas, who subjugated all worldly life under divine law. For experts, a multitude of open and subtle differences surface in the comparison of both scholars' approaches – and they have indeed led to diverse visions of how to implement an Islamic education policy at institutions of learning such as universities. It seems that Al-Attas has been very upset by the contents of publications on the Islamisation of diverse disciplines, by authors from Al-Faruqi's IIIT in Virginia. He considered them a watered-down attempt at Islamising knowledge, lacking in substance and erudition. With a hint at Al-Faruqi's apparent intent to relegate him to the backseat of public international fora, Al-Attas finds that too many vulgarised forms of appropriation of his work have surfaced since 1982: 'plagiarists and pretenders as well as well as ignorant imitators' who encouraged the rise of mediocrity (Al-Attas 1993: xii). On the political and institutional turf, Al-Attas seems to have lost the ideological battle against Al-Faruqi, at least in Malaysia, where the ISTAC became (re-)incorporated into the IIUM as a postgraduate centre in 2002 and is subject to the university's rules and regulations. Another noteworthy anecdote is that at McGill University in Canada, where Al-Fauqi, Al-Attas and Fazlur Rahman all spent time teaching and studying, Al-Faruqi and Rahman seem to have worked together closely. Imtiyaz Yusuf (2012: 3) relates that Al-Faruqui, Rahman, and SH Nasr were *the* three prominent scholars of Islamic studies ('Islamics') in the West in the 1960s, when this field of studies was just about to gain momentum in university research. 'Each of the three men', Yusuf writes in a Festschrift[5] for the late Al-Faruqi, 'made their specialized contributions' to the establishment of this field of study:

> Fazlur Rahman in Islamic thought, Seyyed Hossein Nasr in Islamic mysticism, and Isma'il al Faruqi towards the study of Islam as an area in the academic area of the study of religion and also the Islamization of Knowledge.
> (Yusuf 2012: 3)

The name Al-Attas is not mentioned once in this regard. In view of Al-Faruqi's students who became internationally prominent writers and intellectuals (John Esposito and Imtiyaz Yusuf among numerous others), he has definitely left a stronger impact on the scholars, scholar-activists and activists adhering to his thought than Al-Attas. Moreover, it can be concluded from the number of institutes of research and higher learning that Al-Faruqi managed to establish in different countries of the world (USA, Malaysia, Pakistan and others) that his ideas recorded a bigger transregional spread than those of Al-Attas. The same can probably be said for Al-Attas in comparison to Seyyed Hossein Nasr, whose ideas I will briefly summarise in the following paragraphs.

Seyyed Hossein Nasr: Sacred science

Seyyed Hossein Nasr, a born Iranian (born 1933), left his country after Ayatollah Khomeini's revolution and migrated to the USA, where he had previously been educated for some time. He advocated what became known as the Islamisation of Science, but he is, as we have seen, frequently associated as a main representative of the Islamisation of Knowledge.[6] His thought and writings exerted influence on numerous scholars around the world. I introduce parts of his ideational framework because he was not only a direct communication partner of Isma'il Al-Faruqi and Fazlur Rahman, but because he, too, left considerable traces in Indonesia and Malaysia.

Nasr's œvre is composed of two thematic currents, one relating to the field of Islamic science and the other, considered his main work, to the writings on sacred science or *scientia sacra*. Both currents are rooted in his perception of traditional (e.g. Islamic) science in the function of assisting the intellect in understanding the universe. The basic, general idea pervading Nasr's work is the presupposition that Islam is a comprehensive order for both individuals and for society. Against this background, he tries to examine the foundations underlying the formation of Islamic science. Modern science ('modern' referring to the period after Renaissance) to him is in crisis, or more explicitly, shows deficiencies because it negates the essential aspect of the sacred in science. Science is neither a neutral nor a genuinely Western phenomenon, and once this premise is accepted, it is possible to elaborate on Islamic science. Nasr aligns himself with Al-Attas and Al-Faruqi in the struggle to resuscitate the sense of the sacred (or the divine, the metaphysical). He stresses this with the notion of the *intellectus*. The *intellectus* or intellect, that is the vision of the realities of life, has in Nasr's view, become dull in modern science. This dullness signifies the condition and the development of a modern society that has lost its divine vision. *Intellectus*, as far as Nasr is concerned, is above reason and can receive knowledge directly (Nasr 1993: 4). The intellect connotes the capacity of the heart, the only faculty in human being which can perceive images of God in the universe (Nasr 1981a: 182). Because the modern intellect is dysfunctional in this respect, all knowledge gained by modern mankind is no more than fragmented knowledge, not a horizon of knowledge which will bring about the wisdom to behold the essence of the universe as a single unity, as a mirror of God's unity and almighty power (Nasr 1975).

From the metaphysical point of view, Seyyed Hossein Nasr argues that there was a true relationship between knowledge and being in traditional, religion-affined science. It was the process of secularisation and humanism in the Western world that triggered the process of the separation of knowing from being (Nasr 1981b: vii). Secularised reason, however, cannot cast the full effect of knowing on human studies. All subjects studied using merely reason as a secularised instrument turn out to be void of sacred qualities (Nasr 1981b: 42). Nasr envisages modern science as reducing the notion of quality to quantity and the metaphysically essential to the material sense (Nasr 1984: 523f). In this view, modern science neglects the essential dimensions of science and knowing, which are, in contrast, of particular relevance in traditional science – such as science in the tradition of Islam. Nasr depicts the current condition of modern man as having lost the sense of sacred, whereas in traditional science, this sense was omnipresent:

> The main difference between the traditional sciences and modern science [...] lies in the fact that in the first case the profane and purely human remain always marginal and the sacred central, whereas in modern science the profane has become central and certain intuitions and discoveries which despite everything reveal the Divine Origin of the natural world have become so peripheral that they are usually hardly ever recognized for what they are despite the exceptional views of certain scientists.
>
> (Nasr 1984: 520)

The loss of the sense of the sacred in Western civilisation brings about the segmentation of science into various disciplines and to the separation of science and ethics – which has generated a crisis in the modern world (Nasr 1993: 82). As a consequence of this approach, Nasr argues, logic and mathematics have become alienated from the sacred even though they are used as the main agency of the desacralisation of the process of knowing. For this reason, the process of desacralisation in the West has been marked, among other symptoms, by the diminution of the intellect to reason, and to a limiting of intelligence to mere cunning and cleverness (Nasr 1981b: 45).

As in SN Al-Attas' conception of knowledge, science in Nasr's conception is hierarchical, i.e. subject to a higher order. Without the notion of hierarchy in science, scientific theories and discoveries grow to be merely facts, neglecting the truths that belong to the higher order. In this line of thought, modern science is uncomplete: it deals with certain parts of reality while refuting others. Traditional civilisations emphasise the hierarchy of realities, the primacy of the spiritual over the material, the sacred character of the cosmos, and the unity of knowledge and interrelatedness of beings (Nasr 1993: 75ff). At the epistemological level, traditional science is founded on revelation, intellect, and reason (Nasr 1984: 523f). The importance of revelation and intellect implies that the process of knowing in civilisations that cherish religion is not estranged from the sacred, and human creativity is ingrained in – and therefore should not be separated from – the divine order:

> All of these factors [i.e. the neglect of cosmological order and concentration on human reason in modern science; C.D.] have contributed to forcing a

> re-examination of this most basic problem of the relation between religion and science which encompasses the question of the correct rapport between man and nature not to speak of the ethical implications of so many aspects of the applications of modern science to the life of human beings and their society.
>
> (Nasr 1984: 520)

The required re-examination of the relation between religion and science can be imagined in an Islamisation of knowledge. Nasr, therefore, is truly a forerunner of the IoK project in that he demanded the 'sacred' to be re-integrated into the concept of science – in fact of knowledge. It is of particular interest to investigate the reception of Nasr's ideas in the context of intellectual discourse in Indonesia. As mentioned above, it is hard to measure how the thought of a scholar like Seyyed Hossein Nasr interacted with the ideas of other intellectuals. The place of Nasr's ideas and perspectives can be gauged, however, in the explicit signs of their acceptance and appreciation that have emanated in the intellectual landscape. Asfa Widiyanto, for example, has scrutinised the place of Nasr's ideas in the thought structure of two famous Indonesian intellectuals, namely Nurcholish Madjid – a PhD student of Fazlur Rahman and founder of Paramadina University – and Komaruddin Hidayat, who became the rector of the State Islamic University in Jakarta in 2006 (Widiyanto 2005). Widiyanto's assessment is revealing in that it records the traces of Nasr's thought meticulously. For our purpose, it is sufficient to notice that SH Nasr as well as SN Al-Attas and Al-Faruqi exerted considerable influence on both the intellectual discourse and the institutional manifestations of it in various places. From there, the project of Islamisation trickled down to utterly profane layers of daily life such as consumerism (see Chapter 4). As for the epistemic project, represented by Islamisers like Al-Attas, Al-Faruqi or Nasr, the alternative path proposed is on a higher – metaphysical – level of experience.

Fazlur Rahman: Islam and modernity

As a vital inspirational source for many of his disciples in Southeast Asia, Fazlur Rahman deserves special attention in the context of an Islamisation of knowledge. Rahman was an academic instructor not only to several of ISATC's young visiting researchers, but also to leading figures in Islamic education and idea givers for whole generations of Muslims. This was particularly so in Indonesia, where his significant influence was admitted by almost every of my interlocutors who were consulted for an assessment of the IoK project's standing in the discursive terrain of Islam and knowledge. Fazlur Rahman was always mentioned with unmistakable respect, whereas the Iok project evoked a sceptical mien or a benevolent smile at best. Being far from representative, the reactions I got nevertheless reveal that the big names in the kaleidoscope of renowned scholars of Islam in Indonesia were not convinced about the project's epistemic merit and feasibility. Rather than Al-Attas or Al-Faruqi, Seyyed Hossein Nasr and even more so Fazlur Rahman were the names coming up in conversation; often, both being mentioned in the same breath. Komaruddin Hidayat, Nurcholosh Madjid, Syafi 'i Ma'arif and Abdurrahman Wahid are apparently merely the tip of an iceberg of famous scholars with deep commitment to Rahman (and Nasr).[7]

The appreciation of Fazlur Rahman's thought is to a great deal related to his critical stocktaking of the state of Islamic education in the Muslim world of the 1960s and 1970s, and his liberal ideas on the potential to achieve a 'genuinely democratic interpretation of Islam' (Rahman 1982: 128). While he was outspoken in regard to Western political hegemony in world affairs – from which the 'Muslim lands' should be liberated – he saw the need for the Muslim societies of his time to rethink the issue of education and reconstruct their societies (Rahman 1982: 84f). To him, Islamic education was to get rid of the hard crust of tradition, especially in Indonesia. 'Like Pakistan and Turkey, and almost at the same time, Indonesia had to make a fresh start on Islamic education along modern lines' (Rahman 1982: 126). But the problem of Indonesia, as of all other major Muslim countries for the postcolonial decades, was the lack of adequate personnel for teaching and research. The 'Azharisation'[8] of Islamic education in many countries, to which I will return in Chapter 3, prevented a creative reconstruction of the field. Tolerance of non-Islamic religions coming from within Islam itself formed one element of such a creative reconstruction (cf. Rahman 1982: 128f). Accordingly, he positioned himself as very critical towards the Islamisation of Knowledge.

In Fazlur Rahman's thought, man's intellect and reason enable him to discover knowledge (علم *'ilm*) and to go on doing so. What is not developed properly, however, is a fully adequate sense of responsibility. This applies, in particular, to the sense of moral responsibility. In this regard, man fails most of the time: '[W]hile *'ilm* is there, the sense of responsibility fails. Most of the time when a crucial test comes, man is unable to discharge his trust [which has been offered by God to the entire creation; C.D.]' (Rahman 1988: 4). The central question in view of those entertaining the project of an Islamisation of Knowledge (capital 'K'), then, is how to make man responsible. Interestingly, Rahman includes himself in the group of 'those who entertain this subject, *Islamization of Knowledge*':

> The feeling is that the modern world has been developed and structured upon knowledge which cannot be considered Islamic. Actually, what we should be saying is that the modern world has misused knowledge; that there is nothing wrong with knowledge, but that it has simply been misused.
> (Rahman 1988: 4)

Examples for the misuse of knowledge are plenty, one is the invention of the atomic bomb, the technology for which (generation of nuclear power) is a great success but the effect of which is a burden for mankind. The fatal consequences of the invention should have been thought through before. Using this example as a metaphor, Rahman reasons that an Islamisation of Knowledge is bound to fail when the very tradition of Islamic scholarship itself is not critically thought through before bashing all other (and especially Western) knowledge. This demand to first look into Islam's own tradition merges with his strongest criticism of IoK: Declaring what has to be rejected from other knowledge traditions before having scrutinised one's own. The guiding principles for coming to a point in view of this task are all provided in the Qur'ân. In Fazlur Rahman's words:

> [U]nless we have examined our own tradition very well, in the light of the Qur'ân, we cannot proceed further with Islamic thought. This is because we must have certain criteria to go by and the criteria must obviously come initially from the Qur'ân. First, we must examine our own tradition in the light of these criteria and principles and then critically study the body of knowledge created by modernity. We must also remember that knowledge in Islam exist in order to enable us to act, to change the current events in the world. Islam is an action-oriented book, par excellence. We have to seriously cultivate this procedure and first judge our own tradition as to what is right and what is wrong. Then we must judge the Western tradition.
>
> (Rahman 1988: 11)

It is perspicuous that Fazlur Rahman is not rejecting the Islamisation of Knowledge per se, but that he wants man to use his intellect and reason (عقل *'aql*) to turn to the Qur'ân for guidance on the definition of right and wrong. In other words, instead of going creating Islamic knowledge, he favours the creation of Islamic minds (Rahman 1988: 10). His former student, Indonesian scholar and long-time leader of the mass organisation Muhammadiyah, Syafi 'i Ma'arif, hints at this idea when he disapproves of the IoK project but believes that 'you can Islamise the mind and that is what has to be done'.[9] I will look at other critical stances towards the IoK project in the following section of this chapter.

Evaluations of the Islamisation of Knowledge project[10]

In historical perspective, the drive towards alternative ways of thinking and looking at reality was neither entirely new nor peculiar to Islam. Critical observers like Abaza relate it to

> various modern religious groups which have witnessed revivalism, be they Christian, Jewish or Buddhist, the German intellectual romantics, who, up to the Second World War, advocated similar claims concerning intuitive knowledge and alternative cognitive forms of knowledge. Elitist theories of knowledge, mystical and restricted intellectual circles as advocated by al-Attas, are in fact not restricted to Islam. They rather bear a certain similarity

> with Stefan Georg poetical and mystical circles at the beginning of this century in Germany.
>
> (Abaza 1999: 215)

Abaza's scepticism towards the peculiarity of the IoK endeavour is akin to Farid Alatas' conclusion that the project is not as ground-breaking as is claimed by its proponents, because there is no such thing as Islamising science. In asking 'What are the ways in which a discipline or a field of knowledge that we call social science is defined by Islam in such a way that this field takes on an Islamic or Islamized character?', Alatas brings the central question to the point (Alatas 1995: 98). Is it the methodological approach of, for instance, the Islamic techniques of *tafsîr* and *ta'wîl* (exegesis and commentary) that are applied to interpret the Qur'ân?[11] Alatas doubts it and ponders further in speculating if the exercise of Islamising meant that 'the social sciences are to be defined by Islamic philosophy, that is, Islamic metaphysics and epistemology as they evolved among the Arabs, Persians, Turks, Berbers, Indians, and Malays since the second century A.H' (Alatas 1995: 98). If this were so, Alatas reasons that this 'is insufficient grounds to warrant our reference to such social science as Islamic' because:

> Islamic philosophy affirms the existence of an external world and the possibility of knowledge thereof, and it is this affirmation which makes social science possible. But such an affirmation is common to many philosophical systems and their impression upon the social sciences is of a general nature, not leaving a peculiarly Indian, Greek or Islamic mark on the social sciences.
>
> (Alatas 1995: 98)

The sceptical judgements of social scientists such as Abaza and Alatas should not lead us, however, to do away with project IoK altogether as a temporary intellectual fashion lacking substance whenever the fabric of its products is scrutinised. Farid Alatas himself has elaborated on ways in which social science can be Islamic. 'Social science theories, concepts and methodologies', he writes, 'need to go beyond bringing Muslims and their problems to the foreground' (Alatas 1987: 63). Instead, what is required is:

> systematic bodies of knowledge based on the various Islamic cultures in the same way that the Western social sciences are based on Western culture, especially Western history and philosophy.
>
> (Alatas 1987: 63)

What 'makes social science Islamic is not', in Alatas' view, 'its subject-matter but rather the sources from which its concepts and theories are drawn' (Alatas 1987: 68). He illustrates this by an example of Ibn Khaldûn's political theory. In relating Ibn Khaldûn's study of the concepts of *khalifa* and *mulk* (two types of rulers/political institutions in Islamic history)[12] to Max Weber's legal–rational authority and patrimonialism, he finds that both scholars' reflections are reinforcing each other (Alatas 1987: 65–68). The Islamic notion in Ibn Khaldûn's analysis is that he refers both to the Qur'ân and to Islamic history as his sources, which Weber unsurprisingly does not. Hence, in Alatas' reasoning, Islamic social science can be practiced, but in a much more reconciliatory manner than that proposed in the IoK concept described above. For scholars like Alatas, Western methodology and theory are not axiomatically rejectable because they have diverted from the sacred, the metaphysical or the divine (order).

In fact, the repercussions of the IoK project in the broader international institutional landscape are remarkable and reach beyond the social sciences. The question of success, progress or failure in view of the original goal pursued with IoK put aside, it cannot be denied that the establishment of institutions of knowledge received high-level backing from various corners. In Malaysia, not only SN Al-Attas and his ISTAC, but also the IIUM with its leaning towards Al-Faruqi's version of IoK enjoyed significant political (and financial) backing. In Indonesia, where the New Order regime under president Suharto (1965–98) subdued any noteworthy political influence of Islamic organisations until the 1980s, the intellectual discourse of Islamisation and Islamic resurgence (as a notion more commonly used to designate the demand by Muslim activists to adopt Islam as a 'way of life') nonetheless diffused civil society. Even more remarkable, the repression of political Islam had the effect of sparking off a vibrant Islamic intellectual milieu as Islamic activists moved underground and into the campuses. Through the big two mass organisations Nahdlatul Ulama and Muhammadiyah, but also through other currents associated with intellectual authorities such as Nurcholish Madjid or Komaruddin Hidayat, Islamic views and Islamic values made considerable inroads into Indonesian education under the label of 'cultural Islam'. 'Fast-forward to the fall of Suharto in the late 1990s, this vibrant 'apoliticized' milieu quickly morphed and surfaced as a dynamic terrain of Islamic activism comprising groups with multiple shades of doctrinal affiliations', writes Joseph Chiong Liow (2016). The 'cultural' swiftly transformed into political considerations. 'Many of these [groups] were reformist and liberal groups that embraced democracy and human rights as wholeheartedly as they did Islamic culture and tradition' (Liow 2016).

A number of institutions promoting Islamic values in the natural sciences were set up in different countries under the aegis of the Organisation of Islamic Conference (now Organisation of Islamic Cooperation, OIC) (Siddiqi 2011: 30). Quite different from today, there was no internet when the idea of the IoK was launched (Siddiqi 2011: 32). Therefore, the dissemination of the idea, the global discourse that accompanied it and the institutional arrangements that followed suit are remarkable. It is not surprising that the discourse around IoK embraced a number of controversies and developed into numerous intellectual currents each of which followed their own understanding of what Islamisation should mean and how the resurgence of Islam ought to be implemented and institutionalised. Nurcholish Madjid is an illustrative example of a scholar carrying at least a partial legacy of IoK. He was influenced by Seyyed

Hossein Nasr's ideas as mentioned above, was supervised in his PhD studies by Fazlur Rahman, and later became the founder of Paramadina University (1998) in Jakarta, a prominent higher education institution pursuing the graduation of internationally competitive young leaders for Indonesia while rooted in Islamic ethics and religion. Outright critics in the echelons of tertiary education distanced themselves explicitly from the ideas of IoK. The former rector of Indonesia's first State Islamic University (UIN) and internationally well-known intellectual Azyumardi Azra, for instance, is clear in his judgement. The UIN:

> is not based on the idea of the 'Islamization of knowledge' that has been the subject of discussion and debate among certain Muslim scholars since the early 1980s. [...], from the UIN Jakarta perspective, the idea of the 'Islamization of knowledge' is to a large extent questionable, since all knowledge and sciences are already Islamic. Natural sciences are of course already based on universal principles. If certain theories in the social sciences and humanities are Western-based, then the need is not to 'Islamize' them, but to develop theories that are based on Muslim social and cultural realities.
>
> (Azra 2011: 46)

In Malaysia, Osman Bakar, a student of Seyyed Hossein Nasr in the United States of America, became a professor at Al-Attas' ISTAC. He afterwards joined the International Institute of Advanced Islamic Studies (IAIS) in 2008, which enjoys political backing from the former Malaysian prime minister Abdallah Badawi and promotes the programmatic notion of 'civilizational Islam' (*Islam Hadhari*). Since 2012, Osman Bakar has occupied a chair as professor at the Sultan Omar Ali Saifuddien Centre for Islamic Studies in Brunei, whose declared mission is to generate Islamic thinkers and intellectuals who can share and express their views and thoughts on contemporary issues.[13] While Osman Bakar displays considerable institutional mobility in his academic trajectory, Wan Mohd Nor Wan Daud carried on Al-Attas' mission in a very devoted manner. He was the cornerstone for establishing the Indonesian version of ISTAC in Jakarta and he is also internationally active in political consultancy on Islamic education (see Chapter 3).

The emergence of institutions and the trajectories of political and academic networks behind their establishment already hint at the transnational and transregional offshoots of the intellectual currents of IoK and the Islamic resurgence of the late 1970s and 1980s. I will expand this aspect and unroll the diffusion of Islamisation-inspired thought through political and institutional/educational backing and support; I look into policymaking and policy implementation in the sector of education, trade and economy, and consumerism in Chapters 3 and 4. For the remaining part of this chapter, I put the IoK project into a broader perspective, including the international political situation at the time of its genesis and unfolding.

IoK as a project of its time

Why did the idea of an Islamisation of knowledge come about? Social movement studies looking at the 1970s speak of 'new social movements' coming through during this decade. Sociologist Ronald Inglehart (1981) threw in the notion of 'post-materialist values' when analysing the shared features of those who were active in, supported or sympathised with these new social movements – the 'new' women's movements (the second wave), environmental movements, peace movements, no-nuke movements and others. The attribute 'new' was applied because the preceding ones – the labour movement being the paramount example – were characterised by followers mainly from particular social strata (e.g. the working class), the pursuit of primarily materialist goals (e.g. the improvement of working conditions and higher wages), and an ideological leaning towards the left.[14] It is striking, though, that theories and empirical studies of social movements rarely attended to movements in the Muslim word – or to Islamic social movements for that matter. The late 1960s (1968 in particular) and the 1970s were yielding years for social movement studies in the West – the rise of the Green Party (*Die Grünen*, 1979) in Germany from a movement primarily concerned with environmental protection being a case in point for the intrusion of the grassroots into 'high politics'. The Iranian revolution of 1979 – preceded by what Charles Hirschkind (2006) referred to as Islamic counter-publics via cassette sermons – made no significant inroads into mainstream (Western) social movement studies. Likewise, Islamic resurgence movements led by students in the 1970s and 1980s (as in Malaysia, see Anwar 1987) were hardly known of outside interested or affected circles. As I have discussed elsewhere, a non-Western '1968' can well be discerned from the currents of Islamic revivalism, resurgence, proselytisation (دعوة *da'wa/dakwah*) movements and the like.[15] Islamic resurgence was neither driven by an explicit 'anti-war' mood (as, for example, the anti-Vietnam war movements in Western countries, Japan and elsewhere) nor did it develop into demands for 'love and peace' (catch phrases: 'make love not war'; 'flower power'). The criticism in Muslim-majority states against those in power was directed at the moral decay in politics, the neglect of Islamic values by the political elite, and, from a critical post-colonial perspective, too much voluntary dependence on the (secular) West. Historically, the period of Islamic resurgence in the 1970s and 1980s was a symptom of post-colonial critique of a Western monopoly in various regards, including the scientific monopoly on creating theories, concepts and categories that claim universal validity. On domestic turf, projects such as the IoK served to pluralise religious authority which had for a long time been vested in traditional institutions and organisations (e.g. *'ulamâ'*, mosques, *madrasahs*).

From the perspective of international relations, it is stated that the Muslim world felt politically dependent and weak. In the preceding century, Jamâl ad-Dîn al-Afghânî (1838–97) and others had already thought about ways to overcome this (Riffat Hassan 2007: 175), albeit to little avail on a global level. Discernible displays of Islamic solidarity were triggered politically rather than intellectually. Israel's victory in the Six-Day War of 1967 had been a vital event in this regard (Alles 2016: 52). With the Iranian revolution, ideas of Shi'ite Islamic thought gained momentum in the Muslim world. In Southeast Asia, as in other parts of the world, conversion to Shi'ism increased after Ayatollah Khemeini's rise to power (cf. Abaza 1997: 81). The establishment of the Islamic Republic of Iran was a clear victory for Islam in a world dominated by secularism, but it also met with considerable disapproval among Sunnis in general and Saudi Arabian rulers in particular. The ideological rivalry between Wahhabi Islam and other branches of Islamic religion became an issue of *Realpolitik*, visible, inter alia, in Iranian and Saudi Arabian efforts to spread knowledge in other parts of the world by donating books to religious schools (e.g. to *pesantren* or Islamic boarding schools in Indonesia) and sponsoring institutions (Formichi 2014: 4). Such state-endorsed activities soon advanced to relegating the idea of a united *umma* (unity of all Muslims as a nation) to second rank. As James Dorsey recalls in retrospective:

> To be sure, Wahhabism has been an expansionary, proselytising force from its inception. But the success of an Islamic revolution that could potentially inspire not only Shias but also Sunnis persuaded the Al Sauds, flush with oil dollars in the wake of the 1973 oil crisis, to kick Wahhabi proselytisation into high gear.
>
> (Dorsey 2016)

Although 'the Muslim world' as some coherent entity (as in the concept of *umma*) continued to be an object of reference, the structural international conditions forced governments to implement whatever they deemed necessary in order to gain strength on a nation-state level. This included the care of healthy state-to-state relations via, for instance, Islamic development aid or the sponsoring of schools and other educational institutes (see Chapter 1). In this context, Peter Mandaville's observation is important for understanding how the field of knowledge production (IoK being part of it) interacts with the field of international politics. While Mandaville describes the situation of a decade later, it also applies to the period of intense resurgence and revival movements:

> I want to make the point that the politics of 'Islam and the West' is but one side of the story. Another politics, that of Islam and its own 'internal others', is becoming increasingly important in the translocal climate. Hegemony in its Western guise is not the only obstacle contemporary Islam needs to negotiate; there is also hegemony within.
>
> (Mandaville 2001: 81)

Within this sphere of hegemony from within, different models of Muslim politics were competing with each other. Aside from the regional players in the Middle East and North Africa – Egypt, Iran, Saudi Arabia, Syria – Muslim-majority states in other parts of the world were immersed in balancing their domestic and foreign policies between the bi-polarisation of East and West, non-alignment, and Muslim cooperation. In Southeast Asia, Indonesia and Malaysia were performing in an almost inverse manner. Malaysia's government had embraced Islamisation since the late 1970s and early 1980s as a means to modernise and integrate the force of an Islamic resurgence including the proponents of an Islamisation of knowledge. This had also brought considerable economic investment from Middle Eastern countries. Neighbouring Indonesia, under the administration of General Suharto since 1965, had been extremely reluctant to establish close relationships with the Middle East and to have Islamic organisations exert influence on domestic and foreign policy (Alles 2016). As Delphine Alles points out, the official opening of an office of the Palestine Liberation Organization (PLO) and the granting of full diplomatic status to the PLO took place in Malaysia as early as 1982 (i.e. the year of long-time prime minister Mahathir Mohamad's ascendance to power) (cf. Stark 1999; Derichs 2004), whereas Suharto postponed this gesture of solidarity until 1992 (Alles 2016: 55). Moreover, Indonesia's government sought to avoid an 'Algerian situation' (i.e. political turmoil and civil war in the wake of the denied electoral gains of Algeria's Islamist party FIS [Islamic Salvation Front]) and therefore subdued actors proposing an Islamic or even Islamist agenda on the political turf. It was not until the 1980s that Suharto began to integrate Islamic non-state actors instead of denying them meaningful roles for national politics. The foundation of ICMI (*Ikatan Cendekiawan Muslim Indonesia* or Association of Muslim Scholars of Indonesia) in 1990 is widely held as a symbolic act of Suharto's intent to retard his waning popularity and secure fresh support from Indonesia's Muslims (cf. Liddle 1996). A mere glimpse at other Muslim countries of those decades reveals that Islamic political movements had been dealt with quite controversially throughout the Muslim world. Pakistan's forced Islamisation (including *sharī'a* laws) under Zia ul-Haq (1978–88) or Egypt's suppression of the oppositional Muslim Brotherhood throughout Hosni Mubarak's dictatorial rule (1981–2011) stood against the religiously legitimated monarchy of Saudi Arabia; Malaysia's Islamisation policies at home appeared to sometimes undermine the spirit of regional integration within ASEAN (Association of Southeast Asian Nations, founded in 1967). The continuum depicting Islam's role in formal national politics in the 1970s and 1980s thus stretched from full incorporation to outright subordination and suppression or from state-led Islamisation to its prevention.

In many post-colonial states as well as in those which emerged as sovereign states after decolonization (e.g. most of the Gulf monarchies) Islam became a marker of national identity. Nation-building as an ongoing project required the provision of values and ideational frameworks allowing for a sense of authenticity and distinction from 'others' – especially from the former Western colonial powers. As a matter of fact, the building of the nation went alongside the building of educational systems that nurtured the idea of 'the nation'. Hence the apparatus of knowledge production became designated for generating nation-serving 'Islamic' (read: authentic) knowledge. Non-state actors added volume to the critical tone of post-colonial self-assertion. Algerian Islamist Al Benhadj, for instance, demanded to 'banish France intellectually and ideologically by using the weapon of faith' (Benhadj cited in Kepel 1997: 160). We may assume that attitudes such as Benhadj's met the approval of many IoK activists in other countries, too. Islamisation in the field of knowledge production somehow re-introduced the idea of an *umma* beyond the borders of mundane national political interests – regardless of differences in the actual political treratment of Islamic activism by the political rulers (i.e. support for such activism or repression of it for the sake of nation-building). Indeed, the rejection of Western hegemony in the field of knowledge history seemed to show some repetition of history, reminding of the pan-Islamism of earlier times. As Mandaville recalls, there were:

> Pan-Islamic responses of Muslim thinkers during the colonial era of the late nineteenth and early twentieth centuries, a period marked by Western hegemony in which the umma was reconstituted as an important form of political community in the wider Muslim world.
>
> (Mandaville 2001: 81)

In post-colonial countries with a 'tradition' of questioning 'colonial knowledge' and a discourse of 'indigenisation' of knowledge such as Malaysia, the reception of pan-Islamic initiatives in pursuit of 'authenticity' and distinction from a dominant West were not particularly alien. However, when the IoK project emanated, the overall discourse in Malaysia was primarily driven by reflections of an indigenisation and decolonisation of (social science) knowledge, as discussed in the beginning of this chapter (see also Zawawi and NoorShah 2012). This overarching theme rendered the IoK a part of the 'bigger' struggle and led, as we have seen, to considerable criticism from various currents of concerned scholars, especially social scientists. It also led to a pluralisation of Islamic knowledge, since scholars and lay people alike felt inclined to ponder about the concrete meanings of an Islamisation of knowledge. Irrespective of the approval or disapproval of an Islamisation of knowledge as imagined in the project IoK (or I should rather say 'projects' of IoK), the lines of thought and the argumentation in this discursive period was itself part of a wider circuit of critical development studies – inspired to some extent by the metatheory of dependence (*dependencia*) that originated in Latin America. Zawawi and NoorShah (2012: 194f) see a more-or-less direct relationship between the indigenisation/decolonisation discourse to political economic studies of the time, which had been nurtured by André Gunder Frank's (1969) reflections on development and underdevelopment to treatises of neo-Marxist authors such as Immanuel Wallerstein (1979) or, later on, Ernesto Laclau (1991; 1990). The context of power structures and hegemonies is thus apparent. In the final paragraph of this chapter, I relate this contextual relationship to the issue of knowledge production and disciplines, once again referring to some reflections of Farid Alatas who hints at another deep layer of the motivation for IoK.

From the perspective of 'centre' (the West) and 'periphery' (the non-Western, developing world), as applied by Zawawi and NoorShah (2012; see Chapter 1), hegemonic power lies with the former. Within this power structure, the definition of what is considered scientific or not, what is solid knowledge or not etc. is provided by the 'centre'. The point of view of the Muslim writer in the 'periphery' then is, according to Alatas, 'not considered "scientific" and, as a result, does not have the same currency as one trained in modern social sciences'. (Alatas 1987: 82) This situation has come about because modern (i.e. Western-based) social sciences arrange knowledge in very different ways from traditional styles. This has significant repercussions for scholars' views of their subject matter. For example:

> [U]niversities in Muslim countries have Islamic studies departments in which Islam is simply an object of study and not a point of view of study [as it were, for instance, in the conception of IoK, C.D.]. The scholar trained in in the area of Islamic studies is not regarded as qualified to enter discourse on man and society as this is within the domain of the sociologist, political scientist, and historian. This brings us to another mode of control over ideas and discourses [... and] refers to the organization of the disciplines.
>
> (Alatas 1987: 82f)

The scholar quoted above may be imagined as one convinced of the necessity to assume a divine order above any worldly order. In modern sociology, however, he is not credible as a sociologist when he argues with this idea. 'In order for Islamic sociology to qualify for membership as a discipline, it must deal with a determinate range of objects that should be reducible to "variables"' (Alatas 1987: 83). This is where, understandably, the methodological framework and the research design of the discipline clashes with the presuppositions of the Muslim writer – for he cannot reduce the spiritual component of his analysis to a 'variable' when the approach as such is a 'sociology of faith' (Abaza 1993: 302). Most of the attempts at an Islamisation of particular disciplines by proponents of an Islamisation of Knowledge have therefore not managed to provide alternatives to the dominating methodological toolbox – apart from the application of hermeneutical tools such as *tafsîr* of *ta'wîl* (mentioned above). Al-Faruqi himself conceded that an important concern of the IoK project was the 'specific relevance of Islam to each area of modern knowledge' (Al-Faruqi cited in Abaza 1993: 305), although his approach also claimed to be a holistic epistemological project. In terms of an alternative epistemology, what the project of an IoK has essentially achieved is the provision of key concepts different from the concepts dealt within the dominant disciplines of sciences in the 'centre'. These concepts are taken from Qur'ân and Sunna (the collection of the prophet's statements, declarations, messages, pronouncements, teachings and reported actions) and are usually referred to in their language of origin, i.e. Arabic. I take an example from the publication *Contemporary Islamic Economic Thought*, edited by Mohamad Aslam Haneef (1995), which is quite illustrative of this procedure. In his introduction to the volume, which introduces six representatives of Islamic economic thought,[16] Haneef states that there is, despite differences, 'agreement among Muslim economists and scholars on the basic philosophical foundations of an Islamic economic system' (Haneef 1995: 2). The main philosophical pillars are '*tawhid* (unity), *khilafa* (vicegerency), *'ibadah* (worship) and *takaful* (cooperation)' (Haneef 1995: 2) – apart from the fact that the prohibition of interest is a shared fundamental principle. As differences, Haneef (1995: 2f) points out:

(i) the interpretation of certain terms and concepts found in the Qur'an and Sunnah;
(ii) the approach/methodology that should be followed in building Islamic economic theory and the Islamic economic system; [and]
(iii) as a result of the differences above (mainly in (i)), there are also divergent views on the interpretation of the features of an Islamic economic system.

Looking into the explanations of the said differences: (i) refers, for instance, to the extension of the prohibition of interest – financial interest only or unearned gain in general; (ii) refers to the approval or disapproval of mainstream economic tools, and to the question if Islamic economics is a branch of the science of economics or a separate category in relation to conventional economics; and (iii) hints at the issue of how to position oneself towards private property, the market system, the role of the state, and ownership. What becomes clear from this example is that 'contemporary Islamic economic thought', as introduced by the author, cannot escape the framework of 'conventional' economics as its 'other', as the approach from which it wants to distance itself. Islamised economics need the framework of conventional economics as their comparative counterpart. Since the complete rejection of theories and methods developed in the modern disciplines was thus not fully successful, authors of IoK literature frequently resorted to an 'Islamization of Attitudes and Practices in Science and Technology' (Lodhi 1989) instead of declaring all approaches of modern science null and void.

A second perspective which should not be neglected in the attempt to embed the IoK project in the broader discursive arena of its time is the relationship between the proponents of an Islamisation of knowledge and 'traditional' Islamic scholars or '*ulamâ'* (علماء; plural of عالم *'âlim*). Although I have not elaborated on the biographical background of SN Al-Attas, Al-Faruqi and Seyyed Hossein Nasr, it is quite apparent that all three have been trained both in the West and in traditional local institutions of learning. This is a common denominator of all prominent proponents of the initial IoK project and is a distinctive feature in comparison to most of the local '*ulamâ'* in Muslim countries. 'In terms of production of religious', Abaza writes, 'they [i.e. Al-Attas etc.; C.D.] compete with traditionally trained religious scholars (the *Ulama*) as well as with secular intellectuals' (Abaza 1993: 305). The competition with traditionally trained '*ulamâ*' did not come about by chance (cf. Eickelmann 1992; Kepel and Richard 1990; Rahman 1982). The ongoing efforts in nation-building and framing the idea of the nation by carving out 'authentic' features with which people could identify enhanced the intellectual creativity not only of those who sought to indigenise science, but also of those who were seeking fresh alliances in the pursuit of 'moral capital' (Kane 2001). The double standards applied in politics – referring to domestic as well as foreign policy – were perceived as signs of an increasing moral decay of those in power. As the rise to public acceptance of Islamist forces in several countries demonstrated (e.g. Algeria, Egypt, Afghanistan), the demand for morally sound leaders as opposed to those who were perceived as corrupt and bribable was on the rise. In authoritarian contexts and hence in the context of the majority of the Muslim states of this period in time (1970s –1990s), the '*ulamâ'* would either comply with state authorities (for fear of being sanctioned or simply out of pragmatic reasons) or relegate their role to spiritually guide the average people. Politicisation of the clergy in a revolutionary manner – as happened in Iran – was quite an exception, but all the more impressing (Ismael and Ismael 1980). It does not come as a surprise then that Islamism and Islamic fundamentalism were often referred to as 'political Islam' (Kepel 2006; Salvatore 1997; Esposito 1997; Roy 1994). *'Ulamâ'* were not a priori non-political actors since their teachings were fully rooted in a tradition perceived as morally solid and spiritually inspiring. However, they lacked the desire to actively promote political change and more often than not were not trained in 'both worlds' of science, the 'modern' and the 'traditional'. Motivated by the general mood of (anti-Western) authentication and indigenisation as described above, the proponents of an IoK encourage 'mental revolutions' by tying the moral-*cum*-epistemic project to a moral-*cum*-political one. On moral grounds, they competed with the '*ulamâ* ', on the epistemic level, they competed with Western scholarship as with local critics, and in the political arena, they had to distinguish themselves from those Islamists who were seen as dangerous currents by those in power. It is interesting to observe that politically the most successful promoters of IoK exerted their influence mainly in countries outside the Middle East. Malaysia is a case in point. Even if this Southeast Asian state was a very specific case, it nonetheless serves to illustrate how the drive for authenticity by resorting to Islamic values eventually set in motion what Peter Mandaville (2007: 101) depicted as 'pluralizing authority in the Muslim world'.

This chapter has introduced three protagonists of the initial Islamisation of Knowledge (with a capital 'K'). The three scholars' concept of this endeavour varies, but finds common ground in emphasising the importance of faith, metaphysics, and divine order in science. While they were acquainted with each other, their intellectual and philosophical positions differed and in some cases, led to controversy. These were also nurtured by rivalries over political influence, which was important for the implementation of Islamisation policies and the establishment of institutions of learning and research that would promote the IoK project. The discursive terrain of Iok was shaped by the major currents of Third World critique of dominating theories of development as well as, in the wake of these movements for an indigenisation of science in general and social science in particular. The IoK project can be subsumed into the rubric of movements for indigenising and authenticating knowledge, although this categorisation of IoK is still a contested opinion. The IoK project was criticised and opposed from several corners, particularly from within the Muslim community of social scientists. The promoters of IoK were trained both in local institutions of traditional learning and in Western academic establishments. Moreover, their political *and* educational motivation behind the IoK project distinguished them not only from most traditional Islamic scholars (*'ulamâ'*) of their time, but also from primarily political actors such as members of Islamist parties. They pluralised Islamic knowledge and moved Muslim politics in various regards, although the IoK project never became a clear alternative to dominant knowledge systems and disciplines.

Notes

1 Syed is a title, signifying the dynastic background (descendents of the Prophet Muhammad) of the Alatas family whose ancestors come from the Hasani branch of Hadramaut in Yemen. Farid Alatas' father, Syed Hussein Alatas, is usually referred to by the component Syed, whereas it varies in Farid's case. Hussein Alatas' brother, Syed Naguib, chose to write the family name as Al-Attas; he is referred to as Syed Muhammad Naguib Al-Attas, (Syed) Naguib Al-Attas, or simply SN Al-Attas. Sometimes the family name is written as al-Attas with a lower-case 'A'.

2 ISTAC was founded in 1987 as an academic centre within IIUM. SN Al-Attas, however, preferred ISTAC to be an autonomous entity. The university administration granted it autonomous status in 1991, but since 2002, ISTAC is again attached to the IIUM as a postgraduate research-orientated institute. Available at: www.iium.edu.my/istac/about-us/historical-background (accessed 20 January 2016).

3 The spelling of this name also shows several variants, among them Isma'il Ragi al-Faruqi or Ismail Al-Faruqi. I have chosen the spelling Al-Faruqi with a capital 'A', similar to Al-Attas, except for direct citations where the spelling has been left as in the original.

4 The story could go on, with scholars such as Osman Bakar and Hashim Kamali or politicians like Anwar Ibrahim and Abdallah Ahmad Badawi, in the ideational spectrum of Al-Attas. I consider it natural or at least not surprising that preferences and convictions change over time, so that adherence of a particular line of thought represents a temporary and not necessarily a lifetime affiliation.

5 This Festschrift is an impressive work in itself because of its contributors, e.g. Seyyed Hossein Nasr and Anwar Ibrahim (the Malaysian politician who became crucial for institutionalising IoK).

6 It is, of course, not agreed upon consensually who belongs to these representatives and who does not. Leif Stenberg, for instance, lists Maurice Bucaille, Seyyed Hossein Nasr, Ziauddin Sardar and Ismail Raji al-Faruqi as four intellectuals representing the Islamisation of Science. Stenberg pays less attention to the notion of *scientia sacra*, which is one of Nasr's core ideas (see Stenberg 1996).

7 Syafi'i Ma'arif, for instance, told me that he was a student of Fazlur Rahman in Chicago. To him, Al-Attas is 'too Ghazalian' (i.e. too devoted to the thoughts of Persian theologian Al-Ghazali); regarding IoK, Syafi'i Ma'arif says he 'would not buy it' (Author's conversation with Syafi'i Ma'arif, Yogyakarta, 21 April 2016).

8 This expression hints at the way the four faculties of theology, *sharî'a*, education/teacher training, and *adab* (philosophy, literature) of Egypt's top Islamic university Al-Azhar have been copied by Islamic educational institutions in other countries.
9 Author's conversation with Syafi 'i Ma'arif, Yogyakarta, 21 April 2016.
10 There are countless critical publications on the IoK, including Fazlur Rahman's (1988). I point out two exemplary critiques from authors who have been mentioned in the text before and who look at Iok as social scientists rather than as scholars of Islam, namely Mona Abaza and Syed Farid Alatas.
11 *Tafsîr* and *ta'wîl* can be described as hermeneutical forms of interpretation of the Qur'ân. They take the shape of commentaries (both in Arabic and in local languages) and comprise various methods of analysing the text in light of its divine revelation. As a rough distinction – since there exist countless definitions – the following may suffice: *tafsîr* looks at what has been transmitted (by the prophet and his companions), e.g. in the form of a hadith (a documented saying or action); *ta'wîl* uses reason and personal opinion to arrive at inferences.
12 Khalifa as a political institution refers to the four successors of the Prophet Muhammad who were seen as his substitutes on earth and who ruled in accordance with the requirements of protesting the religion. Mulk is the ruler in a kingdom, a royal authority who is, in contrast to the khalifa, able to rule by force.
13 Available at: http://soascis.ubd.edu.bn/about-us/ (accessed 4 April 2016).
14 For a more precise comparison of 'old' and 'new' social movements see Derichs (1995: 10–39).
15 Derichs, '196X – The Sixites, Women, and Movements', unpublished keynote for the conference *Women – Violence – 1968*, Cambridge, UK: Cambridge University, 14–16 July 2016.
16 These are: Muhammad Abdul Mannan, Muhammad Nejatullah Siddiqi, Syed Nawab Haider Naqvi, Monzer Kahf, Sayyid Mahmud Taleghani, and Muhammad Baqir as-Sadr.

References

Abaza, Mona, 'Some Reflections on the Question of Islam and Social Sciences in the Contemporary Muslim World', *Social Compass* 49 (1993) 2: 301–21.

Abaza, Mona, 'A Preliminary Note on the Impact of External Islamic Trends in Malaysia', *Internationales Asienforum* 25 (1994) 1–2: 149–65.

Abaza, Mona, 'A Mosque of Arab Origin in Singapore: History, Functions and Networks', *Archipel* 53 (1997): 61–83.

Abaza, Mona, 'Intellectuals, Power and Islam in Malaysia: S.N. al-Attas or the Beacon on the Crest of Hill', *Archipel* 58 (1999) 3: 189–217.

Alatas, Syed Farid, 'Reflections on the Idea of Islamic Social Science', *Comparative Civilizations Review* 17 (1987): 60–86.

Alatas, Syed Farid, 'The Sacralization of the Social Sciences: A Critique of an Emerging Theme in Academic Discourse', *Archives de sciences sociales des religions* 40 (1995) 91: 89–111.

Alatas, Syed Hussein, 'The Captive Mind in Development Studies', *International Social Science Journal* 34 (1972) 1: 9–25.

Alatas, Syed Hussein, 'The Captive Mind and Creative Development', *International Social Science Journal* 36 (1974) 4: 691–699.

Alatas, Syed Hussein, *The Myth of the Lazy Native*. London: Frank Cass, 1977.

Al-Attas, Syed Muhammad Naguib, *The Intuition of Existence. A Fundamental Basis of Islamic Metaphysics.* Kuala Lumpur: International Institute of Islamic Thought and Civilization, 1990.

Al-Attas, Syed Muhammad Naguib, *Islam and Secularism.* Kuala Lumpur, Malaysia: International Institute of Islamic Thought and Civilization, 1993 [1978].

Al-Faruqi, Isma'il Raji, *Al Tawhid. Its Implications for Thought and Life.* Herndon, VA: The Institue of Islamic Thought, 1982.

Alles, Delphine, *Transnational Islamic Actors and Indonesian Foreign Policy*, New York: Routledge, 2016.

Anwar, Zainah, *Islamic Revivalism in Malaysia. Dakwah among the Students.* Petaling Jaya: Pendaluk, 1987.

Azra, Azyumardi, 'From IAIN to UIN: Islamic Studies in Indonesia', in Kamaruzzaman Bustamam-Ahmad and Patrick Jory (eds), *Islamic Studies and Islamic Education in Contemporary Southeast Asia.* Kuala Lumpur: Yayasan Ilmuwan, 2011: 43–56.

Derichs, Claudia, *Japans Neue Linke. Soziale Bewegung und außerparlamentarische Opposition, 1957–1994* [Japan's New Left. Social movement and extra-parliamentary opposition, 1957–1994]. Hamburg: OAG, 1995.

Derichs, Claudia, *Nationenbildung in Malaysia als strategisches Staatshandeln* [Nation-Building in Malaysia as Strategic State Action]. Hamburg: OAG, 2004.

Dorsey, James, 'Defeat Islamic State – or become it', *Qantara*, 7 March 2016. Available at: http://en.qantara.de/content/saudi-arabia-and-iran-defeat-islamic-state-or-become-it (accessed 11 March 2016).

Ebrahim, Abdul Fadl Mohsin, 'Ethics of Fertility Treatment: A Case Study of Nadya Suleman's Feat', in Imtiyaz Yusuf (ed.), *Islam and Knowledge: Al-Faruqi's Concept of Religion in Islamic Thought.* London: I.B. Tauris, 2012: 139–56.

Eickelman, Dale F., *Knowledge and Power in Morocco. The Education of a Twentieth-Century Notable.* Princeton, NJ: Princeton University Press, 1992.

Esposito, John L. (ed.), *Political Islam: Revolution, Radicalism, or Reform?* Boulder and London: Lynne Rienner Publishers, 1997.

Formichi, Chiara, 'Contemporary Patterns in Transregional Islam: Indonesia's Shi'a', *Middle East Institute*, 30 October 2014. Available at: www.mei.edu/content/map/contemporary-patterns-transregional-islam-indonesia%E2%80%99s-shi%E2%80%98 (accessed 28 July 2015).

Frank, André Gunder, *Capitalism and Underdevelopment in Latin America.* New York: Monthly Review Press, 1969.

Haneef, Mohamed Aslam, *Contemporary Islamic Thought. A Selected Comparative Analysis.* Kuala Lumpur: Ikraq, 1995.

Hirschkind, Charles, *The Ethical Soundscape. Cassette Sermons and Islamic Counterpublics.* New York: Columbia University Press, 2006.

Ibrahim, Zawawi and NoorShah M.S., 'Indigenising Knowledge and Social Science Discourses in the Periphery: Decolonising Malayness and Malay Underdevelopment', in Zawawi Ibrahim (ed.), *Social Science and Knowledge in a Globalising World.* Kajang: Persatuan Sains Sosial Malaysia, 2012: 165–200.

Inglehart, Ronald, 'Post-materialism in an Environment of Insecurity', *American Political Science Review* 75 (1981) 4: 880–900.

Ismael, J.S. and T.Y. Ismael, 'Social Change in Islamic Society: The Political Thought of Ayatollah Khomeini', *Social Problems* 27 (1980) 5: 601–19.

Kane, John, *The Politics of Moral Capital.* Cambridge, UK: Cambridge University Press, 2001.

Kepel, Gilles, *Allah in the West: Islamic Movements in America and Europe.* Stanford: Stanford University Press, 1997.

Kepel, Gilles, *Jihad: The Trail of Political Islam.* London: I.B.Tauris, 2006.

Kepel, Gilles and Yann Richard (ed.), *Intellectuelles et militants de l'islam contemporain* [Intellectuals and Militants in Contemporary Islam]. Paris: Seuil, 1990.

Laclau, Ernesto, *New Reflections on the Revolution of Our Time.* London: Verso, 1990.

Laclau, Ernesto, 'The Impossibility of Society', *Canadian Journal of Political and Social Science* 15 (1991) 1/3: 24–27.

Liddle, William R., 'The Islamic Turn in Indonesia. A Political Expansion', *Journal of Asian Studies* 55 (1996): 613–34.

Liow, Joseph Chinyong, 'ISIS in the Pacific: Assessing terrorism in Southeast Asia and the threat to the homeland, Testimony', 27 April 2016. Available at: www.brookings.edu/research/testimony/2016/04/27-isis-southeast-asia-liow (accessed 30 April 2016).

Lodhi, M.A.K. (ed.), *Islamization of Attitudes and Practices in Science and Technology.* Riyadh: International Islamic Publishing House, 1989.

Mandaville, Peter, *Transnational Muslim Politics. Reimagining the Umma.* New York: Routledge, 2001.

Mandaville, Peter, 'Globalization and the Politics of Religious Knowledge. Pluralizing Authority in in the Muslim World', *Theory, Culture & Society* 42 (2007) 2: 101–15.

Masud, Muhammad Khalid, 'The Construction and Deconstruction of Secularism as an Ideology in Contemporary Muslim Thought', *Asian Journal of Social Science* 33 (2005) 3: 363–83.

Nasr, Seyyed Hossein, *Islam and the Plight of Modern Man.* London: Longman, 1975.

Nasr, Seyyed Hossein, *Islamic Life and Thought.* London: Allen & Unwin, 1981a.

Nasr, Seyyed Hossein, *Knowledge and the Sacred.* New York: Crossroads Publications, 1981b.

Nasr, Seyyed Hossein, 'The Role of the Traditional Sciences in the Encounter of Religion and Science: An Oriental Perspective', *Religious Studies* 20 (1984) 4: 519–41.

Nasr, Seyyed Hossein, *The Need for a Sacred Science.* Surrey: Curzon Press, 1993.

Rahman, Fazlur, *Islam and Modernity. Transformation of an Intellectual Tradition.* Chicago and London: University of Chicago Press, 1982.

Rahman, Fazlur, 'Islamization of Knowledge: A Response', *American Journal of Islamic Social Science* 5 (1988) 1: 3–11.

Roy, Olivier, *The Failure of Political Islam.* London: Harvard University Press, 1994.

Salvatore, Armando, *Islam and the Political Discourse of Modernity.* Reading: Ithaca Press (UK), 1997.

Siddiqi, Mohammad Nejatullah, 'Islamization of Knowledge: Reflections on Priorities', *American Journal of Islamic Social Sciences* 28 (2011) 3: 15–34.

Stark, Jan, *Kebangkitan Islam. Islamische Entwicklungsprozesse in Malaysia 1981–1995* [Kebangkiatan Islam. Islamic Development Processes in Malaysia 1981–95]. Hamburg: Abera, 1999.

Stenberg, Leif, *The Islamization of Science: Four Muslim Positions developing an Islamic Modernity*, Lund: Lund Universitet, 1996.

Wallerstein, Immanuel, *The Capitalist World-economy.* Cambridge: Cambridge University Press, 1979.

Widiyanto, Asfa, *Seyyed Hossein Nasr on Science and the Reception of His Ideas in Indonesia.* Unpublished Master's thesis, Leiden University, 2005.

Yusuf, Imtiyaz, 'Introduction', in Imtiyaz Yusuf (ed.), *Islam and Knowledge: Al-Faruqi's Concept of Religion in Islamic Thought.* London: I.B.Tauris, 2012: 1–18.

3 Review

Spill-over and diffusion

This chapter looks at collateral momentums, diffusions and the spill-over effects of Islamisation projects in education, politics, and the economy. It provides a preliminary assessment of what has been implemented in terms of Islamisation policies relating to collective societal concerns, and serves to answer the question of how we get from the epistemic dimension of religion to economy and advocacy. The main field for discussion is Islamisation in the field of education with a particular focus on student activism in Indonesia and Malaysia and its transversal connectivities. Corresponding aspects of a faith-sensitive shaping of domestic work and life environments conclude the chapter. More concrete empirical accounts are discussed in Chapter 4.

Islamic resurgence

There is heuristic value in the term Islamisation in general and Islamisation of knowledge in particular. The spill-over from the epistemic discursive platforms of Islamisation to the down-to-earth fields of education, politics, and economy have occurred at a constantly rapid pace in Malaysia since the 1970s and 1980s. It took on a slightly lesser tempo in Indonesia during President Suharto's New Order regime (1965–1998), but accelerated again during political transition and democratisation. In both countries, activists and protagonists from outside the traditional *'ulamâ'* circles emerged as promotors of an Islamic resurgence, entailing not an Islamisation of Knowledge in its purely epistemic sense, but in a much broader understanding comprised in the phrase 'Islam as a way of life'. The resurgence movements – mostly youth-based in the beginning – that emerged during this wave of activism are conventionally called *dakwah* movements (Hamid 2002). The term itself has an Arabic origin, it is spelt *da'wa* (دعوة) and is usually translated as 'call' – hence the call to Islam in a missionary sense. The meaning of *dakwah* as a technical term stretches from proselytisation and missionary work to the spread of principles of how people (ought to) practice Islam. The greater application of Islamic laws and values in one's daily life is a primary goal of *dakwah*; Islamic universities in Southeast Asia have *dakwah* faculties and state-endorsed *dakwah* councils.

DOI: 10.4324/9781315642123-4

After the fall of Suharto in 1998, the formation of an Islamic identity among the country's various Muslim communities became visible in the public sphere. While the international mass media brought the violent clashes between Muslims and Christians (e.g. in Malukku in 1999–2002), bomb attacks of Islamic extremists in Bali (2002) and explosions in Jakarta (the latest one in 2016) to the world's attention, the average Muslim population in Indonesia followed a non-violent form of belief and religious practice, demonstrating their piety in public (e.g. by their attire and desire to use only *halâl* products). Before this tide of commodification, commercialisation mediatisation and aestheticisation of Islam – 'from traditional Islam to fashionable Islam', as Indonesian scholar Muhammad Wildan describes it[1] – gained momentum, the ideational and institutional infrastructure had been prepared by political support for a stronger Islamic self-assertion in the public sphere. In stark contrast to the first three-quarters of the New Order period, when Muslim political activism was curbed and suppressed, the latter decade of Suharto's rule was characterised by an opening of the regime towards Islamic intellectual discourse, responding to an increasing public demand for a more articulate political acknowledgement of Indonesia as a part of the wider Muslim world. Instabilities within the regime and tensions between the presidential circles and the army (who had hitherto worked closely together) had also led Suharto to accommodate Muslim concerns. A general desire among the Muslim population was that Islam should play a greater role in politics. This is understandable since Islam had had been embedded in various cultural (i.e. non-political) expressions because of the repression of its political articulation. Suharto's fierce containment of Islamic political activity in more than two decades of his 32-year rule 'had the effect', writes Joseph Chinyong Liow, 'of catalysing a vibrant Islamic intellectual milieu as Islamic social movements moved underground and into the campuses' (Liow 2016). The policy of eradicating anything that would come close to political Islam thus had a counter-effect; under the surface of a depoliticised Muslim population, intellectual currents were cultivated that preferred a 'cultural' Islam to a 'political' Islam (cultural, however, did not mean 'politically immune'). This cultural engagement was tolerated and could actively be cultivated in education as religious instruction had never been hampered by Suharto, neither in public schools nor in the thousands of private *pesantren* (Islamic boarding schools). During the time of the New Order, numerous *dakwah* groups and Muslim student associations were formed, predominantly in the late 1960s and the early 1970s. Among the more prominent were the Muslim Students Organisation HMI (Himpunan Mahasiswa Islam) or the two student branches attached to the mass organisations NU (Nahdlatul Ulama) and Muhammadiyah. Student movements' activism found expression in the rise of numerous *dakwah* groups and associations in the decades of the 1970s and 1980s. Their activities also flourished partly through transnational and transregional connections, and partly through funding from Saudi Arabia (Liow 2016). HMI, however, was barred from campus activities in the 1980s because of its potential influence on political opinion. Female students were banned from wearing the headscarf (1982 to 1991). The regime thus sought to monitor expressions of religious identity carefully. One successful Muslim movement from the 1980s onwards was the Jamaah Tarbiyah or *tarbiyah* movement (deriving from the Arabic term for education تربية [*tarabîya*]). After the fall of Suharto in 1998, the Jamaah Tarbiyah transformed into the political party PKS (Partai Keadilan Sejahtera or Prosperous Justice Party), one of Indonesia's Islamist parties in the post-New Order political landscape. Forms of 'cultural Islam', despite having been promoted by the generation of the 1960s and 1970s as 'apolitical' practices, had 'by no means neglected the political consciousness of Muslims', writes Yon Machmudi (2008: 67). But political aspirations had been barred from becoming articulated in a religious framing in the ranks of formal politics. Until the opening of the regime towards Muslim intellectuals and advocacy groups in the 1990s and the subsequent liberal climate after the toppling of Suharto, official political backing for ventures such as the IoK was largely absent. Irrespective of the said political handcuffs, Indonesia's 'cultural Islam' unfolded vividly and was neither isolated from developments in the neighbouring countries and the Middle East, nor was it entirely unpolitical. Academic, intellectual and daily communal life in Indonesia was influenced even more by the wider Islamic discourse outside the country than was the case in Malaysia. At the end of the 1990s, neither Indonesia nor Malaysia had escaped the intrusion of former Muslim student activists into the higher echelons of formal politics. Anwar Ibrahim's successful career in Malaysia's main ruling party UMNO (United Malays' National Organization) since the early 1980s had rendered Islamisation in general and the IoK in particular a formally endorsed state project – a component of the national agenda for development and modernisation. Student groups and associations in Indonesia were no less successful in promoting Islamic resurgence, albeit on a broader ideological scale and with more confessional pluralism as was the case in Malaysia. 'Similar to what happened in neighbouring Malaysia, before long graduates of these groups and associations would come to control the levers of power as they entered the bureaucracy and positions of leadership' (Liow 2016). The opening of Indonesia's regime towards Muslims' political concerns in the early 1990s brought about a new relationship between state and Islam. 'Instead of following a pattern of oppression, resistance and co-optation, it offered a new momentum for Muslim groups to express their political identities and orientations' (Machmudi 2008: 101). The difference Malaysia made (in comparison to Indonesia) was the regime's earlier and explicit adoption of Islamic intellectual blueprints for an Islamisation first of the educational sector and later on also the economy – whereas Suharto shied away from such a move for three quarters of his term. The subsequent parts of the chapter compare the developments in both countries during the 1980s, 1990s and 2000s. The comparison reveals that regardless of the amount of official political commitment to Islam's role in shaping society's ideas about a 'way of life', the Islamisation of knowledge (with a minuscule 'k') on a global scale has contributed significantly to these ideas. This finding shines through the hereafter selected manifestations of 'Islamic knowledge's presence' in educational institutions and policymaking.

Islamisation in education and its political reception in Malaysia and Indonesia

The most prominent representatives of an Islamisation of knowledge and science as discussed in Chapter 2 are devoted intellectuals who never thought of pushing their world views through in a militant way. They are far from being associated with the intellectual and ideological currents that paved the way for violent extremist groups such as the Taliban, Islamic State (IS or *Da'esh*), the Al-Nusra front or those who are usually attributed to certain types of *salafism*. Al-Attas and others are also rarely recognised as influential in contemporary compilations of Islamic political thinkers, Nasr Hâmid Abû Zaid, Muhammad Asad or Yusuf Qaradâwî (cf. Hafez 2014). This is due to the fact that, generally, Islamic political thought is (still) first and foremost associated with thinkers of Arab or Iranian origin and writings in Arabic or Persian. The well-known centre-periphery view, which sees the Arabian Peninsula as the centre and homeland of Islam, applies here, too (see Chapter 1). What happened at the periphery (i.e. the non-Arab Muslim world) is less examined in the global mainstream literature; moreover, there is also a centre-periphery dichotomy in terms of what the global mass media prefers to cover. A militant attack or bomb blast, beheadings, abductions and other variants of violent, radical action receive much more attention than the everyday life of the vast majority of Muslims around the world. Hence it often escapes the view of the observer (and also the scholar) that there is an 'Islamic geography' beyond the landscape of militant or violent actors.

The silent majority, as it were, is less the focus of interest, as is the interpersonal connectedness through the mobility of members of this majority across distant geographical spaces. It is this mobility and connectivity across world regions that permeates people's everyday life and shapes the scales of belonging beyond local, national, and regional borders. The manifestations of such scales or faith-based geographies are best captured by looking at the role of Islamic institutions of education for shaping global Islamic discourse. Student mobility, for instance, is emblematic for the translocal, transnational and transregional connectivities among both Muslim individuals and communities. Chapter 2 has already pointed out that scholars such as Fazlur Rahman, Seyyed Hossein Nasr, Syed Naguib Al-Attas, Isma'il Al-Faruqi, or Nurcholish Madjid influenced the establishment of Islamic educational institutions in several countries, among them Malaysia and Indonesia. The institutions they created in the two countries, plus the famous universities in the Middle East where Malaysian and Indonesian students went to study, contributed to the formation of Muslim student associations and movements who proactively disseminated their thoughts on campus as well as in society in general. *Dakwah* groups also deliberately pervaded the 'secular universities', as those institutions offering Islamic religious studies as one subject equal in status to all others – if at all – may be called. Oftentimes, it was through their study abroad that Malaysian and Indonesian students in Western countries (in particular the UK, the US and Australia) had become acquainted with international branches of big activist networks (e.g. the Muslim Brotherhood or Jamaat Tabligh). Back home, they were much more convinced that they needed to 'Islamise' their society than they had been before (cf. Weiss 2011: 218).

In Malaysia, the Islamic Youth Movement ABIM (Angkatan Belia Islam Malaysia) became a protagonist for *dakwah* activities and political reform coated in a religiously inclined agenda for the country's modernisation. ABIM was initially closer to the opposition party PAS (Islamic Party of Malaysia) during the 1970s, but when the main ruling party UMNO (United Malays National Organisation)[2] managed to recruit the movement's charismatic leader Anwar Ibrahim as a member in 1982, ABIM-style Islamisation also entered the official political arena. This was in stark contrast to developments in Indonesia, where no political parties with an explicitly Islamic manifesto were allowed under the New Order regime, but where several Muslim youth and student movements were active on campuses.

Malaysia's Anwar Ibrahim, who assumed several ministerial posts but fell from Prime Minister Mahathir Mohamad's grace during the financial crisis of 1998, was pivotal in the Islamisation of Malaysia's educational sector. His policymaking in this area rapidly evolved when he served as Minister of Education between 1986 and 1991. His support of the IoK project led to the establishment of both the International Institute for Islamic Thought and Civilization (the Al-Attas-orientated ISTAC) and the International Islamic University Malaysia (the Al-Faruqi-orientated IIUM).[3] Al-Faruqi also became an advisor to Mahathir. Against the backdrop of the personal ties between Anwar and Al-Attas on the one hand and Mahathir and Al-Faruqi on the other, it appears legitimate to speculate that ISTAC's re-integration into the IIUM in 2002 had something to do with Anwar's being ousted from the government and his subsequent positioning as opposition leader. After Anwar's arrest and imprisonment, Mahathir distanced himself from Al-Attas and others. Nonetheless, Mahathir pursued the Islamisation agenda at full speed, presumably not because he entirely believed in the IoK project, but more because PAS had never given up being UMNO's strongest competition in elections. UMNO's eternal mission, it seems, is framed in convincing the electorate to abstain from PAS' vision and version of Islam. This is also reflected in UMNO's continuous efforts to monitor and control Islamic discourse in the country and to doctrinally determine the interpretative parameters of a national 'Malaysian' Islam. The race for Islamic credentials between PAS and UMNO led the prime minister to proclaim – curiously enough in view of its (secular) constitution – Malaysia an Islamic state in 2001. The move met with little appreciation from among Malaysia's non-Muslims, some of whom swiftly deconstructed the concept by scrutinising the booklet *Malaysia adalah Sebuah Negara Islam* (Malaysia is an Islamic Nation) which had been published by the government (Martinez 2001: 491–498). Since then, UMNO has not referred to Malaysia as an Islamic state, but has promoted other concepts such as *Islam Hadhari* (civilisational Islam) domestically and internationally, e.g. in the Organization of Islamic Cooperation (OIC) (cf. Chong 2006).

Primary to tertiary education

Islamic education in Malaysia has intensified since the 1970s, when Islamic revivalism became attractive to the Muslim youth and *dakwah* activities spread.[4] The Malaysian government's efforts in the 1980s to Islamicise education, social life and the economy gave Islamic religious education a significant boost. It is worth mentioning that this happened both at the federal and the State (*negeri*) level, because 'the administration of Islamic matters and Malay customs is not centralised at the Federal level but is under the jurisdiction of each *negeri* religious bureaucracy and its ruler' (Shamsul and Azmi 2011: 129). Since religious jurisdiction and enactment of Islamic law lies with the States, their rulers, *'ulamâ'* and bureaucracies do not necessarily have to follow the policies formulated on Islam by the federal Department for the Advancement of Islam (cf. Martinez 2001: 477). This no doubt complicates federal control, even though it does not completely preclude it. It is perceived that the federal government 'controls Islam' in Malaysia not by religious law but by using civil law to discipline Muslims and prevent deviations from the preferred state-defined interpretation (cf. Martinez 2001: 480). Disruptive critiques of the ruling regime are contained by authoritarian governance and hamper state-society dialogue (cf. Weiss 2011: 188f).

In primary education, Malaysia preserved the *pondok* school tradition from pre-colonial times. It is a largely oral-based form of learning with a focus on Islamic theology; most *pondok* schools are private institutions. As in Indonesian *pesantren* (see below), students in *pondok* schools learn Jawi (the Arabic script used for Malay language which was abolished by the British and transformed to Latin script). However, in comparison to the *pesantren*, *pondok* schools are much fewer in number – several dozen *pondok* compared to up to 30,000 *pesantren*. Islamic schooling with a stronger emphasis on reading and writing occurred in *madrashas*, which can be compared to the *madrasahs* in Indonesia, although their trajectory differs. As Shamsul and Azman summarise for Malaysia:

> During the colonial period *madrasahs* were established which taught Islamic theological subjects along with modern science and mathematics. The combination of theological subjects and modern ones was the result of both administrative and market demand. Graduates from such schools were employed in the public service and especially in the religious offices of every province or state. They served the colonial state as well as the Muslim population.
>
> (Shamsul and Azmi 2011: 132)

In the course of state-endorsed Islamisation, the number of additional government-funded primary and secondary religious schools increased considerably. It is therefore not unusual for parents to send their children to both a 'secular' public and a religious school. The boarding-school-type of Islamic education at *pesantren*, which prevails in Indonesia, is less prominent in Malaysia.

This may be attributed, among others, to the concern of the Malaysian government to have the officially sanctioned interpretation of Islam be taught in the country's educational institutions.

In tertiary education, Islamic educational institutions have expanded since the 1980s. Islamic faculties in local public universities became enlarged. This has to be put in perspective, however, since public universities which were primarily meant to cater for the majority population of ethnic Malays are still lower in number than private institutions of higher learning, which have often been established by Malaysians of Chinese descent.[5] With the student population growing, 'new Islamic university colleges specialising in Islamic education have been established' (Shamsul and Azmi 2011: 131). Shamsul and Azmi (2011: 131) also observed that the huge expansion of Islamic education reduced the number of Malaysian students enrolling in Islamic tertiary institutions in the Middle East and South Asia to a considerable extent. In 1983, the International Islamic University Malaysia (IIUM) was set up. It combines religious instruction with modern (secular) subjects and is very much devoted to Al-Faruqi's conception of Islamic knowledge (cf. Chapter 2). At other local universities, this combination of religious and 'secular' subjects is common. Islamic education is offered there in Islamic Faculties. Among the private institutions of higher education, the International Islamic University College in the State of Selangor or KUIS (Kolej University Islam Antarabangsa Islam) has risen to 'one of the most dynamic Islamic private universities in Malaysia', based on its 'mission to become one of the most renowned centres of academic excellence locally and internationally' (Kuis 2016). KUIS is owned by the Selangor Islamic Religious Council and reflects the trend in Malaysia since the 1990s to mainstream Islamic education with Islamic economics, banking and finance. The college hence offers classes in Islamic Studies, Business Management, Islamic Banking, Language Studies, Communication, Information and Communication Technology (ICT), Multimedia and Education. It is 'committed towards providing the best and affordable education in line with the government's aspiration of human capital development' (Kuis 2016). The political role of Islam in shaping the intellectual, economic and social life of Muslims (on structural and agency levels) in Malaysia is quite obvious in view of the trajectory of Islamic education. Islamic financial institutions are nowadays as mainstream as conventional ones; the *halâl* certification sector has advanced to become a business model of transregional outreach (cf. Md Akhir, Kassim and Akhir 2014; Md Akhir et al. 2015). Moreover, '*Shari'ah* lawyers serving the *Shari'ah* courts have also increased in number. Those studying law in Malaysia today can opt to specialise in Islamic law irrespective of one's religion' (Shamsul and Azmi 2011: 132). As in neighbouring Indonesia, Middle Eastern universities have set up campuses in Malaysia. Going abroad to study is still very popular, with Egypt's Al-Azhar usually topping the list of Malaysian students' institution of choice for Islamic Studies. Some authors speak of an 'Azharisation' of Islamic religious training in Malaysia, hinting at the influential role of the university regarding the faculty and curricular composition of Southeast Asian Islamic colleges and universities (Bano and Sakurai 2015b: 15f; see also Shiozaki 2015; Kushimoto 2015).

The situation in Indonesia is more complex than in Malaysia. As described in Chapter 2, the IoK project did not gain as much of a foothold in Indonesia as it did in Malaysia. However, Fazlur Rahman and Seyyed Hossein Nasr were influential thinkers who inspired some of Indonesia's most prominent Islamic intellectual leaders. Indonesia did not establish an International Islamic University as a material site for the Islamisation of knowledge. This was partly due to the regime's repression of Islamic activities that might have carried political weight. Since religious education per se was not barred from public schools and universities and the state had not introduced one particular interpretation of Islam as 'Indonesian', the plurality of Islamic interpretational currents rendered Indonesia a much more vibrant discursive turf than Malaysia. Under the umbrella of 'cultural Islam', the two huge Islamic mass organisations NU and Muhammadiyah stood out as significant structural elements in the nation's Islamic landscape. Abdurrahman Wahid, one of the most prominent NU leaders of recent decades and Indonesian President from 1999 to 2001, embodied the notion of cultural Islam. Abstaining from the propagation of Islamic laws as a substrate of particular religious traditions, Gus Dur (as he is commonly referred to) sought for the conflation of general principles of humanity with the substance of Islamic teachings. This trait also featured the approach of Nurcholish Madjid, who, independent of NU or Muhammadiyah, weaved it into the mission of the institutions he helped to establish.

NU to a large and Muhammadiyah to a lesser extent rely on a religious educational institution called *pesantren* and which covers all school levels (primary to tertiary). The term *pesantren* is commonly translated as Islamic boarding school and there are numerous variants and types. In the wake of political transition and liberalisation after 1998, the number of *pesantren* offering schooling in urban as well as rural areas has doubled, rising to roughly 30,000.[6] What they have in common is a *kyai* as the head of school and the *santri* as 'live-in' students (hence the translation as boarding school). Apart from this structure, the content of what is taught varies, particularly in the informal segments of teaching. 'You cannot understand Islam in Indonesia when you do not study *pesantren*', relates Irfan Abubakar from the State Islamic University Syarif Hidayatullah in Jakarta.[7] In addition to *pesantren*, faith-based day schools named *madrasah diniyah* (religious schools) offer Islamic religious education but follow the state curriculum for instruction in the secular subjects. Sometimes, *pesantren* and *madrasah* types of schools are combined (e.g. a *pesantren* with an integrated *madrasah*). The number of *madrasahs* ranges between 33,000 and 37,000;[8] they are important in the national education system since they target students from families of lower socio-economic strata who often live in rural areas (Parker and Raihani 2011: 716).[9]

In tertiary education, the State Institutes of Islamic Religion (IAIN), and State Islamic Universities (UIN) are the main institutions with an explicit Islamic denomination. Since their beginnings in the 1960s, IAIN have patterned their curricula after Al-Azhar's four faculties of theology, *sharī'a*, education/teacher training, and Islamic humanities (*adab*) (cf. 'Azharisation' above). A particular focus lies on the teaching of Arabic language, so that IAIN students and faculty are usually fluent in reading Arabic and frequently opt for a study period in Egypt to practice their oral conversation. Visiting professors from Al-Azhar have also been quite common at IAIN.[10] During Suharto's time, IAIN were confined to teaching 'Islamic religious sciences'. Offering academic subjects other than those designated as Islamic religious sciences was prohibited. This fact heavily affected their transformation into Islamic universities (UIN), since the status of UIN requires the provision of programmes for all branches of knowledge including Islamic religious studies (Azra 2011). The liberalisation after Suharto facilitated IAINs' transformation to UINs; almost all of the former IAIN have by now (2016) adopted the additional curricular elements and study programmes. Their change of status in recent years notwithstanding, they have been important institutions for the education of the country's talented politicians even during the New Order. As Azra (2011: 44) recalls, 'there is little doubt that the IAIN has played a crucial role in the modernization of Indonesian Muslim society':

> First of all, IAIN has made it possible for the children of *santri* (practising Muslim) families to obtain 'modern' Islamic higher education that allows them to achieve not only educational mobility but also social and economic mobility. IAIN, no doubt, has contributed significantly to the so-called 'intellectual boom' that has been taking place in Indonesia since the late 1970s. Furthermore, one can not ignore the role of IAIN graduates in the modernization of Islamic educational institutions, such as *madrasahs*, *pesantrens*, and *sekolah Islam* (Islamic schools), as well as in the development of other Islamic institutions such as Islamic courts, Islamic banking and others.
>
> (Azra 2011: 44)

The conversion of an IAIN to a UIN is meant to re-integrate the so-called Islamic religious and the secular sciences. But this idea should not be taken as a disengagement of knowledge from its divine origin. As promulgated by IoK proponents, all knowledge is conceived of as coming from God. Taking the example of the leading State Islamic University in the capital Jakarta:

> [In] UIN Jakarta perspective all sciences epistemologically come from God, the All-Knowledgeable, through the '*ayat Qur'aniyyah*' (Qur'anic verses) and the '*ayat kawniyah*', the signs of God that are spread all over the universe. Muslims need to learn the '*ayat Qur'aniyyah*' and the '*ayat kawniyyah*' at the same time, since through the study of the two *ayats*, Muslims will be able to acquire the various kinds of knowledge and sciences that are necessary for their lives.
>
> (Azra 2011: 45)

The proximity to the IoK project's fundamental approach to knowledge is striking, although UIN would never figure as a flagship institution for this endeavour (Azra 2011: 46). Rather than subscribing to an Islamisation of Knowledge/knowledge or to one particular 'school' or tradition of religious knowledge, faculty at UIN Jakarta are affiliated to various local and foreign scholars of influence in contemporary Islamic thought. As mentioned below, the university's rector Komaruddin Hidayat (incumbent 2006–2010) became inspired by the thoughts of Fetullah Gülen during his studies in Turkey, but was also beholden to the ideas of Seyyed Hossein Nasrand Fazlur Rahman. Apart from the State Islamic Universities that became established in several provinces across the archipelago, NU and Muhammadyiah also run their respective universities and colleges. Nurcholish Madjid, the country's famous and influential Islamic intellectual, gave his imprint in higher education with Paramadina University (Universitas Paramadina). First set up as a study centre to disseminate Nurcholish's thought in the Muslim public, Paramadina was less academically inclined.[11] In 1998, Paramadina University commenced its co-educational study programmes; it is a higher education institution with a particular emphasis on science and technology. At the same time, it retains a strong commitment to its founder's religious teachings. Although the number of students is comparatively low (enrolments range from 1,000 to 2,000 students), the university has a strong reputation – calling it an elite institution is probably not an exaggeration.[12]

The landscape of *pesantren*, *madrasahs*, Islamic colleges/universities and mass organisations plus numerous movements and groups in and around campuses have made Indonesia a place for vivid discussion of religious affairs. In the course of political transition, branches of the 'cultural Islam' of Suharto's time quickly transformed into entities of political Islam. According to Liow (2016), the 'vibrant 'apoliticized' milieu quickly morphed and surfaced as a dynamic terrain of Islamic activism comprising groups with multiple shades of doctrinal affiliations'. Their spectrum stretched from groups that welcomed democratic values and human rights (i.e. groups that can be characterised as liberal, progressive and reform-orientated) to those who fought for ideologically narrow, sometimes even anti-democratic principles. Religion in general and the religion of Islam in particular assumed a significant presence after 1998, in particular on the island of Java. As one of the most populous islands, Java became an important religious destination for believers who wanted their religion to grow and disperse. Christianity and Islam are almost competing with one another in view of establishing religious institutions and struggling for a revival of the religions. In this socio-cultural climate, various schools of thought and sects within Islam (and Christianity) have emerged; unsurprisingly, Java represents a fertile land for missionary activism or *dakwah*. University campuses, which have already been an area for *dakwah* activities, have also become an important arena for the recruitment of future politicians. In Machmudi's words:

> The important status of university students in Indonesian society has encouraged political and religious groups to establish their influence upon

> them. For students, being involved in political activities has provided them with political careers in return. Realising this, the focus of Jemaah Tarbiyah, since the beginning, has been to attract students in prestigious secular campuses since they offer the greatest opportunities in terms of vertical and horizontal mobilization. For activists of Jemaah Tarbiyah, students are their greatest assets in the duty of the Islamisation of Indonesia and for the victory of Islam.
>
> (Machmudi 2008: 107)

Making a political career via political action on campus is thus a promising channel for Indonesian students. Islamic-based parties on average account for up to 30 per cent of the votes. But none of the religious parties can be considered a serious challenger to the larger parties such as PDI-P (Party for Democratic Struggle). The political party that emerged from the *tarbiyah* movement (Jamaah Tarbiyah), the Prosperous Justice Party (PKS), made only slight inroads into parliamentary representation in the post-1999 elections (hovering between 6% and 8% of votes) (cf. Hadiz 2014); the parties affiliated to the two mass organisations NU and Muhammadiyah, namely the National Awakening Party (PKB) and the National Mandate Party (PAN) did little better over time. The same can be said from the fourth Islamic party in the national party system, the United Development Party (PPP).[13] PKB member and former NU leader Abdurrahman Wahid became Indonesia's second president after the fall of Suharto (1999–2001). Taken together, because of the rise of religious parties and their affiliation to organisations and movements, religion is nowadays a genuine ingredient in Indonesian politics (as it is in Malaysia). As mentioned before, this did not come about suddenly, but grew and expanded on due to well-organised Muslim student activities on campus, as I will describe in the subsequent paragraphs. Since Indonesia's Jamaah Tarbiyah had the most effective cadre structure in the 1980s, I use this movement to highlight some features of 'campus Islam' and 'campus *dakwah*'.

Campus *dakwah*

Student activism was a driving force for *dakwah* and Islamisation in the most encompassing way. It used Islamic ethical principles as a moral guideline, achieving social justice with Islamic ideals, striving for socio-economic change on the basis of Islamic principles and linking the worldly demands of modern life with an Islamic way of life. In Malaysia and Indonesia alike, students and their on- and off-campus activities made *dakwah* an everyday action which pushed for adherence to the moral and ethical framework of Islam.

Malaysia

In Malaysia, *dakwah* activities accelerated in the 1970s and spread despite the enactment of the University and University Colleges Act of 1974 (UUCA), which contained political campus activism (cf. Weiss 2011: 135–37). Although the Malaysian government was comparatively open-minded towards political Islamic activism from the late 1970s, it disliked practised versions of Islam that showed too high a level of autonomy. While the Suharto regime in Indonesia strove to curb any organised form of political Islam in civil society, Malaysia's government co-opted the main currents of the *dakwah* movement of the 1970s by recruiting its protagonists into the ruling coalition. From the early 1980s, *dakwah* on Malaysian campuses was very much an accompanying element of the state's agenda of Islamic religious revival and resurgence. Islamisation formed a substantial part of the government's developmentalist orientation (Stark 1999). The concomitant institutional infrastructure provided for the training of entrepreneurs and graduates skilled in science and technology and Islamic Studies alike. The Islamisation agenda concatenated these efforts and, as stated above, this led to a huge expansion of Islamic education in Malaysia. The institutional shifts that were particularly linked to the policy of assimilating Islamic values in public institutions (*penyerapan nilai-nilai Islam*) at the same time intensified the racial polarisation in the country (i.e. between Malays who were Muslims as per the Constitution, and non-Malays/non-Muslims the majority of whom were Malaysians of Chinese and Indian origin) (Weiss 2011: 217). The Islamisation agenda took root in the country's first-ever public university – University Malaya, which was established in 1949[14] – by making Islamic Civilisation a compulsory subject in 1984 and introducing new (*shari'a*-compliant) dress codes. As Weiss and Zainah recall, 'By the mid-1980s, around two-thirds of Malay university students (totalling around 40,000) were 'committed to some level or other of *dakwah*' (Zainah 1987: 33–4, cited in Weiss 2011: 218). Both trends – Islamisation as well as racial polarisation – led to a meticulous distinction within the Muslim community between Islamic and un-Islamic (in difference to non-Islamic) be it with regard to dress, attire, public performance, event funding, or any type of popular culture articulation that could be screened for compliance or non-compliance with Islam. *Dakwah* became Malay students' 'parapolitical outlet' (Shamsul 1983: 401) and can legitimately be regarded as an expression of Southeast Asian 'student power'. The missionary, proselyting and moral guidance activities gained so much momentum among the youth (especially on campus) that the main ruling party UMNO hastened to sponsor its own *dakwah* groups and invent control mechanisms for the contents of *'ulamâ*'s' Friday prayers in the local mosques. Some of the *dakwah* movements were linked to political parties (UMNO and PAS) and conducted partisan politics while struggling for the dissemination of the 'right' Islamic teachings. ABIM, for instance, was close to PAS and, later on, also UMNO. Movement organisations such as Jamaah Islah Malaysia, Jamaat Tabligh or Darul Arqam were seen as 'apolitical' and not very interested in anchoring themselves in formal politics. The government nonetheless cracked down on Darul Arqam in the mid-1990s, as it diapproved of its practices.[15] Shi'ite branches were also banned (cf. Formichi and Feener 2015; Marcinkowski 2008) – so Malaysian Shi'ite Muslims now travel to Jakarta to perform their annual rituals (cf. below).

The main external link of the Malaysian *dakwah* movement in the 1970s was with Indonesia – not with Arab countries, Iran or India (Shamsul 1983: 401). There was an increase in the number of Malaysian students studying abroad; against general expectation, more of them returned with a stronger commitment to their being Muslim than before. This also applied, as mentioned above, to those who went to Western countries like Australia, Britain, or the USA (Weiss 2011: 218). Transregionally, the ties to international branches of the Egypt's Ikhwân al-Muslimîn (Muslim Brothers, conventionally known as the Muslim Brotherhood) were particularly tight. Regional ties between Malaysian and neighbouring student and youth groups were built on the notion of solidarity among Islamic and Islamist movements. ABIM sent members for training to Indonesia and linked up with the local HMI (Muslim Students Association [of Indonesia]); Malaysia's PMI (Persatuan Mahasiswa Islam or Muslim Student Society) launched solidarity demonstrations for fellow Muslim students in both Thailand and in the Philippines (Weiss 2011: 166f). The Yom Kippur War of 1973, the Russian invasion of Afghanistan in 1979, the Sabra and Shatila massacres with huge losses on the Palestinian side in 1982, and the Palestinian liberation struggle itself were other events which showed international Muslim affectedness.

Indonesia and the tarbiyah movement

Since 1967, religious instruction as part of strengthening Indonesian national identity was mandatory in public secular schools. Muslim leaders worked hard to train Islamic teachers and to participate in this national agenda. Mohammad Natsir, who had been Indonesia's prime minister from 1950 to 1951 and was widely recognised as a religious leader, together with others established the Indonesian Council for Islamic Propagation (Dewan Dakwah Islamiyah Indonesia or DDII). As we will see below, the DDII had strong transnational relations, all the more so because it was the formal representative of the (Saudi-based) Muslim World League in Indonesia (Hefner 2003: 165). With the assignment to practice religious education in public institutions of learning, secular campuses turned into centres for *dakwah*. The 1980s were a difficult time for Muslim activists on campus since the regime had established a system of close control and monitoring of Friday prayers, public sermons and preachings to prevent any political *dakwah*. The government sponsored its own *dakwah* groups, and there was a remarkable increase from the numbers in the 1970s (Hefner 1987: 546). Propagation in university-based Islamic study groups called *halaqah* (arab. حلقة, circle) appeared to be a safer mode for the promotion of the Islamic cause than mosque sermons. These *halaqah* were the predecessors of the prayer room meetings with trained cadres – usually senior students – of Jamaah Tarbiyah in later years. Machmudi describes those who attended such meetings and joined the *halaqah* as students of high religious and spiritual interest. They were 'able to develop close contacts with one another and consider[ed] themselves and their fellow Muslims as one family' (Machmudi 2008: 110; see also Hadiz 2014). The concept of the family was important in several regards since it conveyed a feeling of belonging as well as security, all framed in notions of satisfying students' spiritual needs. It also reflects the programmatic proximity of the *tarbiyah* groups to the Muslim Brotherhood, whose very name – *ikhwân* (اخوان) or 'brothers' in Arabic – hints at the notion of familial ties. Moreover, the strong regularity which is inherent in *tarbiyah*'s rituals of prayer and worship structures the day and provides an emotional hold:

> There is a practice of sharing material goods and a sense of security in these newly Islamic environments. Spirituality, piety, the regular observance of Islamic duties, solidarity and togetherness are the features that draw students to join these circles.
>
> (Machmudi 2008: 110)

Machmudi (2008: 112) also calls the strictly organised forms of campus *dakwah* that directly emerged from the *halaqah* 'the most successful Islamisation processes on secular campuses [that] have taken place since the 1990s'. Apparently, these were much more responsive and successful than other on- and off-campus activities of Muslim groups and organisations. Hence, *halaqah* circles, study groups and study clubs on secular campuses flourished and amplified the caderisation of the Jamaah Tarbiyah. There was great appreciation of the organisational tactics of Egypt's Muslim Brotherhood, for the latter also had to strike a balance between public outreach and escaping the regime's security apparatus. The fact that the *tarbiyah* groups had 'better-structured materials of the Muslim Brothers than others' made their emphasis on 'the need to develop individual morality and piety' even more convincing (Machmudi 2008: 115). Reading materials were largely composed of translations from books written in Arabic by Muslim Brotherhood members. Later, when liberalisation allowed for open public activity the Turkish party AKP (the Justice and Development Party) became a role model for *tarbiyah* and PKS activists (Hadiz 2014). The study of AKP literature followed suit. The shift made sense in that the Muslim Brotherhood model had served the *tarbiyah* movement to survive authoritarianism, while after the fall of Suharto and the founding of PKS, the AKP model provided useful means 'to emphasize adherence to democratic methods of contesting power and political inclusiveness' (Hadiz 2014).

In sum, it is true that any political Islamic activity during the New Order period was severely curtailed and hardly possible. Despite this feature of authoritarian restriction, however, the exercise of cultural Islam, (cultural) Islamic education and clandestine campus *dakwah* by *tarbiah* cadres was conducted more or less constantly, so that neither the formation of Islamic political parties after 1998 nor the open articulation of demands for *sharî'a*-compliant policies came as a surprising occurrence. If anything is surprising, then it might be the speed with which the proliferation of popular religious leaders took place in Indonesia. As described in Chapter 4, this became ultimately linked to the prominence of Islamic consumerism, for instance in the tourism sector where pilgrimages to Mecca can be conducted with a celebrity. In terms of the diffusion of Islamisation from campuses into politics and into consumers' daily life, there is next to no difference between Malaysia and Indonesia. Catering to the spiritual needs of mostly young people (on campuses and elsewhere) recruiting activists for further *dakwah* work was a remarkably effective strategy to promote the pursuit of a 'true' Muslim identity. The agenda behind the campus and *dakwah* struggle was connected to generating social change. In this regard, students from high-ranking secular universities were a preferred target:

> Students of the prestigious institutions were seen to have more potential to bring about social and political change in Indonesia, and efforts to cultivate the seeds of activism on the campuses were believed to be the fastest ways to bring about change in the society.
>
> (Machmudi 2008: 112)[16]

At least for Indonesia, this meant that the restraint of Muslim activism under Suharto led to *dakwah* activities flourishing on the campuses that were commonly considered to be secular. The more plural ideational and ideological setting in Indonesian Islamic discourse – compared to Malaysia – came about through an Islamic educational infrastructure that was virtually uncontrollable even by an authoritarian political regime. The state-endorsed religious institutes of higher learning (former IAIN now UIN) were meant to strive for an Islamic renewal that embraces secular ideas and stresses that 'liberal' thought is in accordance with Islamic principles. While their impact was driven by respected intellectuals with considerable public outreach (such as Nurcholish Madjid), the *pesantren* followed their own traditional or modernist curriculum (depending on the *kyai*). The outreach of reform-orientated Islamic study clubs such as those organised by Nurcholish Madjid should not, however, be underestimated. Equally important for the spread of what is called neo-modernist Islamic thought in Indonesia (currently underlining the accordance of democracy with Islam) is the fact that prominent leaders such as Nurcholish Madjid, Abdurrahman Wahid, Syafi'i Ma'arif and others were able to disseminate their ideas to politicians and general audiences because they were respected public intellectuals.

Transregional connections

The agency of orthodox *tarbiyah* groups and reform-orientated circles on the secular campuses nurtured the movement-countermovement constellation. While the cadres of Jamaah Tarbiyah had the Muslim Brotherhood as their early role model, others found the Iranian model more appealing and some also adhered to SN Al-Attas. Others were inspired by the local Indonesian leaders of legally operating mass movements (Abdurrahman Wahid, Syafi'i Ma'arif), or respected intellectuals like Nurcholish Madjid (who had been chairman of the HMI in the 1960s). Students were not confined to studying at home, but frequently incorporated a study period abroad – in the Middle East, including Iran, in Malaysia, and also in the USA. In fact, as Vedi Hadiz (2014) recalls, the *tarbiyah* movement in Indonesia 'was initiated by a small collection of activists that had returned to Indonesia from studies in the Middle East'. This included Saudi Arabia, 'where many Indonesians went to study' and where 'a melding of Wahhabi doctrinal rigidity and Muslim Brotherhood organizational discipline and capacity introduced by the latter's substantial diaspora' had already taken place (Hadiz 2014). Others preferred Iran as their study destination and, not surprisingly, converted to Shi'ism upon their return, married Iranian wives and raised bilingual children (Formichi 2014). The following paragraphs shed light on the transnational and transregional student mobility and the repercussions for their home country that emanate from this type of mobility.

Since the mid-1980s, Indonesian Muslim students who had graduated in the Middle East returned with an energetic commitment to practicing Islam in another way than they used to do before. Quite often they had got in direct contact with well-known activists of the Muslim Brotherhood. Through study circles such as the *halaqah* of the *trabiyah* movement on Indonesian campuses, they transferred the ideas of prominent Brotherhood ideologues of Islamic revival (Hasan Al-Bannâ; Sayyid Qutb) to their local environment. The 1980s Islamic resurgence threw Islamic publications and translations into the publishing market. The era 'witnessed the translation of hundreds of books from Arabic into Indonesian' and most books 'were not just about ritual obligations but carried a concern for social and political problems as well' (Machmudi 2008: 30). Because Malaysian and Indonesian languages are relatively close to each other and can be mutually understood, Malaysian students made use of the Indonesian translations, too. In Malaysia, it was mainly ABIM who functioned as the connecting rod between the global Muslim Brotherhood organisations and local activists. In Indonesia, the Indonesian Council for Islamic Propagation (Dewan Dakwah Islam Indonesia or DDII) and its leader Mohammad Natsir facilitated the participation of Indonesian students in study programmes at Middle Eastern universities through personal ties. As mentioned by Hadiz (2014), Saudi Arabia provided the space where rigidity of Wahhabi school could synergistically merge with the Brotherhood's discipline and the organisational capacity of its cadres. DDII as the formal representative of the Saudi-based Muslim World League in Indonesia could benefit from links not only to donors in Saudi Arabia, but also Kuwait and Pakistan 'to finance its domestic programs' (Machmudi 2008: 29).

The prominent Middle Eastern universities – Al-Azhar in Egypt, Al-Mustafa in Iran and the Islamic University of Madina (Al-Madina) in Saudi Arabia have been significant for what Masooda Bano and Keiko Sakurai (2015a) identify as the shaping global Islamic discourses. Other universities and famous institutions (e.g. Dar ul-Ulum Deoband in India or the Fetullah Gülen schools in various continents) notwithstanding, these three universities claim centre stage in the 'ivy league' of Islamic universities and are prime examples for an alternative to the traditional, orthodox centres of learning, i.e. mosques and *madrasahs*, in their region. Their distinct status derives from the support of the respective state authorities in Egypt, Iran and Saudi Arabia. 'These three universities are unique in the sense that they all have direct or indirect links with their governments and their student base comes from across the globe' (Bano and Sakurai 2015b: 2). In ideological terms, Al-Madina and Al-Mustafa indeed relate to each other like their governments in the realm of international relations:

> Al-Madina and al-Mustafa have, in particular, come to act as the central locations for the promotion of Wahhabi-infused Salafism ad Iranian-styled Shi'ism, respectively: the former particularly associate with encroachment on alternative religious spaces and erosion of the localized Islam of Sufi veneration and folk religion; the latter associate with transmitting a particularly Iranian brand of Shi'ism, [...].
>
> (Bano and Sakurai 2015b: 2)

The political dimension is inextricably linked with the desire of the governments to have these elite institutions of higher education exert their influence on the direction of global Islamic discourses. Al-Azhar has therefore 'survived' the political turmoil in Egypt after 2011 and can, under a new military regime, still present itself as a moderate university whose religious worldview adapts to transition and change – the 'protector of the middle-way Islam' (*al-wasatiyya*), as Bano (2015: 73) calls it. While Al-Azhar attracts around 30,000 students from more than 100 countries, al-Madina is reported to host about 13,000 students from 160 countries, and al-Mustafa lists about 12,000 students from countries outside Iran (Bano 2015: 73; Sakurai 2015: 41 – numbers given for 2011ff). These numbers, however, do not reveal too much since the overseas outreach of the universities (see below) is not taken into account. Furthermore, the numbers do not tell us anything about how ideas, thoughts and convictions are transmitted from one locale to another by transregionally mobile students. How exactly returning graduates 'perform' as agents of a particular missionary inclinations of the said institutions is almost impossible to measure – the interplay of personal, individual dispositions, local and global contexts as well as opportunity structures back home is way too complex for the task of systematic analytical mapping. What is observable and traceable is either based on rich ethnographic material deriving from fieldwork and case studies (cf. Zulkifli 2015; Reid 1993), or else, as practiced in the present study, on accumulated accounts of years of research in the home countries of the returnees. One very general account is that the opportunity to study abroad has enabled ordinary students in Southeast Asia to uplift their status among peers by working as agents of Islamisation upon their arrival back home. Having said that, we should be mindful, too, of those who studied at Western universities. As mentioned above, they were no exceptions in the ranks of influential role models for young Muslim scholars and activists. On the one hand, the global networks of organisations such as the Muslim Brotherhood were strong enough to attract Muslim students worldwide – despite or maybe just because these organisations lacked the state backing that the elite institutions enjoyed. On the other hand, a highly influential current emerged from the intellectual appeal of Muslim scholars who pursued the Islamisation of knowledge and science.

The 'big names' of Islamic intellectual leaders who have been affiliated with the Islamisation of knowledge all spent time abroad during their studies. This exposure to international Islamic discourses frequently furthered their cooperation and opened up new ways of thinking which influenced numerous students at home. The multiplier effect was huge, particularly when the political backing for certain variants of Islamisation facilitated an institutionalisation of some kind (as, for instance, in the case of the IIUM, ISTAC or Paramadina). As mentioned in Chapter 2, a number of personal ties can be traced with discernible consequences in the realm of Islamic education. Within the 'first generation' of IoK proponents, Fazlur Rahman, Seyyed Hossein Nasr and Isma'il Al-Faruqi met at McGill University in Canada and together developed the 'Islamics' as a field of study there in the 1960s. Al-Attas also studied at McGill, but was not among this group. All four, however, secured a significant following in the years to come. Fazlur Rahman exerted a strong influence on Nurcholish Madjijd (who had previously been influenced by Mohammad Natsir) and Syafi'i Ma'arif; both attended Fazlur Rahman's teachings at the University of Chicago.[17] Abdurrahman Wahid, too, was attracted by what is called Fazlur Rahman's neo-modernist thinking, but probably even more so by Seyyed Hossein Nasr, whose book *Ideals and Realities of Islam* (Nasr 1981) he translated into Indonesian. Likewise, Komaruddin Hidayat was devoted to Seyyed Hossein Nasr (and to Fazlur Rahman). Komaruddin's studies in Turkey contributed to his appreciation of Fetullah Gülen's Sufi-based educational approach. Syed Naguib Al-Attas' ideas have taken effect in Indonesia through Wan Mohd Nor Wan Daud's advocacy work and the establishment of the Indonesian version of SN Al-Attas' Institute for the Study of Islamic Thought and Civilization (ISTAC) which operates under the acronym INSISTS.[18] The Malaysian scholar Wan Daud himself is one of the best-known disciples of SN Al-Attas. His biography displays a highly impressive career from high-ranking positions at leading Malaysian universities (including the National University of Malaysia, UKM) to an international advisor for numerous academic institutions abroad (e.g. Australia, Turkey).[19] Unsurprisingly, Wan Daud did his PhD under the supervision of Fazlur Rahman in Chicago and became deputy director of ISTAC. Given his credentials and those of other contemporaries who advanced to the elite of higher education, the offshoots of the IoK project at leading universities in the Muslim-majority countries of Southeast Asia are manifold. Osman Bakar, who also traces his career back to, among others, Temple University in Philadelphia (USA), ISTAC and IAIS (International Institute of Advanced Islamic Studies) (Malaysia), assumed a professorship in Brunei in 2012. Inspired by Seyyed Hossein Nasr, his mission is the conception of science in Islam rather than the IoK.[20] Together with the founder of INSISTS in Indonesia, Hamid Fahmy Zarkasyi, Osman Bakar published a book on *Islamic Science* in 2016. Taken together, the 'second generation' of scholars who ascended to high-ranking positions in educational institutions or even in formal politics, and who established study centres, research institutes and universities, had multiple sources of inspiration from their transnational and transregional connections. The networking between Malaysian and Indonesian scholars continues and has partly become consolidated via 'sister institutions' such as ISTAC and INSISTS.

Another perspective on the spectrum of transregional ties and connections lies in looking at those students and scholars who prepared the soil for the establishment of (branches of) international Islamic institutions in their home countries. In the student tier of tertiary education in the late 1970 and 1980s, international mobility facilitated and enhanced the flow of thought and strategies for *dakwah* activities across continents. A rather typical example of a career of an Islamic activist through his international connectedness is that of Imaduddin Abdulrahim, a highly respected Indonesian *dakwah* activist and lecturer based at the Salman Mosque of the prestigious Bandung Institute of Technology (Hadiz 2014; see also Chapter 5). His transnational credentials evolved through his active engagement in the 1960s in the domestic Indonesian student association HMI, which was then chaired by Nurcholish Madjid. Machmudi describes the trajectory as follows:

> In 1963 Imaduddin went to the USA to pursue his studies towards a master's degree at the University of Iowa. During his stay there he became involved with international Islamic propagation, making contact with other Muslim students from various countries. His Islamic orientation and his vision of struggle became more international in scope. It was also in the USA that he established his first contact with Muslim Brothers who were students in the university. Imaduddin developed this contact until he finally became a member of Muslim Students Association (MSA) of the USA and Canada. After his return home to Indonesia in 1966 he was appointed chairman of the Central Board of Islamic Education and Propagation (PB LDMI, Lembaga Dakwah Mahasiswa Islam) a campus missionary institution under HMI. Through LDMI Imaduddin became close to Nurcholish Madjid, then chairman of HMI. During the time Imaduddin was chairman of LDMI he was sent to attend a (sic) international seminar organised by the International Islamic Federation of Student Organizations (IIFSO), which finally led him to be elected secretary-general of this organization. Now he enjoyed interaction with Muslim leaders from around the world.
>
> (Machmudi 2008: 114)

The International Islamic Federation of Student Organizations (IIFSO) embodied most of the youth in the global Muslim Brotherhood. The accession of Imaduddin to a high-ranking post within IIFSO shows two things. On the one hand, a Muslim activist from the 'margins' of the Islamic world (the Arab world being taken as the 'centre') ascended to secretary general of an international Islamic association a few years after his first period of study abroad. On the other hand, the very fact that this international student organisation recruited its members globally is a strong indicator of the successful networking of the Muslim Brotherhood in those days. Another influence from the 'centre' derived from Saudi Arabia (for the Sunni branch) and Iran (for the Shi'a branch). In the mid-1980s, graduates from Saudi Arabian universities returned to Southeast Asia and introduced contemporary Wahhabi interpretations of Islam to home audiences. The Iranian revolution, which had generated a wave of conversions to Shi'ism even in Sunni-dominated regions of the Muslim world, made Qom a prominent destination for Islamic studies abroad (shifting from Najaf in Iraq which had become a rather uncomfortable place for Shi'ites after Saddam Hussein came to power). The cross-regional affiliations that were established by students and graduates returning from the Middle East soon evolved into the establishment of branch campuses of big Middle-Eastern universities in Southeast Asia. As a branch of Muhammad bin Saud University in Riyadh, Saudi Arabia, the college LIPIA (Lembaga Ilmu Penggetahuan Islam dan Arab, Islamic and Arabic College) opened a campus in Jakarta in 1980.[21] Lectures are delivered in Arabic and the majority of teachers at LIPIA come from Saudi Arabia. In Malaysia, Al-Madinah International University started its business in 2006. The university's parent institution is Al-Madinah University in Saudi Arabia, although the website text of Al-Madinah International University abstains from emphasising any close affiliation. Shi'ite ties to Iran have been strenghtened in Indonesia since the late 1990s, although the tolerance of religious pluralism including intra-Islamic pluralism has declined and Shi'ites are increasingly facing discrimination. Shi'ite Islamic studies were introduced in the Islamic College (IC), one of 24 colleges of Al-Mustafa International University in Qom (Iran), and the Islamic Cultural Center (ICC, est. 2000).[22] Before its re-naming, the IC was known as ICAS (Islamic College for Advanced Studies), which had become established in Jakarta in 2003 after the signing of a Memorandum of Understanding between Nurcholish Madjid (then rector of Paramadina University) and the representative of ICAS London, Ali Movaheddi (Zulkifli 2015: 138). The spirit behind the IC was to establish a Shi'ite sister institution to Paramadina University (Formichi 2014). The Islamic Cultural Center (ICC) also forms a hub of Shi'ite Islamic education in Indonesia. Shi'ism is banned in Malaysia, so Malaysian Shi'ites travel to Jakarta to perform their rituals.

Diffusion into policymaking and economic practice

Translocal, transnational and transregional connections among Sunnis, Shi'ites, (former) students at local or returnees from foreign universities have transformed into well-established networks. One impact of this trend is a mushrooming of teaching and preaching Islamic knowledge across the country – in Malaysia and Indonesia alike. Schools, foundations and endowments facilitate the resurgence of religiously grounded identity formation. This also invites those with mobilising skills and charisma to cultivate the role of religious leader. This may go along with the acknowledgement of the leader (by his or her followers) as a religious authority on a particular field of exegesis or a specific tradition. As Ismail F. Alatas (2014) points out in regard to the resurgence of Sufism in the plethora of Islamic religious orientations in Indonesia, some popular leaders explicitly target the wealthy urban middle-class elite. During the presidency of Susilo Bambang Yudhoyono (2004–2014), Aa Gym was a particularly successful and popular religious leader. He ran a *pesantren* in Bandung (Java) and drew his ideas from intellectual and ethical elements of classical Sufi texts 'as well from the global genre of 'self-help' and 'successful management'' books. Supported by politicians and business people, Aa Gym acquired popstar status:

> The new forms of Sufism enjoyed unprecedented popularity across society, mediated by especially by Islamic programs on television. Business people and celebrities engage in *dhikr* (ritual chanting) activities, which are also serving to support political events linked to the regime.
>
> (Alatas 2014)

The spread of religious information through new Islamic media has increased rapidly since the 1990s, as has the physical mobility of people. Alatas (2014) identifies two 'industries' which he says have 'experienced a considerable boom in the 1990s in Indonesia' – one of them being the ever-increasing desire of Indonesian Muslims to undertake the pilgrimage (*hajj*) to Mecca, the other the migration of workers from Indonesia to the Middle East. In the case of the *hajj*, the number of pilgrims allowed to perform this ritual is limited per the quota system for each country. In the case of labour migration, the number of migrants is limited by a quota system; the Gulf states are the main destination and they have implemented the *kafâla* system (i.e. a regulating sponsorship system for foreign employees). Both male and female workers leave their country hoping to better their families' situation by sending money home. The fact that they migrate to a Muslim-majority country often comforts their relatives back home. In education, learning Arabic has become an utterly pragmatic activity driven by economic considerations (labour migrants) as well as faith-based inclinations (pilgrims). I will discuss the impact that such trends and 'industries' have for the increasing commercialisation and commodification of Islam in Chapter 4. For the remaininder of this chapter, I will concentrate on the spill-overs of Islamisation to policymaking and economic practice.

Laws and verdicts

One indicator for the successful input of dedicated Muslims' concerns into politics is the increase in laws and policies serving particular Muslim interests. I have already raised the example of Malaysia being officially declared an Islamic state. While this move of the Malaysian government did not unfold according to plan, the developments in law-making and jurisdiction of recent decades nonetheless display a constant tendency of strengthening the rights of the Malaysian

Muslim community (cf. Yeoh 2011; Derichs 2014; Lee 2010). One of the more spectacular judicial verdicts in this regard has been the prohibition of non-Muslims from using the word 'Allah' when referring to (their) God (Derichs 2016). Other legal issues relate to the interpretation of constitutional rights, religious freedom, religious conversion, sexual orientation, or the omnipresent issue of Malay supremacy. In fact the question of whether or not Malaysia's Constitution is 'secular' has occupied a great deal of public discourse over the years (Khoo 2014; Hoffstaedter 2013; Abdul Aziz 2010; Kessler 2008). The case of physical punishment (caning with six lashes according to Islamic law) for a Malaysian Muslim woman who had been caught drinking a beer in 2009 was eventually transformed into community service; but the issue fuelled the debate on the country's Islamisation (cf. Abdul Aziz 2010). The so-called religious bureaucracy on the State (*negeri*) level has expanded its monitoring portfolio continuously. Post-Suharto Indonesia shows similar tendencies to control public morale through laws and decrees that often run counter to official commitments towards religious pluralism and tolerance. Apart from the influential role of the Indonesian Council of Ulama' (MUI), which, among others, issued a *fatwa*[23] in 2005 opposing pluralism, liberalism, and secularism (Gillespie 2007; Kaptein 2004), public intellectuals, religious leaders, the Islamic political parties and the authoritative figures in NU and Muhammadiyah are important actors on the input side of policymaking. Among the laws and decrees that became particularly contested in and outside parliament and showed a considerable leaning towards particularistic Muslim concerns are the 'Anti-Pornography and Anti-Porno-Action Law' of 2007 (Ottendörfer and Ziegenhain 2008; Sherlock 2008) and the 2008 ban on the country's Ahmadiyah community. The former sanctions the production of pornographic material and the spread of pornography. It was a fiercely debated law, however, since the first draft also contained some dozen paragraphs on 'pornographic behaviour' (*porno aksi*) and could have been applied to, for instance, wearing traditional local dress (with sleeveless tops) in Bali or other regions. These paragraphs were deleted after protests from opponents of the law. The latter was a joint decree (generally referred to as the 'Ahmadiyah ban') of three ministries stipulating that all activities of Ahmadiyah outside its own community be curtailed because it was a deviant Islamic sect if not totally non-Islamic.[24] Heavy pressure from MUI, the Prosperous Justice Party (PKS) as well as hardline groups led to the decision to enact the decree ordering.

Female perspectives on 'Islamised' policymaking

The examples of legislation mentioned above suggest that the mood of Islamic resurgence beginning with the 1970s and translating into remarkable responsiveness by the political authorities over the years was met preponderantly, but not exclusively by applause. Aside from those communities who have to cope with discriminatory policies because of certain basics of their faith (like Ahmadiya on Indonesia), a feeling of uneasiness also emerged among Muslim women. There is a particular gender dimension to the narrative of Islamisation. The fomented push for Islamising all worldly spheres of life was frequently accompanied by a patriarchal framing of the agendas for change. As early as in the 1970s, 'women reacted to the pressure of Islamisation and realised that the religion is used to repress rather than liberate them', states Riffat Hassan (2007: 179).). She relates this insight directly to the Islamisation processes described above, of which, she reasons, women have been the primary targets:

> Since the nineteen-seventies, largely due to the pressure of anti-women laws which have been promulgated under the guise of 'Islamisation' in a number of Muslim countries, women with some degree of education and awareness have begun to realise that religion is being used as an instrument of oppression rather than as a means of liberation from unjust social structures and systems of thought and conduct. This realization has stemmed from the fact that the women have been the primary targets of the 'Islamisation' process.
> (Hassan 2007: 179f)

Laws restricting women's rights – family laws in particular – were promulgated under the guise of Islamisation and made women the primary targets of the 'purifying' efforts by protagonists of religious resurgence and revival (Derichs 2010). Against this trend, women organised themselves and took advantage of transnational and transregional networking (Derichs 2013; Mir-Hosseini 2006). The resurgence of religion and religious affiliation as a marker of identity and authenticity (starting in the 1970s) added a significant tier to the complex task of reconciling the demand for equal rights with religious principles. The claim for authenticity put many women's activists in Muslim-majority countries on the defensive, particularly since full equality between men and women is frequently declared by Islamist activists to be a Western value, and therefore unacceptable for non-Western societies. The apparent – if constructed – 'dilemma' of being a believing individual and yet a supporter of equal rights has been addressed by various currents of what is usually referred to as Islamic feminism (see Chapter 4). Although there is common ground in using Islamic sources to legitimise Muslim women's demands, activists differ completely in acknowledging who has the right to define what is or is not Islamic. Frederik Holst and Saskia Schäfer (2014) illustrate how this conflict evolved in Malaysia, where the popular NGO Sisters in Islam (SIS) were condemned as un-Islamic by Islamist critics. SIS activists, who perceive themselves to be legitimate feminist advocates of Muslim women's concerns, have since raised the question of who has the right to define such 'truths'. Who has the right to declare a particular interpretation to be the one-and-only valid source for legal pronouncements? This question was (and is) relevant to women, as it is mostly men who claim the legitimacy to determine what is correct and what is unacceptable – what is right and what is wrong. For women who are convinced of gender equality as opposed to a complementary understanding of men's and women's roles, the crucial issue is not whether a Sufi theologian defends another position on divorce than a member of the Muslim Brotherhood. When both men insist on the exclusive right of divorce for husbands, women/wives have not gained much in terms of gender equality.

During the Suharto period in Indonesia and the pertinent 'state feminism' in the aftermath of the crackdown on the women's movement Gerwani (predominantly carried by women affiliated to the Communist Party), particular concerns of Muslim women were glossed over and subsumed under the concept of *kodrat perempuan* (the 'natural' features of womanhood) (Kusmana 2015). Women's political role was more or less restricted to a supportive one; that is women were expected to physically and morally assist in the nation's development. The end of the New Order regime brought with it new windows of opportunity to organise on interest platforms independent of the national ideology. The government's post-New Order democratisation agenda earmarked several institutional and administrative sites for reform to strengthen political participation. The decision of the government to carry out the transformation of the IAIN to State Islamic Universities (UIN), for instance, was taken as a reflection of the:

> long-standing aspiration within both government circles and Muslim society generally to have modern Islamic universities that will in turn make a greater contribution to the creation of a modern and democratic Indonesia.
> (Azra 2011: 47)

The decentralisation programme of 2001 was another step in this direction, envisaging people's appreciation of the country's democratisation through active participation in local politics (e.g. in direct elections of district heads). Administrative decentralisation and the possibility to form faith-based political parties and interest organisations encouraged citizens to launch advocacy groups and openly articulate their concerns. Contrary to the positive expectations, however, some instruments of the decentralisation policy aroused opposition from Muslim women activists. A number of local regulations (by-laws) commonly known as *peraturan daerah* or *perda* came under attack because provincial and district authorities made rather arbitrary use of the permission to legislate independently from the central government in Jakarta. Decentralisation also allowed for individual provincial legislation in the field of social policy – social policy in its broadest sense because it included clauses such as the 'banning and eradication of amoral behaviour' (Noerdin 2002: 183). Once they turned into regulations, such policies imposed on women how they should dress and behave, whereas men's appearance was of no major interest. Although the term *sharī'a* is not mentioned in these regulations and by-laws, their impact is in many cases a clandestine implementation of *sharī'a* law on the local level (see Hadiz 2010). Developments such as these have led observers to doubt if democratisation is by default a process conducive to the strengthening of women's rights (Schröter 2014). It pays to be cautious, however, in issuing quick judgements concerning such questions because 'women' is a plural category. As Kristina Großmann

(2011; 2013) has analysed, in the Indonesian province of Aceh (i.e. the only province allowed by the central government to implement *sharî'a* law), many women are perfectly fine with the *sharî'aisation* of the legal framework that regulates their lives.

Irrespective of the factual female proportion among those who supported the patriarchal moves of those venturing to restrict women's rights in the name of women's protection, Muslim women's organisations in Southeast Asia as well as elsewhere coalesced to counter the trend of discriminating attempts at *sharî'aisation* of their rights (cf. Maznah 2014; Othman 2005). Riffat Hassan's statement about a repression of women rather than their liberation by Islamisation (see above) is thus a dimension in the context of Islamic resurgence that merits distinct attention. The Islamisation of knowledge is a central source of friction in the kaleidoscope of Muslim feminist approaches to claim their right to define right or wrong. Transnational Muslim women's organisations such as Musawah (founded in Malaysia), systematically collect information on Qur'anic and Islamic jurisdiction concepts to provide 'alternative' knowledge (see Chapter 4).

Diffusion into economy

A lot of the political responsiveness towards certain Muslim concerns in Malaysia and Indonesia was related to the rise of a Muslim middle class that exacted its toll for contributing to the nation's wealth and being loyal to the regime. Vali Nasr's term 'Meccanomics' and his analysis of the rise of the Muslim middle class on a global scale (Nasr 2009; 2010) may be read critically, but his observation of a causal relationship between this shift in social stratification and the popularity of Islamic finance, trade and commerce is hard to reject.[25] The forms of Islamic capitalism that Nasr describes have at least not come about by chance or all of a sudden. In Indonesia, for instance, Hadiz observed that activists of the *tarbiyah* movement were quite successful in entering the business world. 'By the late 1990s and early 2000s cohorts of Tarbiyah activists had become encroached in the world of small businesses, government, or the professions and had their own social security as well as upward mobility in mind' (Hadiz 2014). The author considers the movement as 'stubbornly urban middle class' and less skilled in catering to the broader (and poorer) segments of civil society through charities and social services (Hadiz 2014). But the diffusion of particular faith-related demands did not stop at the junction between urban and rural. Rather, it marched forward and urged the state to take note of believers' concerns. As Alatas (2014) points out exemplarily, the Indonesian Ministry of Tourism had to respond to the new demand of Muslim pilgrims wanting to visit the graves of saints outside the urban context by 'restoring and building the necessary infrastructure'. In the corporate world, the reflection on Islamic economic alternatives to the dominant Western ones materialised in a tremendous increment in institutions offering Islamic banking services, *sharî'a*-compliant products, medical services, *halâl* certifications and shop-floor environments that are compatible with and conducive to Muslim employees' demands. Chapter 4 introduces such tangible manifestations of an Islamic identity that are not meant to reject Western patterns of work and life, but, more often than not, erase the juxtaposition of Islam versus West in conciliatory and productive ways.

Conclusion

On- and off-campus *dakwah* movements, the huge expansion of Islamic education and the institutional infrastructure that was built up through the policies of following and furthering Islamisation contributed to the flourishing of Muslim intellectual activity. Given this environment, it is not surprising that an endeavour such as the IoK fell on fruitful soil. The tradition of Islamic learning in Southeast Asia has a long and rich history. The interpersonal relations traced above are but a recent outcome of cross-regional intellectual inspiration. Globally enhanced and technically facilitated mobility of students since the 1970s served the expansion of knowledge acquisition beyond national borders on a mass level. The impact credited to the three top universities for Islamic Studies in the Middle East for the shaping of global Islamic discourses is most obvious in numbers of Indonesian and Malaysia students applying for enrolment in their programmes. What Azymardi Azra found out for historical times sounds familiar for the contemporary situation, too. Tracing Malaysian and Indonesian *'ulamâ'* networks, he arrives at the conclusion that the tradition of Islamic learning in Indonesia at both socio-cultural and intellectual levels cannot be separated from the religio-intellectual traditions developed in Mecca and Medina (Azra 2011: 48; 2004 – one might add the name Cairo). This is not to suggest, however, that traditions of Islamic learning in Southeast Asia have developed in almost the same way as they did in their lands of origin or, in other words, that Islamic Studies in Southeast Asia were a mere mimicry of Middle Eastern Islamic Studies. As the rise of the IoK project as well as the pluralisation of inspirational sources among the subsequent generations of Muslim students show, Islam outside the Middle East found its own distinctive intellectual traditions. These were translated into action through the spectacular proliferation of *dakwah* movements – in Indonesia and Malaysia certainly an expression of student power comparable to that of the '1968' movements in the Western world. The newly emerging Muslim intellectuals – socialised locally or internationally at secular or Islamic educational institutions or both – swiftly embodied the political and professional ranks. They were indeed different from earlier ones and their reputation and status was different from the traditional representatives of learned religious authorities (*'ulamâ'*, *kyai* etc.). Yet they would not reject traditional religious authorities but pluralise religious authority – including those figures who acquired a celebrity-like image as popular religious leaders. In non-academic environments, the rise of the Muslim middle class became particularly apparent in the financial and services sector. Vedi Nasr's dictum of Islamic capitalism and 'Meccanomics' reflects the broad recognition of this development. Again, transnational and transregional connections owe their part to the

Islamisation of economic concepts and performance. Virtually all segments of consumers' worlds have become affected by the tide of explicit assertion of religious identities. The political response to faith-based demands and concerns of citizens – voters – was generally accommodative if not proactively supportive, i.e. expediting *sharī'a*-compliant policies and providing for the concomitant institutional infrastructure.

Apart from the harvest generated by successful advocacy work in the name of Islamic resurgence, the implementation of allegedly faith-friendly policies was not unanimously welcomed in the Muslim community. The gender dimension of Islamisation, Islamic resurgence and *sharī'aisation* is a case in point for the formation of domestic as well as transnational Muslim women's rights movements. The social control that saw the introduction of monitoring instruments for moral correctness (dress codes etc.) established Islamic standards in society which affected women's and men's daily lives differently – and curbed women's rights in the guise of democratisation. At the same time, urban and rural middle-class concerns grew out of a demand for the establishment of standards compatible with people's religious identity. This pertained to immediate services (medical, tourist, food, clothing etc.) as well as to the broader economic sector (finance, trade, commerce). I will attend to the visible and practice-related implications and impacts of Islamisation in Indonesia and Malaysia in the next chapter, focusing on the themes of Islamic economy and Islamic feminism.

This chapter has outlined the trajectory of Islamisation projects in education, politics, and economy. Concrete examples for the 'presence of Islamic knowledge' in these fields of inspection were the predominantly student-based *dakwah* movements in Indonesia and Malaysia, from where the spirit of Islamic resurgence spilled over into the higher echelons of the political and academic world. In the field of knowledge, the chapter showed the importance of transnational and transregional mobility for shaping of Islamisation processes 'back home'. Transversal connectivity in a general and transregional connections between Southeast Asia and the Middle East in particular have drawn the demarcations of faith-based geographies which escape the scales of nation-states and regions (e.g. in the case of Qom, al-Mustafa University and its overseas outreach).

Notes

1 Phrase in a presentation by Muhammad Wildan to the International Conference *Trans-L Encounters: Islamic Religious Education and Popular Culture*, Marburg University, Germany, 26–28 May 2016.

2 UMNO is the dominant party within the ruling coalition BN (Barisan Nasional or National Front). But because of its hegemonic position, it is often conceived of as *the* ruling party.

3 Mona Abaza (1999: 205) underscores this view: 'One could view ISTAC as a symbol of the Malaysian government's vision of 2020, with its intentions to promote economic prosperity as one of the leading Asian tigers and to cultivate an Islam with money, status and the means to acquire rich collections of books from Europe

and various parts of the Western world, an Islam of power and wealth and lavish institutions.'

4 It is interesting in this context to recall that SN Al-Attas devoted his book '*Islam and Secularism*' to the Muslim youth.

5 As of 2008, 21 public universities had been established.

6 This number was mentioned to me in a meeting with the Director General of Islamic Education, H. Kamaruddin Amin, in the Ministry of Religious Affairs, Jakarta, 21 April 2016. Other estimates are more cautious and suggest from 26,000 to 27,000 schools.

7 Personal meeting with the author, Jakarta, 19 April 2016.

8 An estimation given by Chaider S. Bamualim from the Center for the Study of Religion and Culture (CSRC) at State Islamic University Syarif Hidayatullah, personal communication, Jakarta, 19 April 2016.

9 On *madrasah* before and after the New Order period see Parker and Raihani (2011: 714–16).

10 These impressions are primarily based on visits to IAIN and STAIN (Sekolah Tinggi Agama Islam Negeri or State Islamic College) in Java between 2011 and 2014.

11 Personal conversation with Irfan Abubakar, Yogyakarta, 19 April 2016.

12 Paramadina University is particularly acknowledged for its study programme in the pursuit of preventing corruption. I have a personal impression of the institution through several visits to Paramadina's campuses and a guest lecture on corruption prevention.

13 The distribution of votes in parliamentary elections 1999 to 2014 are available at: www.ipu.org/parline-e/reports/2147_E.htm (accessed 3 June 2016). In 1973, all Islamic parties were forced to merge into the United Development Party (Partai Persatuan Pembangunan or PPP). PPP survived the fall of the New Order regime.

14 The establishment of the university in 1949 took place in Singapore; a branch campus was set up in Kuala Lumpur in 1959. The latter is commonly referred to as University Malaya after the separation of Malaysia and Singapore in 1965.

15 For a detailed narration of the banning of Darul Arqam in Malaysia see Hamid (2005). The group is still active in Malaysia and other countries; the 'Obedient Wives Club' and activists with an explicitly anti-Jewish agenda are said to be linked to it (cf. Derichs 2012).

16 For concrete examples of how *tarbiyah* missionary work on campuses was carried out, see Machmudi (2008: 113ff).

17 The criss-cross relations described here are condensed from various conversations with Indonesian and Malaysian university colleagues. I have double-checked them with information available from numerous biographical accounts on the internet.

18 INSISTS was founded by Hamid Fahmy Zarkasyi, who received his PhD from ISTAC in Malaysia and has served as *kyai* for the prominent *pesantren* Gontor in his home country Indonesia.

19 For an overview of Wan Daud's biography and professional record see the unauthored pdf document 'Prof. Dr. Wan Mohd Nor Wan Daud'. Available at: www.gmomf.org/wp-content/uploads/media/1474.pdf (accessed 30 June 2016). For his standing at INSISTS see 'Prof. Dr. Wan Mohd Nor Wan Daud: Dari Neo-Modernisme ke Islamisasi Ilmu'. Available at: https://insists.id/prof-dr-wan-mohd-nor-wan-daud-dari-neo-modernisme-ke-islamisasi-ilmu/ (accessed 30 June 2016).

20 An overview of Osman Bakar's biography is available at: www.cis-ca.org/voices/b/bakar.htm (accessed 30 June 2016).

21 Available at: www.lipia.org (in Arabic www.gmomf.org/wp-content/uploads/media/1474.pdf) (accessed 28 June 2016).
22 For a more comprehensive yet succinct overview of Shi'ite transregional ties between Indonesia and Iran see Formichi (2014); for Shi'ism in in Southeast Asia see Formichi and Feener (2015).
23 A *fatwa* is a scholarly opinion expressed by a religious authority.
24 The claim against Ahmadiyah refers to the belief that Mohammad was not the last prophet in Islam. This is seen as a deviation from the principal teachings of Islam.
25 For tracing personal ties and relations it is interesting to note that Vali Nasr is the son of Seyyed Hossein Nasr.

References

Abaza, Mona, 'Intellectuals, Power and Islam in Malaysia: S.N. al-Attas or the Beacon on the Crest of Hill', *Archipel* 58 (1999): 189–217.

Abdul Aziz, Zarizana, 'Malaysia – Trajectory towards Secularism or Islamism?' in Claudia Derichs and Andrea Fleschenberg (eds), *Religious Fundamentalisms and Their Gendered Impacts in Asia*, Berlin: Friedrich-Ebert-Stiftung, 2010: 44–67.

Alatas, Ismail Fajrie, 'Contemporary Indonesian Pilgrimage to Hadramawt, Yemen', *Contemporary Patterns in Transregional Islam* (Middle East Institute), 24 October 2014. Available at: www.mei.edu/content/map/ziarah-hadramaut-contemporary-indonesian-pilgrimage-hadramawt-yemen (accessed 23 November 2014).

Azra, Azyumardi, *The Origins of Islamic Reformism in Southeast Asia: Networks of Malay-Indonesian and Middle Eastern 'Ulamā' in the Seventeenth and Eighteenth Centuries.* Honolulu: University of Hawai'i Press, 2004.

Azra, Azyumardi, 'From IAIN to UIN: Islamic Studies in Indonesia', in Kamaruzzaman Bustamam-Ahmad and Patrick Jory (eds), *Islamic Studies and Islamic Education in Contemporary Southeast Asia.* Kuala Lumpur: Yayasan Ilmuwan, 2011: 43–56.

Baharuddin, Shamsul Amri, 'A Revival in the Study of Islam in Malaysia', *Man, New Series* 18 (1983) 2: 399–404.

Baharuddin, Shamsul Amri and Azmi Aziz, 'Colonial Knowledge and the Reshaping of Islam, the Muslim and Islamic Education in Malaysia', in Kamaruzzaman Bustamam-Ahmad and Patrick Jory (eds), *Islamic Studies and Islamic Education in Contemporary Southeast Asia.* Kuala Lumpur: Yayasan Ilmuwan, 2011: 113–35.

Bano, Masooda, 'Protector of the 'al-Wasatiyya' Islam: Cairo's al-Azhar University', in Masooda Bano and Keiko Sakurai (eds), *Shaping Global Islamic Discourses. The Role of Al-Azhar, Al-Madina and Al-Mustafa.* Edinburgh: Edinburgh University Press, 2015: 73–90.

Bano, Masooda and Keiko Sakurai (eds), *Shaping Global Islamic Discourses. The Role of Al-Azhar, Al-Madina and Al-Mustafa.* Edinburgh: Edinburgh University Press, 2015a.

Bano, Masooda and Keiko Sakurai, 'Introduction', in Masooda Bano and Keiko Sakurai (eds), *Shaping Global Islamic Discourses. The Role of Al-Azhar, Al-Madina and Al-Mustafa.* Edinburgh: Edinburgh University Press, 2015b: 1–18.

Chong, Terence, 'The Emerging Politics of Islam Hadhari', in Swee-Hock Saw and K. Kesavapany (eds), *Malaysia: Recent Trends and Challenges.* Singapore: ISEAS, 2006: 38–42.

Derichs, Claudia, 'Islamische Familiengesetze: Vom Zankapfel zum Reformobjekt' [Islamic Family Law: From Bone of Contention to Object of Reform], in Fritz Schulze and Holger Warnk (eds), *Islam und Staat in den Ländern Südostasiens* [Islam and State in Southeast Asia]. Wiesbaden: Harrassowitz, 2010: 127–45.

Derichs, Claudia, Islamischer Feminismus und Emanzipation [Islamic Feminism and Emancipation], in Carmen Birkle et al. (eds): *Emanzipation und feministische Politiken. Verwicklungen, Verwerfungen, Verwandlungen* [Emancipation and Feminist Politics. Entanglements, rejections, transformations]. Sulzbach: Ulrike Helmer Verlag, 2012: 165–80.

Derichs, Claudia, 'Transnationale Netzwerke Muslimischer Frauen – Eindrücke am Beispiel von Musawah for Equality in the Family' [Transnational Networks of Muslim Women – Impressions from Musawah for Equality in the Family], in Ina Wunn and Mualla Selcuk (eds), *Islam, Frauen, Europa* [Islam, Women, Europe]. Stuttgart: Kohlhammer, 2013: 225–40.

Derichs, Claudia, 'Constitutional Rights in Multiethnic States –The Case of Malaysia', in Dirk Ehlers, Henning Glaser and Kittisak Prokati (eds), *Constitutionalism and Good Governance. Eastern and Western Perspectives*. Baden-Baden: Nomos, 2014: 255–80.

Derichs, Claudia, 'Participation, Legal Discourse and Constitutional Rights – the 'Allah' Issue in Malaysia', in Noorhaidi Hasan and Fritz Schulze (eds), *Indonesian and German Views on the Islamic Legal Discourse on Gender and Civil Rights.* Wiesbaden: Harrassowitz 2016: 121–32.

Formichi, Chiara, 'Indonesia's Shi'a', *Contemporary Patterns in Transregional Islam* (Middle East Institute), 30 October 2014. Available at: www.mei.edu/content/map/contemporary-patterns-transregional-islam-indonesia%E2%80%99s-shi%E2%80%98 (accessed 28 July 2015).

Formichi, Chiara and Michael Feener (eds), *Shi'ism in Southeast Asia. 'Alid Piety and Sectarian Constructions*. Oxford: Oxford University Press, 2015.

Gillespie, Piers, 'Current Issues in Indonesian Islam: Analysing the 2005 Council of Indonesian Ulama Fatwa No. 7 Opposing Pluralism, Liberalism, and Secularism', *Journal of Islamic Studies* 18 (2007) 2: 202–40.

Großmann, Kristina, 'Women as Change Agents in the Transformation Process in Aceh, Indonesia', in Claudia Derichs and Andrea Fleschenberg (eds), *Women and Politics in Asia. A Springboard for Democracy?* Singapore: Institute of Southeast Asian Studies, 2011: 97–121.

Großmann, Kristina, *Gender, Islam, Aktivismus* [Gender, Islam, Activism]. Bielefeld: regiospectra, 2013.

Hadiz, Vedi, *Localising Power in Post-Authoritarian Indonesia. A Southeast Asian Perspective.* Stanford: Stanford University Press, 2010.

Hadiz, Vedi, 'Islamic Politics in Indonesia: Domestic Challenges, Cross-National Inspirations', *Contemporary Patterns in Transregional Islam* (Middle East Institute), 21 November 2014. Available at: www.mei.edu/content/map/islamic-politics-indonesia-domestic-challenges-cross-national-inspirations (accessed 12 December 2014).

Hafez, Farid, *Islamisch-politische Denker. Eine Einführung in die islamisch-politische Ideengeschichte* [Islamic-Political Thinkers. An Introduction to Islamic-Political History of Ideas]. Frankfurt am Main: Peter Lang, 2014.

Hamid, Ahmad Fauzi Abdul, 'The Formative Years of The *Dakwah* Movement: Origins, Causes and Manifestations of 'Islamic Resurgence' in Malaysia', *IKIM Journal* 10 (2002) 2: 87–124.

Hamid, Ahmad Fauzi Abdul, 'The Banning of Darul Arqam in Malaysia', *Review of Indonesian and Malaysian Affairs* 39 (2005) 1: 92–93.

Hassan, Riffat, 'Religion, Ethics and Violence: Developing a New Muslim Discourse', in Berma Klein Goldewijk (ed.), *Religion, IR and Development Cooperation*. Wageningen: Wageningen Academic, 2007: 161–85.

Hefner, Robert, 'Islamizing Java? Religion and Politics in Rural East Java', *The Journal of Asian Studies* 46 (1987) 3: 533–54.

Hefner, Robert, 'Civic Pluralism Denied? The New Media and Jihadi Violence in Indonesia', in Dale F. Eickelman and Jon W. Anderson (eds), *New Media in the Muslim World. The Emerging Public Sphere*. Bloomington, IN: Indiana University Press, 2003: 158–79.

Hoffstaedter, Gerhard, 'Secular State, Religious Lives: Islam and the State in Malaysia', *Asian Studies Review* 14 (2013) 4: 475–89.

Holst, Frederik and Saskia Schäfer, 'Anti-Feminist Discourses and Islam in Malaysia: A Critical Enquiry', in Claudia Derichs (ed.), *Women's Movements and Countermovements. The Quest for Gender Equality in Southeast Asia and the Middle East*. Newcastle-upon-Tyne: Cambridge Scholars Publishing, 2014: 55–77.

Kaptein, Nico J. G., 'The Voice of the Ulamâ': Fatwas and Religious Authority in Indonesia', *Archives de Sciences Sociales des Religions* 125 (2004): 115–30.

Kessler, Clive S., 'Islam, the State and Desecularization: The Islamist Trajectory During the Badawi Years', in Norani Othman, Mavis C. Puthucheary and Clive S. Kessler, *Sharing the Nation: Faith, Difference, Power and the State 50 Years After Merdeka*. Petaling Jaya: Strategic Information and Research Development Centre, 2008: 59–80.

Khoo, Gaik Cheng, 'The Rise of Constitutional Patriotism in Malaysian Civil Society', *Asian Studies Review* 38 (2014) 3: 325–44.

Kuis [Kolej Universiti Islam Antarabangsa Selangor], 'Introduction'. Available at: www.kuis.edu.my/en/kuis-info/introduction (accessed 24 April 2016).

Kushimoto, Hiroko, ''Azharization' of 'Ulama Training in Malaysia', in Masooda Bano and Keiko Sakurai (eds), *Shaping Global Islamic Discourses. The Role of al-Azhar, al-Madina and Al-Mustafa*. Edinburgh: Edinburgh University Press, 2015: 190–218.

Kusmana, '*Contemporary Interpretation of Kodrat Perempuan: Local Discourse of Muslim Women's Leadership in Indonesia*', unpublished PhD thesis, Erasmus University Rotterdam, 2015.

Lee, Julian C. H., *Islamization and Activism in Malaysia*. Singapore: Institute of Southeast Asian Studies, 2010.

Liow, Joseph Chinyong, 'ISIS in the Pacific: Assessing terrorism in Southeast Asia and the threat to the homeland, Testimony', 27 April 2016. Available at: www.brookings.edu/research/testimony/2016/04/27-isis-southeast-asia-liow (accessed 30 April 2016).

Machmudi, Yon, *Islamising Indonesia: The Rise of Jemaah Tarbiyah and the Prosperous Justice Party*. Canberra: ANU Press, 2008.

Marcinkowski, Christoph, 'Aspects of Shi 'ism in Contemporary Southeast Asia', *The Muslim World* 98 (2008) 1: 36–71.

Martinez, Patricia A., 'The Islamic State or the State of Islam in Malaysia', *Contemporary Southeast Asia* 23 (2002) 3: 474–503.

Md Akhir, Md Nasrudin, Siti Rohaini Kassim and Azmi Mat Akhir, 'Issues of Halal Interpretation and its Enforcement in Malaysia', in Kazuaki Sawai, Yukari Sai and Hirofumi Okai (eds), *Islam and Multiculturalism*. Tokyo: Organization for Islamic Area Studies (Waseda University), 2014: 1–10.

Md Akhir, Md Nasrudin, Siti Rohaini Kassim, Nor Nazihah Abd Ghani and Nurulaida Ramli, 'Halal Executive as a Measure for Standardization: The Role of Higher Learning Institutions', Takayuki Yoshimura and Satoshi Katsunuma (eds), *International Seminar on Islam and Multiculturalism: Islam in Global Perspective*. Tokyo: Organization for Islamic Area Studies (Waseda University), 2015: 11–12.

Maznah Mohamad, 'Women's Empowerment in Religious Contexts: Competitive Modernity and the Feminized Public Sphere in Malaysia', *Asien. The German Journal on Contemporary Asia* 132 (2014): 81–97.

Mir-Hosseini, Ziba, 'Muslim Women's Quest for Equality: Between Islamic Law and Feminism', *Critical Inquiry* 32 (2006) 4: 629–45.

Nasr, Seyyed Hossein, *Islam dalam Cita dan Fakta/Ideals and Realities of Islam*, translated by Abdurrahman Wahid and Hashim Wahid. Jakarta: Leppenas, 1981.

Nasr, Vali, *Forces of Fortune: The Rise of the New Muslim Middle Class and What It Will Mean for Our World*. New York: Simon and Schuster, 2009.

Nasr, Vali, *Meccanomics: The March of the New Muslim Middle Class*. Oxford: Oneworld Publications, 2010.

Noerdin, Edriana, 'Customary Institutions, *Syariah* Law and the Marginalisation of Indonesian Women', in Kathryn Robinson and Sharon Bessell (eds), *Women in Indonesia. Gender, Equity and Development*. Singapore: Institute of Southeast Asian Studies, 2002: 179–86.

Othman, Norani (ed.), *Muslim Women and the Challenge of Islamic Extremism*. Petaling Jaya: Sisters in Islam, 2005.

Ottendörfer, Eva and Patrick Ziegenhain, 'Islam und Demokratisierung in Indonesien: Die *shari'ah*-Gesetze auf lokaler Ebene und die Debatte um das Anti-Pornographie-Gesetz' [Islam and Democratization in Indonesia: Local *shari'ah* By-laws and the Debate on the Anti-Pornography Law], in Fritz Schulze and Holger Warnk (eds), *Religion und Identität. Muslime und Nicht-Muslime in Südostasien* [Religion and Identity. Muslims and Non-Muslims in Southeast Asia]. Wiesbaden: Harrassowitz, 2008: 43–64.

Parker, Lyn and R. Raihani, 'Democratizing Indonesia through Education? Community Participation in Islamic Schooling', *Educational Management, Administration and Leadership* 39 (2011) 6: 712–32.

Reid, Anthony (ed.), 'The Making of an Islamic Political Discourse in Southeast Asia', *Monash Papers on Southeast Asia* 27. Clayton: Centre of Southeast Asian Studies, Monash University, 1993.

Sakurai, Keiko, 'Making Qom a Centre of Shi'i Scholarship: Al-Mustafa International University', in Masooda Bano and Keiko Sakurai (eds), *Shaping Global Islamic Discourses. The Role of al-Azhar, al-Madina and Al-Mustafa*. Edinburgh: Edinburgh University Press, 2015: 41–72.

Schröter, Susanne (ed.), *Geschlechtergerechtigkeit durch Demokratisierung? Transformationen und Restaurationen von Genderverhältnissen in der islamischen Welt* [Gender Equality through Democratization? Transformations und Restaurations of Gender Relations in the Islamic World]. Bielefeld: transcript, 2014.

Sherlock, Stephen, 'Parties and Decision-Making in the Indonesian Parliament: A Case Study of RUU APP, the Anti-pornography Bill', *Australian Journal of Asian Law* 10 (2008) 2: 159–83.

Shiozaki, Yuki, 'From Mecca to Cairo: Changing Influences on Fatwas in Southeast Asia', in Masooda Bano and Keiko Sakurai (eds), *Shaping Global Islamic Discourses. The Role of al-Azhar, al-Madina and Al-Mustafa*. Edinburgh: Edinburgh University Press, 2015: 167–189.

Stark, Jan, *Kebangkitan Islam: islamische Entwicklungsprozesse in Malaysia von 1981 bis 1995* [Kebangkitan Islam. Islamic Development Processes in Malaysia from 1981 to 1995]. Hamburg: Abera, 1999.

Weiss, Meredith L., *Student Activism in Malaysia. Crucible, Mirror, Sideshow.* Singapore: NUS Press, 2011.

Yeoh, Seng Guan, 'In Defense of the Secular? Islamisation, Christians and (New) Politics in Urbane Malaysia', *Asian Studies Review* 35 (2011) 1: 83–103.

Zainah Anwar, *Islamic Revivalism in Malaysia: Dakwah among the Students*. Petaling Jaya: Pendaluk, 1987.

Zarkasyi, Hamid Fahmy et al. (eds), *Islamic Science. Paradigma, Fakta dan Agenda* [Islamic Science. Paradigm, Facts and Agenda]. Jakarta: Institute for the Study of Islamic Thought and Civilization, 2016.

Zulkifli, 'Qom Alumni in Indonesia: Their Role in the Shi'i Community', in Masooda Bano and Keiko Sakurai (eds), *Shaping Global Islamic Discourses. The Role of al-Azhar, al-Madina and Al-Mustafa*. Edinburgh: Edinburgh University Press, 2015: 117–141.

4 Empirical case studies

Islamic economy and Islamic feminism

This chapter turns to concrete case studies to trace the diffusion of Islamisation into everyday life. Chapter 3 addressed the spill-over effects and the implementation of policies and agendas that derived from the attempt to create epistemic authority through a religiously inspired worldview. The effects reached out to the public and the private, the collective and the individual dimensions of everyday life. This chapter focuses on two thematically organised empirical studies of spill-over effects in (a) the corporate world (Islamised corporate culture) and (b) the field of rights advocacy (here: equality from a Muslim feminist viewpoint). Both cases illustrate the pluri-local grounding of the knowledge that informs individuals' interactive behaviour.

The implementation of policies and agendas that are, ultimately, driven by a desire to have one's faith play a bigger role in the shaping of 'the good life' is reflected in various arenas of human interaction. The integration of Islamic principles into corporate culture is one example; another is the harmonisation of Islamic and non-Islamic frames of reference in advocacy work for equality and women's rights. The subsequent paragraphs discuss ideas of corporate culture in an 'Islamic economy' and of religious reference in the quest for 'equality in the Muslim family'. The material is taken from numerous fieldwork travels to Muslim-majority countries over the last ten years. The fieldwork is supplemented by publicly accessible scholarly studies, as well as other documents related to the topic which I obtained from conferences and on public websites. Before turning to the empirical cases, I share some reflections on religion as a conceptual term because the sociological understanding of it is helpful to relate the project of Islamisation with the notion of lived religion.

Assessing religion, economy and advocacy

Religion is frequently associated with culture, sometimes even treated like a synonym. The never-ending discussion about the definition of culture and religion notwithstanding, the two concepts have adopted different meanings at different points in time. They have a history in the very sense of Reinhart Koselleck's 'conceptual history', changing according to context (Koselleck 2002). In order to avoid the pitfalls of narrowing down complexity by providing a reductive

DOI: 10.4324/9781315642123-5

definition with limited explanatory scope, culture and religion should be treated as pivot terms that allow for negotiation of meaning. Siding with Malvin Richter, who reflected on the 'contestability' of concepts, it is useful to stress that meanings are seldom free from disagreement; they are contested:

> First, the term [contestability] indicates that disputes about such concepts as 'democracy' involved their central rather than their marginal meanings. [...] Second, in 'contestable' concepts, disagreements form an indispensable part of the meaning. [...] Third, [...] the meanings of some concept derive from controversy rather than from any consensus about their meaning. Certain concepts are valuable, not despite disputes about their meaning, but just because of such disagreements.
>
> (Richter 2000: 138)

The conceptual terms culture and religion are cases in point for the difficulty of achieving definitional consensus. Defining the terms has been a highly contentious task of the social sciences both past and present, and the study at hand will not pretend to make any further contribution to this debate. A disclaimer that has to be made is that religion in the present study is not identified as the core of culture – the reason being that doing so bears the tendency to associate cultural fault lines with religious ones, which is misleading. Since the focus of the present study lies on lived religion and its social and local manifestations, any direct identification of religion as the essential heart of 'a culture' would lead to a mismatch of scopes and scales. While a Muslim woman in China can relate easily to a fellow Muslim woman in France, both would probably state that they are living in very different cultures. As for the term religion, it:

> has been defined as a worldview; belief system; system of symbolic actions, rituals and ceremonies; normative framework for justice; sustain to the local and global order; uphold of human flourishing or interior human impulse towards God.
>
> (Klein Godewijk 2007: 34)

All such definitions, Klein Godewijk continues, 'introduce important approaches', but lack important elements that come to the fore in the shape of 'many different and ambiguous, powerful and ordinary aspects of the sacred and the spiritual in people's everyday lives' (Klein Godewijk 2007: 34). Instead of adding another aspect to the discursive issue of defining religion and attempts at associating or dissociating culture and religion with /from one another, it is consequential to apply Monica Miller's perspective and seek to 'understand how religion is constructed (socially), understood (contextually), translated (historically), and negotiated' (Miller 2013: 2). How religion is negotiated in human cooperation on a transregional, transnational and translocal scale is worth analysing for numerous reasons, among them the fact that 'we currently witness the revitalization of cultural and religious traditions as one of the most significant contemporary global trends' (Miller 2013: 11).

Applying a comprehensive understanding of religion, the sacred, the spiritual and faith, so the argumentative direction of this chapter, allows for the identification of variables that determine to a considerable extent why believers act in the way they do. As determinants of action and interaction, the connecting capacity of religion and faith for visions of 'the good life' oftentimes passes unnoticed by those who cannot relate to the concepts and principles behind them – be it because of linguistic unfamiliarity, different epistemic and experiential backgrounds or socialisation.

Mainstream theoretical approaches in the field of International Relations (IR) rarely give space to religion and faith – to the sacred and the spiritual – and to the individual mindset as elements of cooperation in the 'international system'.[1] Moreover, the terminology of global cooperation, development, human rights and the like does not match the vocabulary of ontological registers other than those generated in the West or the global North. An Islamically informed register of communication is a case in point. The underlying epistemologies differ and the hegemony of Western knowledge production on the global scale provides little room for a shift towards another lexicon or other frames of reference. While, for instance, *nushûz* (نشوز; 'disobedience' [of wife towards husband]/ 'marital disharmony')[2] as a conceptual term is immediately clear and comprehensible to a Muslim feminist in the discourse on gender equality, a women's rights activist not familiar with the term *nushûz* can barely relate to its semantic scope. At the same time, the distinction between the *English* terms equality and equity has served to create tremendous division among Muslim feminists (as explained below) – whereas others would probably not regard this distinction a fundamental issue in the 'global sisterhood'. The problem at stake, however, is not purely verbal or linguistic, but one that is deeply concerned with codes, scales, conceptualisations, and the production of knowledge.

Commodification, commercialisation and aestheticisation of religion

An Indonesian friend of mine frequently relates to me the information she receives via social media from her female Muslim friends. 'Lately, the hype are *Gucci* handbags made of *halâl* leather' she said. 'My friends recommend them and tell each other the shops in Jakarta where you can find them.'[3] Similarly en vogue was the exchange of *halâl* recipes for healthy dishes, and of addresses of posh coffee shops and restaurants serving *halâl* food. My friend insists that this trend is quite recent; a few years ago nobody cared about the Islamic correctness of a handbag from a famous international brand. But nowadays upper-class women who can afford expensive consumer goods do care. They also meet in private or public places for *majlis ta'lim*, learning sessions dedicated to enlarging one's religious knowledge. According to my friend, there is a lot of social pressure to join in these activities – so much so that it has become tough to, for instance, resist the donning of the headscarf (*tudung*) for women. The headscarf itself has become a faith-related fashion item of prime rank (cf. Lewis 2015). Competition among designers is fierce, and business is booming all across the Muslim world. The community of *hijabers* (from the Arabic term *hijab* حجاب for veil) which emerged in 2010 in Indonesia hosts many promising young designers. They associate the veil with a classy head covering and elegantly designed clothes (Rahayu 2016). 'In the 1970s and 1980s, and even well into 1990s, wearing the *hijâb* was considered as extremist in Indonesia – out of fear of a spill-over of the Iranian revolution' says Munid Rahayu (2016). This has changed rapidly, so that *hijâb* and Muslim fashion designers have become prominent respected personalities. But it is not entirely about fashion. 'The *hijâbers* make strong efforts in terms of piety and want to accomplish how to be a good Muslim' (Rahayu 2016). The faith dimension accompanying the headscarf as a commodity and commercial item is still recognised.

Other forms of commercialisation have found their way into the pilgrimage ritual. In metropolitan Southeast Asia, posters and billboards advertise the *umra* (small *hajj*) using a celebrity – a musician, actor etc. Such pilgramages can be booked in tourist offices like any other holiday tour. Performing the *hajj*, Indonesian colleagues say, has nowadays to be shared with those staying at home. A party before or after the pilgrimage, often celebrated in big hotels, is the norm among Indonesian middle-class Muslims. Pilgrimages to the Hadramaut in Yemen (an important destination for adherents of Sufism) have risen in popularity since the 1990s among Indonesian Muslims. As a result, Ismail Alatas (2014) observed, 'several Arabian airline companies including Emirates and Yemenia Airways began opening up direct routes between Jakarta and their respective capitals in the hopes of seizing this lucrative market'. 'Islamic sermons are not only religious teachings any more but have become part of formal programs and social functions'(Wildan 2016). Religious sermons are given on TV, in fancy hotels and other places that guarantee a huge audience. Female preachers such as Mamah Dedeh present their wisdom in various formats (see Mamah Dedeh 2009); the social media are naturally among them. This form of popular piety, states Muhammad Wildan (2016), speaks of the 'aestheticisation and privatisation of religion, alongside its commodification and capitalisation'. The importance for the consumer is a steady supply of *halâl* products, a concern that has led Malaysian companies to employ their own *halâl* executives (Md Akhir et al. 2015). Not unlike the conventional quality control in production, these executives conduct product checks, monitor packaging procedures, cleanliness and the like, i.e. they overlook the whole process of *halâl* production in order to fulfil the criteria for certification. Proper Islamic consumption (Fischer 2008) plus the necessary financial services (Islamic banking), gastronomical or medical (*tibb al-nabawî* or prophetic medicine) regard is as much a lifestyle signifier as it is an indicator of an increased religious consciousness.

As far as Islam's commercialisation is concerned, the business relies on trans- and multinational enterprises just like any other secular global business. A distinction can, however, can be made by what Daromir Rudnyckyj (2010) calls spiritual economies and Patricia Sloane-White (2011) calls the Islamic economy. I discuss this in more detail below. In view of the theme of knowledge in the lived religion, the following thoughts address what may be understood as a first approximation towards a cohesive picture of (mental, emotional, ideational) connectivities that are based on an Islamically informed epistemic space – the basic principle being that all knowledge derives from God. The procedural framework employed for this undertaking is the Islamisation of knowledge as introduced in Chapter 2, mainly in the broad sense, but also acknowledging the epistemic project with its origins in the late 1970s and early 1980s, when it was written with a capital K and accompanied the heyday of Islamic resurgence in various parts of the world. From the brief reiteration of the core ideas of the project and how it became criticised in the following decades (indicated by changing to the minuscule k), I move to empirical cases that serve to illustrate how 'Islamisation' may translate from intellectual discourse into practice. In distinction to the preceding chapter, I concentrate on cases of diffusions from intellectual discourse into practical everyday life which are no longer characterised by a mission of Islamisation (as was the case with *dakwah* and Islamic resurgence initiatives). Rather than having to stress that Islam is 'the' way of life, the actors introduced here are already fully immersed in the reality of a faith-conscious life. In other words, what motivated the *dakwah* and IoK protagonists of the 1970s and 1980s is now a given, a common good. By way of an example: Islamic banking is not something that has yet to be established and lobbied for, but is as natural and familiar as other forms of banking. The issue is which concepts of Islamic banking are applied in what way and how ambiguous or inconclusive concepts are dealt with in the sector (e.g. profit sharing agreements or equity participation) (cf. Iqbal 1997), is a matter of interpretation. For the 'in-group', taken here as the global community of Muslim people who to Islam is a way of life, there is no need to explain which Islamic principles are relevant for the individual and the community. It is the explanation and interpretation itself – relying on experts' exegesis and interpretation of the sacred sources – which may differ from person to person since there is no ultimate human authority to define right and wrong. This goes for financial and medical services, for the supply *sharî'a*-compliant tourism, the supply of *halâl* products and for virtually any kind of immaterial commodity. An overarching yet non-universal normative approval is *halâl* certification, which is a business in itself and no less important for consumption-conscious believers than a fair-trade certificate for advocates of global economic justice. It is a non-universal norm because the scope of what is still *halâl* and what is already *harâm* (forbidden) differs significantly, depending on who decides. Some traditional beverages containing alcohol in Central Asia, for instance, have been declared *halâl*, although alcohol consumption is conventionally inhibited for Muslims.[4]

The examples of a religiously informed perspective on 'economy' and 'equality' discussed below put forward an alternative frame of reference for human development, interaction and cooperation, albeit not by coining a term for an explicit alternative development model such as the Latin American 'buen vivir' or the de-growth model. The two selected empirical cases are:

(1) Islamic economy (اقتصاد اسلامي) and '*sharī'aised*' workplaces.
(2) Gender justice (عدالة النوع الاجتماعي) and transnational Islamic/ Muslim feminism.

The geographic scale – with regard to the terms transregional, transnational, translocal and pluri-local – stretches from the MENA region (Middle East and North Africa) to the Muslim-populated parts of Southeast Asia (the Muslim-majority countries Indonesia and Malaysia in particular) and, to a lesser extent, to other parts of the world. I concentrate mostly on Southeast Asia, extending the view from the MENA region which usually occupies centre stage as a reference region for Islamic thought and practice since it is regarded as the heartland of Islam (cf. the centre-periphery dichotomy adverted to in previous chapters). In the conflation of the two empirical examples I introduce and discuss what I think is oftentimes 'falling through the cracks' in assessments of Southeast Asian economies and the struggle of Muslim women's rights initiatives. Bearing in mind the plurality of the category 'Muslim' in ideological, confessional and many other regards, the case studies nonetheless reveal the wealth of common denominators among actors whose sense of belonging is very much linked with faith-related shared value orientations.[5] This sharing caters to the perception of 'emotional geographies' (faith-based geographies), hence cognitive and emotional spaces providing mutual understanding – an invisible transversal connectivity built on shared values, norms, principles and concernments. Religion and faith as well as the knowledge concepts related to them play a key role in this regard.

The subsequent sections try to capture the connecting features of transnational and, even more prominently, translocal Muslim activities. These activities are embedded in pluri-local ontological registers that reveal themselves most noticeably in the lexical merger of Islamic and Western vocabulary. Studying empirical cases of lived religion is a step towards drawing the wider picture. This wider picture, which is catered to in the present study, pertains to the potential transformative power of such forms of connectivity in the field of development policies, global cooperation and – last but not least – the scholarly activity named Area Studies.[6] It will be discussed in Part III. The empirical material is structured according to different themes, but relates to the subjectivity of individual Muslim lives and collectively shared ideas of lived Islam as overarching topics. The case of Islam in the economy tackles the theme of Muslim's professional organisation, while the case of equality in the Muslim family discusses the theme of women's rights and gender justice.

The Islamisation of Knowledge and its repercussions

The intellectual and epistemic project of an Islamisation of knowledge[7] originated, as we have seen, in ideas put forward by internationally mobile reformist thinkers. It was in the late 1970s and early 1980s when reformist ideas were picked up and freshly shaped in an endeavour to create epistemic unity between reason and faith, or the interlinking of knowledge with worship. These efforts bear witness of an ambitious philosophically inclined project of an Islamisation of Knowledge with a capital 'k'. Most commonly associated with the origins of this project are the Muslim intellectuals that have been introduced in Chapter 2, (i.e. Syed Naquib al-Attas, Isma'il al-Faruqi, Seyyed Hossein Nasr and also Fazlur Rahman) albeit not in the narrow context of Islamising knowledge but with a more 'liberal' touch. In Malaysia, Al-Attas and Al-Faruqi became the most vital promoters in the shaping of an Islamic epistemology, succeeded by devoted scholars like Wan Mohd Nor Wan Daud. By the 1990s, the project had spread quite extensively, advocated by Muslim intellectuals in the West as well as elsewhere. Egyptian sociologist Mona Abaza, who examined the project from a critical point of view, was led to ascertain that '[...] with minor variations in its application, this phenomenon seems to have taken a global dimension in the Muslim world' (Abaza 1993: 301). While critics disapprove of the exercise of 'infusing knowledge with spiritual insights' (Siddiqui 2011: 18), its proponents stress the value-added of an alternative Islamic approach to knowledge.

Islamisation of Knowledge in Al-Attas' sense adhered to a strong belief in an antagonistic relationship between religion (Islam) and secularism. It was a project seeking to expose a language of difference of Islam 'in terms of legalization, Islamic politics, state Islamization, education and ecology' (Abaza 1993: 306). This is still being pursued today by certain ideological currents in and beyond Southeast Asia (e.g. in Southern Asia) (cf. Siddique 2011). The opposite of the antagonistic is the reconciling approach, proponents of which prefer to propitiate the religious with the secular and live up to a Muslim identity even in environments where religion is not a frame of reference (e.g. the Wall Street business sectors, as referred to below) or in secular surroundings in general. Their orientation for spiritual guidance in everyday life is based on principles and concepts of faith, but is at the same time brought in line with the requirements of a manageable work–life balance. Obviously, there is no direct link between the project of an Islamisation of Knowledge in Al-Attas' sense and those who opt for a conciliatory relationship between the religious and the secular. There is, however, an indirect link between the 'capital K' and 'lower-case K' Islamisation project, since the latter comprises considerable criticism of the former. In the light of the discussion in Chapter 3, the purpose of the subsequent paragraphs is to become cognisant of the ways in which knowledge production with the vantage point of relating all knowledge to a divine power translates into lifestyles and professional activity. The preceding chapter ventured to capture the landscape of institutions of knowledge production and dissemination – from primary to tertiary level – which operate on a religious base. The proliferation of such institutions since the late 1970s and their consolidation as an important pillar of national education systems was directly linked with the political will to promote Islamic education – be it in the form of 'cultural Islam' like in Indonesia, or in the straightforward institutionalisation of an Islamisation of knowledge, as in Malaysia. Why was Islamic education acknowledged and fostered? The domestic political context is of importance in this context because the handy explanation that in both countries the Islamic resurgence movement had to operate in an authoritarian political surrounding glosses over too many aspects that merit recognition beyond political-systemic or regime-focused analysis.

Domestic political contexts

In retrospective of the two countries' domestic politics, the moves of enhancing Islamic education were perfectly in line with the overall political agenda of the time. In Indonesia, President Suharto had shattered the Communist Party PKI and subsequently purged the communist movement (1965ff), including anybody who appeared to sympathetic to it (e.g. the women's movement Gerwani). The vacuum that was left by the hundreds of thousands who fell victim to the regime's atrocities had to be filled somehow, all the more because a lot of social services had been carried out by supporters of PKI.[8] Directing the orientation of the Muslim majority in the nation towards Islamic values (i.e. religious values which had allegedly been shunned by communists) was a policy to fill the void. Organised Islamic activism was hence welcome, provided its surfacing occurred in the shape of cultural Islam and abstinent from any political inclination. In the 1980s, when the Suharto regime itself came under pressure and, as mentioned in Chapter 3, sought to secure the loyalty (= votes) of the masses, it seemed advantageous to sponsor the opening of channels for public Islamic discourses and positively respond to the demand for a more credible political commitment to Indonesia's role in the Muslim world. The clandestine *dakwah* work of the *tarbiyah* movement during most of the New Order period and the mushrooming increase of Islamic boarding schools after the fall of Suharto are but two tangible signifiers of the transition from pre- to post-New Order times. In the liberalised post-New Order climate, the *dakwah* generation could make full use of the opportunities of upward social mobility. The swift ascendance of former Muslim student activists into the higher echelons of politics and economy is an indicator for the successful consolidation of a Muslim middle class and its professionalisation.

In Malaysia, the New Economic Policy (NEP) formed the main framework for the stipulation on the domestic political agenda. Enacted and implemented in the wake of the racial riots of 1969, the NEP pursued two essential objectives: the eradication of poverty among the entire population; and the elimination of the identification of race with economic function (Hng 1998; Mahathir 1991). These objectives were paramount since the imbalance in economic strength and status between ethnic Chinese (the numeric minority) and ethnic Malays (the numerical majority) had been identified as the root cause of the 1969 riots. The Malay majority felt deprived against an economically powerful minority. Increasing the economic standing of the nation's most populous ethnic group (i.e. Malays who are Muslims qua constitutional definition) was thus the core task of the ruling parties for the sake of preserving political stability. When Mahathir Mohamad assumed the post of Prime Minister in 1981, he too committed himself to this task and took advantage of two simultaneous currents in Malaysian society: one that proactively sponsored the notion of 'Malay supremacy' in respect of political power and social privileges, and one affiliated to the broader movement of Islamic resurgence and *dakwah*. In a most logical combination, Mahathir attended to the concerns of both by aligning Islamic values with entrepreneurial skill and economic achievement. Accordingly, the debate about Asian values which occupied international discourses on the 'Asian miracle' and the like in the late 1980s and well in to the 1990s (virtually until the regional financial crisis struck several countries in Southeast Asia) was largely informed from the Malaysian side by notions of the importance of Islamic (rather than Confucian) values for economic progress. Hence, the motto *kebangkitan Islam* (Islamic awakening or resurgence) matched the national political goal of furthering successful economic performance, thereby utilising and appropriating citizens' religious sentiments (see Stark 1999). Even more consequential in the pursuit of this goal was the recruitment of leading figures of the Islamic resurgence movement into the main ruling party UMNO (United Malays National Organisation). The active embrace of the *dakwah*, resurgence and Islamisation of knowledge movement by Malaysia's authoritarian regime in the 1980s – embodied in the establishment of numerous institutions of Islamic education, as described before – explains why there not emerged a direct pendant to the Indonesian *tarbiyah* movement. Although the youth movement ABIM was strongly inspired by the Muslim Brotherhood, its affiliation to both the ruling party UMNO and the biggest opposition party PAS allowed its members to act openly and articulate political demands directly. For ABIM, neither the strategies and operating tactics of the Brotherhood nor those of the Jamaah Tarbiyah had to be employed on Malaysian soil.

Beyond domestic politics

The domestic political context just sketched out suggests that national specificities dominated the way in which policies of Islamisation were able to unfold. Consequently, the present study does not propose to make any definite statements on universal patterns. Having said that, it nonetheless seeks to supplement currently limited knowledge by analysing cases that could prove emblematic of a broader trend –Islamic resurgence in past decades as well as those of commodification, commercialisation, aestheticisation and mediatisation of Islam in the public sphere. Particular forms of organising by individual actors who subscribe to a Muslim identity reflect on behavioural features that often escape the conventional gaze at the corporate world and global advocacy networks. I therefore approach the case studies from a 'knowledge angle' which I consider salient for the argument of an epistemic adhesive that connects actors translocally, transnationally, and transregionally.

In terms of academic disciplines, the early project of an Islamisation of Knowledge was not confined to the social sciences or the humanities, but encompassed the natural sciences, mathematics, economics, engineering and so forth (cf. Lodhi 1994).[9] This trend can be traced back through publications that appeared in various languages, among them English. During fieldwork periods in Malaysia in the 1990s, I came across a broad range of books with titles such as *Towards an Islamic Theory of International Relations: New Directions for Methodology and Thought*, or *Islamization of Attitudes and Practices in Science and Technology*.[10] The latter covered several topics on the natural sciences and mathematics (e.g. in food and nutrition sciences, computer science education, earth science, groundwater hydrology or embryology). From the space that these and other books of similar orientation occupied a decade ago on the shelves of urban Malaysian bookshops, one can tell that they covered topics of considerable public interest. The mid-1990s, however, were a time when many of my interlocutors in Malaysia would tell me that the project of the Islamisation of Knowledge had failed – indicating that these books could be considered shelf-huggers and leftovers from a period when they were in high demand. In retrospect, I would not fully agree with this evaluation. Regardless of their loss of appeal, the books are remnants of a time when the project of the Islamisation of Knowledge enjoyed considerable political backing. By the 1990s, the integration of Islamic knowledge in academia had translated thoroughly into the establishment of institutions of higher learning: international Islamic universities, research institutes, think tanks and the like (see Chapter 3). Proactive political intervention putting Islam high on the agenda of national value-orientation facilitated the emergence of activists propagating a narrow-minded ideological 'tauhid worldview' (Ibrahim 2014: 47)[11] in which Islam stood as an 'all-embracing system of life' (Ibrahim 2014: 36). These ideological currents gained currency under the label of 'revivalists', whereas their opponents criticised their weak intellectual grounding and inability to deliberate seriously on the rich knowledge of Islamic intellectual tradition. Actors portrayed in the present chapter fit the latter rather than the revivalist current. They appear to intentionally dissociate themselves from epistemic hair-splitting or little more than grandiose pietistic rhetoric, and prefer an attitude that is primarily geared towards integrating religious principles and Muslim identity into their daily lives.

Over the course of time, the global wave of Islamic resurgence in general and the endeavour to Islamise the corpus of scholarly knowledge in particular, transformed into more practical, tangible and palpable fields. The transformative trajectory from the Islamisation of Knowledge to an Islamisation of knowledge (understood as the merger of Islamic and non-Islamic knowledge) is remarkable. Through the supply of educational institutions offering Islamic studies, the gain of Islamic knowledge in society grew. Augmenting one's knowledge about Islam soon advanced to a status marker, particularly in urban surroundings, as Sylva Frisk (2009) has analysed for Malaysia. Processes of Islamisation gradually pervaded the practical dimension of everyday life, including the corporate world. The term 'Islamic economy' conveys this development and hints, as we will see, at more than the rapid spread of Islamic banking and insurance institutions. In the realm of jurisprudence, Islamic family laws became a rallying point for contestation. The implementation of 'reforms' of family laws and personal status codes (i.e. laws pertaining to divorce, child custody, inheritance etc.), which did not always work out in favour of equal rights for men and women, was a frequent concomitant in several Muslim-majority countries. Consequently, women who disapproved of the shrinking of their rights in the guise of legal reform mobilised support for legal codes which are nurtured by more progressive registers of (Islamic) judicial knowledge – ultimately reconciling secular notions of gender equality with Islamic ones. Another concomitant was the re-imagination of the *umma* (the community of Muslims all over the world) brought about by a 'variety of global sociocultural transformations which serve to disembed political identities from national contexts and also to stretch social relations across time and space' as Peter Mandaville (2001: 2) put it. The cases introduced below illustrate some repercussions of this transformation in Muslim lives in a globalised world.

Islamic economy and sharî'aised workplaces

Walking through Indonesian or Malaysian bookstores in the 2010s, most of the books on the Islamisation of Knowledge are gone. Instead, one finds many lifestyle-orientated works referring to an 'Islamic way of XYZ'. These range from guidebooks on Islamic parenting; fashion magazines for *hijab*-wearing women; cartoon-style training booklets for studying the Qur'ân and the life of the prophet; manuals for men, women and children for praying in the mosque; tool kits to prepare for the pilgrimage to Mecca to comic books with male or female heroes/ heroines who represent the ideal Muslim. Comics addressing children feature young Muslim *Manga*- and *Anime*-style figures as moral role models. The business and management section contains numerous books on Islamic leadership and management skills. Women are increasingly included in this target group, with books giving advice about Muslim women's careers in the corporate world. These provide guidance for the managers and leaders in what is perceived as the Islamic economy (or الاقتصاد الاسلامي in Arabic). They promise to make the reader familiar with the fundamentals of the prophet's leadership model, style, strategies, skills, features, character and morale.[12] They draw from international studies on types of leadership (charismatic, paternalist, military, autocratic, laissez-faire, populist, administrative, executive, democratic, delegating and others) and relate them to features of prophetic leadership found in Qur'ân and Sunna (the collection of the prophet's statements, declarations, messages, pronouncements, teachings and reported actions). For those who are not yet familiar with Arabic script, language kits for self-learning can be found nearby. The main language is the respective national tongue (Malaysian and Indonesian in the cases studied here), but hardly any publication in the field can do without citations in Arabic, as exemplified below.

In the Islamic economy, enterprises are found in the segment of banks, insurance companies, human resources and training consultancies, accountancies and auditing firms (Sloane-White 2011: 305). The board members, directors, and owners of such enterprises are usually well equipped in the conventional wisdom of managing and leading a corporation. The conventional (secular) knowledge lacks an Islamic frame of reference. As an Indonesian informant put it, it 'does not live *sharî'a*'.[13] From an Islamic perspective, the conventional guidebooks promote principles that are useful to a certain extent, but are not fully compatible with those of Islam. They detract from faith-based values and care, for example, little about gender segregation or the double function of leading and serving. In theological terms, they ignore the principles that are seen by Islamic economists as being crucial: *tauhîd* (توحيد unity, cf. the 'tauhîdic worldview' in Chapter 2), *rububiyya* (ربوبية God's guidance to success), *khilâfa* (خلافة man as God's vicegerent on earth), and *tazkiyya* (تزكية growth and purification of man) (Alatas 1995: 93). 'The putting into practice of these principles results in *falah* [فلاح], that is, prosperity in this world as well as the hereafter' (Alatas 1995: 93; italics added).

In both the Islamic economy and the Islamic workplace, the spiritual dimension of an organisation becomes important. The principles and values attached to an Islamic corporate culture derive from Qur'ân and Sunna (i.e. the revelation on the one hand and the corpus of the reports and teachings of the prophet which have been complied as *ahâdîth* (احاديث, pl. of *hadîth* حديث) on the other). The knowledge network that is created around the idea of an appropriate Islamic leadership (prophetic leadership), for instance, is based on the information drawn from selected *ahâdîth* and *sûras* (verses) of the Qur'ân. Their content is interpreted in view of the topic at stake – let us say 'the theory of the prophet's leadership'. The interpretative procedure for a non-Arab readership usually takes three steps. First, the chosen phrase of the selected *sûra* is presented its original Arabic spelling, e.g. واجعلنا للمتقين اماما. The reference is given (here: QS al-Furqaan [25]: 74) and is usually followed by the translation into the language of the targeted reader (e.g. Malaysian or Indonesian).[14] Since there is no single, agreed-upon scholarly authority in Islam, there is no universally accepted translation of the phrase. Common English translations range from '… and make us leaders of those who guard against evil' via '… and keep us in the forefront of the righteous' to '… [let] ourselves [be] examples of the pious ones' or '… and give us [the grace of] leading the righteous'. The essence of the phrase, however, becomes quite clear. It is meant to convey that a proper Islamic leader is a 'righteous' one, a role model for the pious and an opponent of all evil. The notions derived from the sources shape, as Rudnyckyj (2010) has described it, a 'spiritual economy'. Rudnyckyj's most telling empirical evidence stems from fieldwork with Indonesian managers of the Krakatau steel corporation, who used Islamic training courses to 'transform the pieties and dispositions of employees to shape them into globally competitive personnel for the neoliberal economy' (Rudnyckij quoted in Sloane-White 2011: 309).[15] '[D]eveloping faith' Rudnyckyj (2010: 3) argues:

> refers to concrete initiatives designed to intensify religious practice under the presumption that doing so will bring the work practices of corporate employees in line with global business norms and effect greater productivity and transparency.

Islam is never against trade and profit, since, as is pointed out frequently in interviews with Muslim scholars and practitioners, the prophet himself was a trader and his first wife Khadija was a highly successful business woman. The goal of the corporate project is thus not to escape from profit-orientated business, but to 'decolonise' oneself from the (Western) mainstream of leadership merits and 'connect directly to Islam's Arab roots and its global brotherhood' (Sloane-White 2011: 310). Quoting from the website of the *Islamic Economy Award*,[16] the goal of Islamic economic action is indeed geared towards welfare and prosperity:

> Now in its second year, the annual award recognizes innovative world-class business initiatives and ideas that have contributed to the social and economic welfare of the Muslim population. These initiatives and ideas must prove to enhance bilateral trade and investment relations between Islamic nations and forge closer economic ties with the rest of the world towards fostering prosperity, harmony and well-being for all.
>
> (Reuters 2015)

The transnational, transregional and translocal connection between Muslims around the world is symbolised by the increasing language proficiency of Muslims from non-Arab countries in Arabic. Knowledge of the Arab lexicon in script and speech is a status symbol and a value on its own. Performing the *hajj* (pilgrimage to Mecca), which usually requires not only a lot of money but years of waiting since each country is allocated only a limited annual quota of pilgrims, adds to the individual's status credentials. The title of *hajji* (male noun) or *hajja* (female noun), which one becomes eligible for when the pilgrimage has been performed successfully, can be likened to a PhD in academia. It lifts one's social status and becomes part of the personal name, even for the children of the pilgrim who are referred to as 'son of' or 'daughter of' (*bin* or *bint*) a *hajji*. Increasing global mobility and digital modes of communication have facilitated not only the performance of the pilgrimage but also the acquisition of language skills for students. From Southeast and Central Asia, several thousands of students migrate to Middle Eastern countries each year.[17] They return with a particular lexical repertoire which helps them to build up local educational networks and implement their ideas in their home environment (organising study circles, building mosques etc.).[18] When they enter the corporate world, the observation of rules, procedures, and disciplinary norms coated in Qur'anic terminology and a faith-compliant interpretation, is what many employees want. A manager who caters to the notions of a religious identity is more likely to become a respected and accepted leader (often referred to by the Arabic term *khalîf* خليف) than one who ignores the religious/faith-related dimension of workers' wellbeing.

Khalîfa-inspired leadership may generate blessings (بركة *baraka*) and trust from God, when the duties and obligations of *fard al-'ain* (فرض العين individual duties) and *fard al-kifâyah* (فرض الكفاية community duties) are met. The concept of *khalîfa* is matched by the concept of *'abd* (عبد) or servant. A leader is expected to be a respected authority and at the same time submit himself to divine authority. As Mohamed Aslam Haneef and Hafas Furqani (2009: 180) point out:

> The *khalîfa-'abd*, unlike the rational economic man of modern economics, is not only interested in maximizing his own utility and preserving his self-interest but also in building an intimate relationship with God, his fellow human beings and the universe.

The relationships of man and god, man and man, and man and universe form the basis for an assessment of the ethical foundations of Islamic economics, 'i.e. the "behavior" of man related to the economic problem of scarcity, resource allocation, and decision making in consumption, production, distribution, exchange, etc' (Haneef and Furqani 2009: 180). While the vertical relationship between man and God does not play a role in conventional economics, it plays a crucial role in Islamic economics. Although there is no universally accepted definition of Islamic economics, most scholars agree on the importance of the behavioural dimension in the conceptual framework. How Muslim economic actors organise their resources, 'which are a trust' counts for the evaluation as 'true' Muslims in their society (Haneef and Furquani 2009: 183). Islamic ethical doctrine in Arabic and Qur'anic diction pervades the knowledge about leadership and management skills. The very notion of moral and ethical fidelity which Islamic orientations add to the conventional secular guidebooks on leadership renders the Islamic corporate leader a respected *khalîf*. During fieldwork in the *hajj* season in Malaysia in 2006, I got a first-hand idea of how the *khalîfa-'abd* model translates into corporate life. A manager of a medium-sized enterprise in Kuala Lumpur was preparing to travel to Mecca, the transport to the airport being scheduled for later in the day. The manager, let us call him Osman, had already donned the white cloth of the pilgrims (which is a typical Southeast Asian *hajj* gear), and family and friends had gathered to pay their farewell respects to him. One of those who had come was an employee of Osman's firm. He did not seem to be a very high-ranking person, but a trusted man; let us call him Aslam. He was weeping when he took Osman's hands to say goodbye. It was a solemn moment. Later on, he related to me that he had never experienced so much sorrow for the temporary absence of his boss and at the same time so much pride. Aslam was proud not only because his boss was performing the pilgrimage, but because he himself had been designated as caretaker of the firm during Osman's absence. Aslam transformed from *'abd* to *khalîf* for roughly six weeks. He was most grateful for the trust and confidence Osman had placed in him, but he was also aware of the task before him. His *khalîf* was leaving, and although traveling to Mecca had become a rather safe and all-inclusive package tour, he feared for his boss going to this faraway place. The intensive man-to-man relationship and the accompanying relationship of both to the higher authority of God were revealed in both men's firm belief in doing 'the right thing' for 'the sake of Allah' (في سبيل الله/*fî sabîl illah* in Arabic).

The application of the principles derived from Qur'an and Sunna has particular repercussions on the working conditions on the shop floor. To exemplify this, a glimpse at how the Islamisation and *sharî'aisation* of the workplace relates to the issue of gendered spaces in the factory is helpful. In her study of Malaysian firms in the Islamic economy, Sloane-White (2011: 324) states that 'all of the companies I studied enforced a hijab (head covering) policy for women'. Note that here the term *hijab*, the Arab term for the headscarf, is intentionally used instead of the local Malay term *tudung*. The creation of an Islamic workplace frequently includes having separate working spaces for men and women to avoid any close proximity that violates *sharî'a* norms. Close proximity encompasses handshaking and touching (not ultimately, but according to certain interpretations). The atmosphere of separation is welcomed by many female employees, as Sloane-White shows using the example of a woman who had changed her workplace to become an employee of an Islamicised[19] firm:

> One woman told me that she came to work each day with a sense of peace and calm inside her; these feelings sharply contrasted with those she felt in other jobs she had held. She pointed to the Qur'anic phrase on her computer screen and said that in this job she was reminded of God all day long. God's words were there when she turned her computer on in the morning; and because of the prayers which played on the loudspeaker in the morning, 'even the walls heard God'.
>
> (Sloane-White 2011: 323)

Sharî'a regulates the relationship between men and women in the family, too. The rules are usually codified in Islamic Family Law or the Personal Status Code. Most family laws grant husbands the right to guide their wives. This might also be transferred to the workplace, in that a husband can withdraw his wife from employment if he thinks that the employer treats her improperly or prevents her from taking care of her husband (cf. the term *nushûz*/نشوز mentioned above). The influence of *sharî'aisation* of the workplace is far-reaching; it does not stop at the management level to produce 'benevolent leaders'. The revitalisation of faith and religious identities in the corporate world, the connectivity to the Arab world, created by using a common language, and the moral and ethical commensurability of the Islamic workplace all count as merits in comparison to the secular world which is perceived to be lacking these features.

The secular world poses certain challenges to Muslim employees who would like to perform in a *sharî'a*-compliant way. I will briefly reflect on the conditions of working as a believing individual in a non-religious environment, using the case of professionals in the financial service sector, which will also be mentioned in the following section of conceptual reflection. For Muslims working on, for instance, Wall Street, several issues have to be pondered. Beginning with the observance of five prayers a day, abstention from alcohol, fasting during Ramadan, and handshakes with the opposite sex are central issues that require individual decision-making – never mind the fact that Wall Street financial institutions deal with interest (*riba* ربا), which is considered usury and is forbidden according to certain interpretations of the religious doctrine. Muslims coping with these challenges on a daily basis find ways to organise their lives around forbidden (*harâm* حرام), permissible (*halâl* حلال; *mubâh* مباح) or recommendable (*mustahabb* مستحب) behaviour by forming interest groups and associations that allow for consultation, mutual assistance, and exchanges of opinion. While the physical workplace stays the same, the individual actor *sharî'aises* his or her performance in a subjective, often invisible, manner as the institutional framework is a-religious and not easily adjustable to the requirements of lived religion. As one employee of the finance sector of Thomson Reuters Corporation explained in an interview with the *New York Times*, the underlying concept is called 'the law of necessity', requesting one to 'abide by the laws of the land you happen to reside in, whether it's the formal laws or the unwritten laws'. (Roose 2012) Simply put: When there is no designated space for praying available at the workplace, do not complain: any vacant room can serve the purpose.

The examples raised lead to some conceptual reflections on actors' *sharî'a*-compliant behaviour in the global economy. Within the framework of integrating religion and faith into corporate life and professional performance, the Islamic economy and the *sharî'aised* workplace can be conceptualised as a feature of a collective 'conscientisation' of Muslim professionals. Bridget Welsh (2008) has analysed the political and economic setting in which Muslim professionals expanded their presence in Malaysian society. While specific circumstances in the case of Malaysia led to the growth and assertion of Muslim professionals in this country, Welsh (2008: 37) also discerns general patterns of the phenomenon:

> Throughout the Muslim world professionals play a vital role in influencing political values, often serving as a conduit that feeds into the formal political elite. From Egypt to Indonesia, lawyers, professors, doctors, journalist, and businessmen are role models and leaders in everyday life and have considerable influence in shaping norms and setting the public agenda.

Muslim professional organisations – lawyers' associations, chambers of commerce, medical bodies and the like – are captured by the idea of bestowing their very professions with a particular Islamic spirit, oftentimes based on individual piety and a belief in the duty to fulfil the obligations of the individual (*fard al-'ain*). From a political analytical perspective, the forming of professional and other interest organisations is a typical feature of proactive political participation. This counts for democracies and non-democracies (authoritarian and hybrid systems, even dictatorial regimes) alike. Malaysia, as a case in point for an authoritarian system until the mid-1990s,[20] saw the 'narrowing of political space in the wake of the 1969 race riots' in the 1970s, leading to 'the emergence of political Islam as the populace's main vehicle for organizing and voicing concerns' (Welsh 2008: 37). The deepening of religious identity and the global trend of an assertion of an Islamic identity through and beyond the decade of the 1970s (epitomised by the Iranian revolution in 1979) facilitated the manifestation of Islam as a way of life in Muslim communities. Issues such as setting 'appropriate professional standards for *sharia* law' (Welsh 2008: 37) occupied the agendas of Muslim professionals. The trickle-down effects onto the shop floor and the shaping of whole economic sectors such as banking or insurance are the result of a concerted form of interest aggregation in the pursuit of favourable conditions for one's own professional well-being.

Muslim professional organisations do not always have to be coated in a religious diction. Members of the international organisation of Muppies (Muslim Urban Professionals, founded in 2006), for instance, prefer to focus on professional success and community service without putting forward the terms of the sacred sources (cf. Muppies 2014). The organisation's activities are dedicated to the advancement of Muslim professionals all over the globe. As stressed in its 2014 annual report, the vision and the mission of Muppies relate to both global networking and the development of leadership:

> Our vision is to create a global network of professionals that supports the advancement of Muslim leaders in private, public and non-profit sectors. Our mission is to provide a platform for current and future Muslim professionals to develop leadership in their careers.
>
> (Muppies 2014)

While there is no mention of religion or faith in the self-portrait of Muppies, the members' community service is often linked to work with mosques and other religiously based institutions. Members also exchange opinions on how to handle challenging situations such as shaking hands with persons of the opposite sex who are not relatives, or whether or not to join colleagues in visiting establishments serving alcohol. The top industries in which Muppies members are working cover consulting, financial services, investment and commercial banking, private equity, and law (Muppies 2014). Applications for membership are competitive and have to meet a highly focused set of membership criteria. The application guide of the organisation's website points out that '[m]any applications are declined because they are incomplete or inaccurate, or the applicant does not come from one of the career fields' that have been designated as acceptable: industry, entrepreneurship, consulting, finance, and social enterprise – some of them further specified (see Muppies 2015). Geographically, Muppies members are concentrated in the United States of America; Canada, the United Kingdom, the United Arab Emirates and Pakistan comprise have lower proportions (6 to 1 per cent of the 2015 total [Muppies 2014]). With this composition, the organisation caters to what Peter Mandaville (2001: 110) calls the 'cross-fertilization between local experience and intellectual resources developed in global settings'.

The examples of national and international professional Muslim organisations and interest aggregation shows the re-configuration of Islamic knowledge in Muslim lives and practices. Conceptualised in this way, the Islamic economy is on the one hand comparable to other normative models of economic order such as the 'social ecological market economy' (following the principles of ecological sustainability), and on the other hand displays the results of a global communication process that brings with it 'the opportunity to critically engage with the question of who, what, and where Muslim [...] community can be in the time of translocality' (Mandaville 2001: 4).

Gender justice and transnational Islamic feminism

The preceding case of *sharî'a*-compliant workplaces and Muslim professionals illustrated how scientific and technocratic approaches to common tasks and services in the corporate world become wrapped in ethical notions of Islamic thought and tradition. I conceive of this as an outcome of intensified efforts to Islamise dimensions of 'knowledge' that have gradually been translated and diffused into individual lifestyles. The second case study represents a project that also aims at an explicit reconciliation between the religious and the secular. Similar to the Muppies' approach, the dichotomy of religious and secular is not abandoned or denied, neither does it lead to antagonisms or contradictions (at least not *within* the group of activists that are portrayed). I introduce a single empirical example, namely a transnational Muslim women's rights initiative which engages in projects of 'knowledge building' (بناء المعرفة) around core concepts in Islamic thought. It is the network Musawah for Equality in the Muslim Family – musawah (مساواة *musâwâa*) being the Arabic word for 'equality'. Musawah for Equality in the Muslim Family is an ever-present participant the contentious debate on Muslim women's rights and the even more contentious discourse on Islamic feminism. It positions itself clearly by pursuing an understanding of equality that rejects the notion of a complementary relationship between men and women (which is associated with traditionalist views and attitudes venerated by Islamists and Salafists), and subscribes to the notion of heteronormativity. Previous research on the network has been conducted (cf. Derichs 2013; 2010),[21] but relating it to the issue of knowledge opens up a new perspective.

The network is usually referred to as Musawah. The name indicates that the central issue it addresses is that of equality – in particular in the framework of law and jurisprudence, which is a major concern for many Muslim women. Musawah is backed by leading Muslim reformers and regards itself a 'global movement for equality and justice in the Muslim family' (Musawah 2015a). It was founded by eleven internationally prominent representatives of Islamic women's and women's rights movements, who in 2007 formed Musawah's planning committee.[22] The committee members' list looked like a Who's Who of the feminist Islamic women's movements – among them well-known women's rights activists such as the late Cassandra Balchin from Great Britain. The initial planning committee was dissolved in favour of an International Advisory Group, founded in February 2010 in London.[23] Musawah concentrates on the incorporation of principles of equality in the family and urges governments around the world to uphold them. The principles are:

- Equality, non-discrimination, justice and dignity as the basis of all human relations;
- Full and equal citizenship for every individual; and
- Marriage and family relations based on equality and justice.

(Musawah 2015c)

Musawah activists wish to accelerate the pressure for reform of the Islamic/Muslim Family Law[24] in their respective nation-states. Accordingly, transnational networking serves the strengthening of initiatives on the national level. The importance of the transnational dimension, however, should not lead us to underestimate the relevance of local and national conditions and context. Malaysia stands as a case in point, because the mix of ethnic and religious affiliations, the context of a post-colonial and semi-authoritarian political system[25] as well as the regional and international competition for reputation and foreign investment renders the country an arena for fierce contestation. Malaysia reflects what Tilly and Tarrow (2007) have theorised as 'contentious politics'. Since Islam has become extremely politicised in this amalgamation of traits, the women's movement is sometimes torn between demands from diverse groups that claim ethnic, religious or political loyalty (cf. Ng, Maznah and tan 2007). The official launch of Musawah in February 2009 revealed the contentious politics into which the network was dragged even before it formally existed (cf. Derichs 2010: 408). Here, the meaning of the term translocal surfaces in a specific manner. The understanding of 'local' is that of a subnational geographical, but also an emotional or ideational space. Musawah activists in a country such as Malaysia form a minority by number (taking the nation-state as the scale to measure), but they are connected tightly to activists in other countries and enjoy the above mentioned emotional and faith-based geography and sense of belonging with fellow activists in other local parts of the world.

Musawah offers an example for an association of actors who base their argument on the conviction of a 'humane' Islam. For Musawah's activists as well as scholars and public intellectuals in this field, Islamic principles are perfectly in line with 'secular' international conventions on women's rights. A humane Islam symbolises, and this is remarkable, a result and not a beginning of intra-Islamic dialogue and integration. Starting from the vantage point of this achievement (i.e. a shared understanding of what equality in the family should incorporate) and of the principles of Islam as a source of justice and equality, Musawha's supporters have entered their struggle for family law reform. The intra-religious debate on concepts and identity markers such as 'Islamic', 'Muslim', and 'feminism' is nonetheless ongoing. Conventionally, the emergence of a 'new feminism' in Muslim-majority countries was attributed to initiatives of the mid-1980s, when Muslim women engaged in attempts to prove that equality is an inherent concept of Islam. In Riffat Hassan's words:

> Having spent almost thirty years in doing research in the arena of Women in the Qur'an, I know that the Qur'an does not discriminate against women. In fact, in view of their disadvantaged and vulnerable condition, it is highly protective of their rights and interests. But this does not change the fact that the way Islam has been practiced in most Muslim societies for centuries has left millions of Muslim women with battered bodies, minds and souls.
>
> (Hassan, 2007: 181)

Over the years, many women's rights organisations and networks organised themselves nationally as well transnationally with the common goal of implementing gender justice and gender equality within an Islamic environment. This endeavour became associated with the term Islamic feminism. Yet, as Ziba Mir-Hosseini (2006: 640) observed, there is no unitary definition regarding these concepts of gender justice and gender equality, and even the approaches to reaching a consensus in understanding differ from one local context to another. The diversity of the many different currents of feminists, along with the frequent objection of activists to being labelled 'Islamic feminists', has made it virtually impossible to define what kind of feminism is meant or desired.

In one of the recent bulletins of Musawah's parent organisation, the Malaysian women's NGO Sisters-in-Islam (SIS), the topic 'Islam and feminism' was raised (again) and the spectrum of its understandings summarised (Sisters in Islam Forum 2014). While some actors in the global movement that is usually referred to as 'Islamic feminism' distance themselves from the term 'feminism' (e.g. Amina Wadud), others are more inclined to embrace it (e.g. Ziba Mir-Hosseini or the late Fatima Mernissi). Most of the prominent authors and activists in Islamic feminism, however, explain their differentiating stance explicitly (e.g. Asma Barlas). Zeenath Kausar, a 'scholar-activist' in Islamic thought and women's rights, strongly advocates for women's empowerment through the Islamisation of Knowledge (Sisters in Islam Forum 2014: 27). The spectrum of opinions and personal convictions is thus broad and complex. The notion of Islamic feminism can only hint at some shared features and forms an utterly vivid discursive turf. The members of Musawah, however, agree upon central themes of gender equality and have built a framework of action around it covering knowledge building, capacity building, international advocacy and outreach (see www.musawah.org).

The knowledge-building project Musawah began to engage with in 2012 is focused on two core concepts of Islamic legal interpretation and jurisprudence: *qiwâma* (قوامة; male authority over women) and *wilâya* (ولاية; male guardianship of women and children). These are concepts 'which are commonly understood as sanctioning men's authority over women' (see Eshkevari 2013 for details). In the networks' own words:

> As interpreted and constructed in Muslim legal tradition, and as applied in modern laws and practices, these concepts play a central role in

> institutionalising, justifying and sustaining a patriarchal model of families in Muslim contexts. In Muslim legal tradition, marriage presumes an exchange: the wife's obedience and submission (*tamkin*)[26] in return for maintenance (*nafaqah*) and protection from the husband. This theoretical relationship, which still underlies many family law provisions in our contexts as Muslims today, results in inequality in matters such as financial security, right to divorce, custody and guardianship, choice and consent in marriage, sexual and reproductive health and rights, inheritance and nationality laws. This inequality is at odds with the underlying ethical principles of Islamic [sic!] as articulated in the Qur'an. It also clashes with contemporary notions of Islamic and human rights principles, and with the reality that men are often unable or unwilling to protect and provide for their families.
>
> (Musawah 2015d)

The aim of Musawah's knowledge-building initiative is two-fold. On the one hand, it is meant to show that patriarchal and discriminating interpretations of *qiwâma* and *wilâya*, which are still frequently applied in Muslim jurisprudence and *sharî'a* courts throughout the Muslim world, are outdated and 'no longer reflect the justice of Islam' (Musawah 2015d). On the other hand, a fresh and unbiased understanding of the terms in legal contexts renders them perfectly compatible with principles advocated in international conventions such as CEDAW (Convention on the Elimination of All Forms of Discrimination against Women). Interpretations other than the ones presented in traditional Islamic jurisprudence 'are both possible and more in line with human rights principles and contemporary lived realities' (Musawah 2015d). The connectivity between Musawah's activists from all over the world is based on their shared experience as 'women living under Muslim laws',[27] which leads them to argue in their own terms for equality rather than echoing the language of the 'secular' women's movement.[28]

Perceiving Musawah in conceptual categories leads us to social movement theory. Following the typology of Margaret Keck and Kathryn Sikkink (1998), Musawah can be typified as a *transnational advocacy network* or TAN. TANs as networks encompass 'relevant actors [who are] working internationally on an issue, who are bound together by shared values, a common discourse, and dense exchanges of information and services' (Keck and Sikkink 1998: 2). Another important notion is that activists in TANs 'try not only to influence policy outcomes but to transform the terms and nature of debate' (Keck and Sikkink 1998: 3). According to Valerie Sperling, Myra Marx Ferree and Barbara Risman (2001: 1157), they 'mobilize smaller numbers of individual activists who use more specialized resources of expertise and access to elites'. Hence their supporters are usually not gathering in mass demonstrations, but carry out their networking in formal or informal organisations. This description of transnational advocacy networks matches with transnational Islamic women's networks which are 'organized around principles of challenging gender hierarchy and improving the conditions of women's lives' (Sperling, Ferree and Risman 2001: 1157). Bearing these features in mind, Musawah can be taken as an example of a TAN that engages in a field of jurisdiction which applies predominantly to Muslims (Islamic/ Muslim Family Law).[29] It addresses the issue of equality within the Muslim family in particular, but invites non-Muslim supporters who subscribe to the network's principles and framework for action to join. The framework for action is deliberately integrative in that it bases its content on both religious and universal (secular) values. Founded in the late 2000s, Musawah is one of the younger associations in the spectrum of women's networks organising beyond national borders. Against the backdrop of an increasing global trend of strengthening Muslim's piety and juxtaposing religious against secular values and orientations, Musawah may also be seen to represent a countermovement towards retrograde or revivalist tendencies in Islamic thought – assuming a counter position towards IoK. Yet it takes part in a specific form of integrating elements of Islamic sources into the conventional body of knowledge since it legitimises the struggle for gender equality from an Islamic religious point of view. The effort of building knowledge is geared towards an updating of religious knowledge, presented in clear distinction from the early endeavour of an Islamisation of Knowledge which would reject the idea of making secular notions of gender equality consistent with notions of Qur'ân and Sunna. This is achieved by conceding, for instance, that 'Islamic jurisprudence and positive law (*fiqh* فقه) is an historical development, socially constructed and embedded in diverse social contexts, and not a sacred, revealed and unchangeable part of religion' (Mir-Hosseini et al. 2013: 4). Producing new knowledge about traditional Islamic terms and concepts is expected to reach out to both the Muslim community as well as the non-Muslim community. The non-Muslim community is usually not familiar with the terms and concepts that derive from religious sources, whereas the Muslim community maybe familiar with them, but has learned about their meaning only in the framework of conservative interpretations. Moreover, notions such as gender equality are 'newly created issues' in Islamic juristic tradition (i.e. 'issues for which there is no previous ruling' (*masâ'il mustahdatha* مسائل مستحدثة)); 'Muslim jurists have not had to address [them] until the twentieth century' (Mir-Hosseini et al. 2013: 1). Muswah's effort is thus bi-directional in terms of its epistemic compass.

Pulling the strings together

The topography of Islamisation has expanded transnationally, transregionally and translocally. The 'prominence of identity politics among Muslims' (Weck, Hasan and Abubakar 2011: 2) feeds into an ongoing increase of Islamic symbols in the public sphere, or put more succinctly, 'the florescence since the 1970s of Islamic piety and religiosity in conjunction with diverse manifestations of a resurgent or revitalized Islam in various public arenas' (Peletz 2013: 604). While the claim of a direct causal relationship between the epistemic project of an Islamisation of Knowledge and the empirical cases introduced in this chapter is not discernible, mutual influence and reciprocal effects may well be assumed. It seems indeed legitimate to speak of a transformative trajectory from an Islamisation of Knowledge to an Islamisation of knowledge just because the ideological framework of the former was rejected by so many Muslims during the decades. I have taken the Islamisation of knowledge as a vantage point for this study since the production of knowledge and the modes of knowledge production *per se* inform our way of analysing. I have done this in a preferably non-normative manner, last but not least because I fully agree with Michael G. Peletz (2013: 604) in the confession that a:

> defensible middle ground or balance in the study of Muslim politics and culture is exceedingly difficult to achieve. This is especially so if one seeks to produce descriptions and analyses that are robust, nuanced, empathetic, and aspire to objectivity, yet are simultaneously geared toward laying bare and critiquing structures of inequality and social processes that involve alienation or dehumanization.

A first attempt to escape the pitfalls of normative judgements about and achieving a balance in the study of affairs connected to a particular religion is to simply not approach the topic from a normative point of view. Yet a decision has been made here, since the phenomena described above are subsumed here under the rubric of Islamisation or even *sharī'aisation*, whereas others would probably categorise them as 'manifestations of processes involving the de-privatization of religion or the desecularization public life' (Peletz 2013: 605). I have chosen to take the former approach (Islamisation) as my point of departure and relegate the latter (desecularisation) to second rank because I feel uncomfortable with the strong juxtaposition of religious and secular. Islamisation in the case studies introduced above does not ignore the accomplishments of non-Islamic corporate leadership, secular judicial knowledge or UN-backed women's rights struggles over time. On the contrary, the embedding of existing ideas about economy, professionalism, jurisprudence, and equality in Islamic frames of reference is much more palpable than their outright rejection and substitution.[30] Metaphorically speaking, Islamisation along this line gives the dress new cut and colour, but does not reject it as an element of human attire or substitute it by something completely different.

There is, to my mind, heuristic value in the term Islamisation in general and Islamisation of knowledge in particular. I have showed that a religiously informed perspective on economy and rights advocacy puts forward an alternative frame of reference for human interaction and cooperation. In development studies' terms, inter-Islamic cooperation across borders does not represent a type of South-South cooperation. Rather than linking actors and institutions of the South under an explicit paradigm, cooperation in what can be called 'Muslim worlds' (Freitag 2013)[31] is spiritually anchored, yet intentionally mercantile-orientated in economic terms, and more subtle in scale, linking the Arab-Islamic world (parts of which belong to the global North) with non-Arab Muslim worlds. The connectivity is to a significant extent supported by the command of not only the Arab language, but also the semantics which are put into service for the creation of a particular feeling of having something in common and having something to share – hence of belonging. This feeling of belonging stretches across continents, so that the individual 'comfort zone' adopts emotional quality and can easily become detached from the geographical locality of people's 'home' (Stephan-Emmrich 2013); home becomes a pluri-local place and space: the mosque in Qom is as much home as the one in Jakarta. If emotional well-being and spiritual feeling-at-home is meant to form a component of a vision of 'the good life' and thus of a comprehensive concept of interaction, the frequently articulated need to bestow this dimension of life with more attention and respect in the reflection on international cooperation (cf. Brigg 2014) is intelligible. My own observation of how Islamic concepts and the mastery of their usage in trans- and international communication underpins the relations between 'Islamic nations' leads me to the inference that the view of global cooperation that I have been socialised with glosses over a huge amount of modes of cooperation which had simply escaped my awareness. These modes have not been addressed in any textbook I read. The task is to access them analytically and relate them critically to the overarching scholarly exercise of getting to know about other approaches to knowledge (i.e. approaches that are not underlying the hegemonic apparatus of conceptual reasoning found in mainstream books and journals of the various disciplines).

As for the variables that determine to a considerable extent why believers act in the way they do, which I purported to identify in this chapter, the following three can form a first tentative set: principles of human interaction; rootedness of human values in religious values; and moral/ethical commensurability with one's faith. As the case studies revealed, an alternative frame of reference for human behaviour, interaction and cooperation is shaped by the importance that is granted to the spiritual and emotional dimension of 'the good life' (including lifestyle questions), and by the embedding of personal and collective goals in a religiously grounded worldview. In the following chapter, I draw from the empirical case studies discussed here. I analyse the findings from the perspective of producing not only knowledge in general, but *area knowledge* in particular. I show that 'new' geographies (or areas) emerge when the focus of analysis shifts from conventional area boundaries towards boundaries defined by particular concepts, norms, and principles that are shared across geographical distances. It jumps the conventional scales of areas (van Schendel 2001) and emphasises the inclusion of pluri-local settings in the study of areas.

Notes

1 As far as I can oversee the literature, this is the case in theoretical approaches focusing on state and non-state cooperation alike.
2 The translations can only give a rough idea of what is actually associated with the respective terms in daily life as well as jurisprudence.
3 Private conversation, Jakarta, April 2016.

4 This example was raised by Aisalkyn Botoeva in her presentation 'Imams as business ethicists in Kyrgyzstan' to the international workshop on *Mobile Muslim Professionals. Trans-regional Connectedness and (Non-)State Cooperation in Central Asia, Southeast Asia and the Middle East*, Berlin, 14–15 April 2016.

5 I explain in more detail why I use the term 'Muslim' instead of 'Islamic' in Chapter 7, referring to the notion of 'Muslim world'.

6 In this regard, the denotatum and the boundaries of 'regions', 'areas' etc. come under scrutiny. As the recent re-introduction of the Mediterranean as a geographical area of study shows, regions can be demarcated quite differently at different points in time. For Asia, Willem van Schendel was one of the first to hint at the sometimes skewed definition of 'regions' and 'areas' in academia and politics (see van Schendel 2001).

7 It is worth mentioning that the 'globalisation of knowledge' is currently pushed as an attempt to re-consider or even re-write a global history of knowledge and to thereby avoid the eurocentric approach of taking Europe and the USA as the centres from where knowledge spread into other parts of the world.

8 There is not much untainted literature available on the PKI and an open public debate on '1965' is still, by-and-large, taboo in Indonesia. Concerning the social engagement of Gerwani before the purge see Keller (2015).

9 The chapters in Lodhi 1994 cover topics such as 'Use of Islamic Beliefs in Mathematics and Computer Science' (by Muhammad Ishaq Zahid); 'A Blueprint for the Islamization of Attitude and Practice in Earth Sciences with Special Emphasis on Groundwater Hydrology' (by Abdel A. Bakr); 'Islamization of Attitude and Practice in Embryology' (by Ali Kyrala); or 'The Making of a Scientist: The Islamization of a Muslim Scientist' (by M.A.K. Lodhi).

10 The first edition by Abdul Hamîd A. AbûSulaymân, was published as early as 1989 and reprinted in 1994; the second, by M.A.K. Lodhi, appeared in 1987, had a second edition in 1993, and a third in 1994. Both are publications from the International Islamic Publishing House in Riyadh, Saudi Arabia, which distributed the volumes, and the International Institute of Islamic Thought in Herndon, Virginia, USA (see AbûSulaymân 1994; Lodhi 1994).

11 *Tauhîd* literally means 'unity' and is often referred to when the unity (i.e. non-separation) of state and religion is emphasised.

12 This is basically the content of Shoni Rahmatullah Amrozi's Indonesian publication *The Power of Rasulullah's Leadership* (see Amrozi 2012).

13 Conversation with an academic from Universitas Islam Nasional (National Islamic University), Yogyakarta, 22 November 2014.

14 The example is taken from Amrozi (2012: 57).

15 Part of Rudnyckyij's findings, summarised in Sloane-White (2011: 309).

16 Since 2013, the United Arab Emirates offers a special *Islamic Economy Award*. The award is divided into eight key Islamic economy categories: money and finance; food and health; media; hospitality and tourism; waqf and endowments; SME development; Islamic economy knowledge infrastructure; and Islamic arts. For details see Reuters (2015).

17 Cf. the numbers mentioned in the previous chapter for foreign students at the three big universities Al-Azhar, Al-Mustafa and Al-Madina.

18 Interview with Jowel Conudaw, Manila/Philippines, 4 September 2014. It should be mentioned that Middle Eastern students going to Southeast Asia (Malaysia

in particular) is equally popular; an estimated 80 per cent of student migrants in Malaysia come from Muslim-majority countries (cf. Killian 2013).

19 Sloane-White uses the term 'Islamicized', whereas my preferred term is 'Islamised' in reference to the Islamisation of Knowledge. The meanings are similar.

20 Political scientists are not unified in designating a term to today's political system in Malaysia. Harold Crouch's (1996) categorisation as 'semi-authoritarian' is widely accepted and I use it in the present study.

21 For (Muslim) women's networks and movements other than, but similar to Musawah see Derichs (2014).

22 The link to the planning committee (see Musawah 2009) is no longer available. Members of the planning committee were Amal Abdel Hadi (Egypt), Amira Al-Azhary Sonbol (Egypt/Qatar/USA), Asma'u Joda (Nigeria), Azza Soliman (Egypt), Cassandra Balchin (Great Britain), Isatou Touray (Gambia), Kamala Chandrakirana (Indonesia), Pinar Ilkaracan (Turkey), Rabéa Naciri (Morocco), Sohail Akbar Warraich (Pakistan/GB), Zainah Anwar (Malaysia) and Ziba Mir-Hosseini (Iran/GB).

23 For the names of the International Advisory Board, see Musawah (2015b).

24 Islamic and Muslim Family Laws are deliberately distinguished. Those who speak of Muslim Family Law stress the 'man-made' dimension of making and codifying laws, thus rejecting the idea that Family Law is revealed, sacred and unchangeable – which the term Islamic Family Law tends to suggest.

25 On the semi-authoritarian system see endnote 19.

26 The term *tamkîn* (تمكين) has several meanings and is sometimes also used to refer to the concept of 'empowerment'. It can, however, also be translated as self-restriction or self-discipline. It is the latter meaning which is depicted by Musawah in reference to mainstream Islamic jurisprudence.

27 This is, in fact, the name of another famous international women's rights network, abbreviated as WLUML.

28 The 'shift' in argumentation that has taken place in the Muslim feminist movement of recent years was succinctly formulated by Rafia Zaman in a conference statement: 'What we demand is compatible with Islam' shifted to 'What we demand is *in* Islam' (Conference 'Islam, Youth, and Gender in South and Southeast Asia', Berlin, 20–21 April 2012). Another example is that the term 'gender justice' is often preferred to 'gender equality' in Islamic feminist discourse, since justice is an Islamic concept whereas equality has the smack of a western or 'un-Islamic' concept. Musawah's use of the word equality is thus a statement of its own.

29 I have elaborated on this in more detail in Derichs (2010).

30 tan beng-hui, for instance, verifies more commonalities between British Common Law and Malaysian Shari'ah Law than between the Qur'ân and Shari'ah (cf. tan 2012).

31 The term 'Muslim worlds' was coined by Ulrike Freitag, the director of *Zentrum Moderner Orient* (ZMO) in Berlin, where the focus on a profoundly plural landscape of Muslim identities forms the paradigm of the institute's current research programme. See also Chapter 7.

References

Abaza, Mona, 'Some Reflections on the Question of Islam and Social Sciences in the Contemporary Muslim World', *Social Compass* 40 (1993) 2: 301–21.

AbûSulaymân, Abdul Hamîd A. (ed.), *Towards an Islamic Theory of International Relations: New Directions for Methodology and Thought*. Herndon: International Institute of Islamic Thought, 1994.

Alatas, Ismail Fajrie, 'Contemporary Indonesian Pilgrimage to Hadramawt, Yemen', *Contemporary Patterns in Transregional Islam* (Middle East Institute), 24 October 2014. Available at: www.mei.edu/content/map/ziarah-hadramaut-contemporary-indonesian-pilgrimage-hadramawt-yemen (accessed 23 November 2014).

Alatas, Syed Farid, 'The Sacralization of the Social Sciences: A Critique of an Emerging Theme in Academic Discourse', *Archives de sciences sociales des religions* 40 (1995) 91: 89–111.

Amrozi, Shoni Rahmatullah, *The Power of Rasulullah's Leadership. Menelusi Perilaku Uswah Sifat Fundamental Kemimpinan Rasulullah Saw.* Jogyakarta: Sabil, 2012.

Brigg, Morgan, 'Culture, 'Relationality', and Global Cooperation', *Global Cooperation Research Papers* 6. Duisburg: Käte Hamburger Kolleg/Centre for Global Cooperation Research, 2014.

Crouch, Harold A., *Government and Society in Malaysia*. Ithaca, NY: Cornell University Press, 1996.

Derichs, Claudia, 'Transnational Women's Movements and Networking: The Case of Muswah for Equality in the Family', *Gender, Technology and Development* (Special Issue: Women in National Politics in Asia: A Springboard for Gender Democracy?) 14 (2010) 3: 405–21.

Derichs, Claudia, 'Transnationale Netzwerke Muslimischer Frauen – Eindrücke am Beispiel von *Musawah for Equality in the Family*' [Transnational Networks of Muslim Women – Impressions from *Musawah for Equality in the Family*], in Ina Wunn and Mualla Selcuk (eds), *Islam, Frauen, Europa* [Islam, Women, Europe]. Stuttgart: Kohlhammer, 2013: 225–40.

Derichs, Claudia (ed.), *Women's Movements and Countermovements. The Quest for Gender Equality in Southeast Asia and the Middle East*. Newcastle-upon-Tyne: Cambridge Scholars Publishing, 2014.

Eshkevari, Hassan Yousef, 'Rethinking Men's Authority over Women: Qiwâma, Wilâya and their Underlying Assumptions', in Ziba Mir-Hosseini, Kari Vogt, Lena Larsen and Christian Moe (eds), *Gender and Equality in Muslim Family Law. Justice and Ethics in Islamic Legal Tradition*. London: I.B. Tauris, 2013: 191–211.

Fischer, Johan, *Proper Islamic Consumption. Shopping among the Malays in Modern Malaysia*. Copenhagen: NIAS Press, 2008.

Freitag, Ulrike, 'Researching 'Muslim Worlds'. Regions and Disciplines', *ZMO programmatic texts* (2013) 6: 1–10.

Frisk, Sylva, *Submitting to God. Women and Islam in Urban Malaysia*. Copenhagen: NIAS Press, 2009.

Haneef, Mohamed Aslam and Hafas Furqani, 'Developing the Ethical Foundations of Islamic Economics: Benefitting from Toshihiko Izutsu', *Intellectual Discourse* 17 (2009) 2: 173–99.

Hassan, Riffat, 'Religion, Ethics and Violence: Developing a New Muslim Discourse', in Berma Klein Goldewijk (ed.), *Religion, IR and Development Cooperation*. Wageningen: Wageningen Academic, 2007: 161–85.

Hng, Hung Yong, *CEO Malaysia. Strategy in Nation-Building*. Kuala Lumpur: Pendaluk, 1998.

Ibrahim, Azhar, *Contemporary Islamic Discourse in the Malay-Indonesian World*, Petaling Jaya: Strategic Information and Research Development Centre, 2014.

Iqbal, Zamir, 'Islamic Financial Systems', *Finance & Development* 34 (1997): 42–45.

Keck, Margaret and Kathryn Sikkink, *Activists Beyond Borders. Advocacy Networks in International Politics*. Ithaca NY: Cornell University Press, 1998.

Keller, Anett, *Indonesien 1965ff. Die Gegenwart eines Massenmordes* [Indonesia 1965ff. The Presence of Mass Murder]. Bielefeld: Regiospectra, 2015.

Killian, Olivia, 'Doing Religion in a Malaysian Apartment Block – Religion and Ethnicity in the Context of Educational Migration from the Middle East to Malaysia'. Paper presented to the Conference *Mobilizing Religion: Networks and Mobility*, Bonn, 18–19 July 2013.

Klein Godewijk, Berma, 'Introduction', in Berma Klein Godewijk (ed.), *Resurgence of Religion, International Relations and Development Cooperation*. Wageningen: Wageningen Academic Publishers, 2007: 23–54.

Koselleck, Reinhart, *The Practice of Conceptual History. Timing History, Spacing Concepts*. Stanford: Stanford University Press, 2002.

Lewis, Reina, *Muslim Fashion. Contemporary Style Cultures*. Durham: Duke University Press, 2015.

Lodhi, M.A.K., *Islamization of Attitudes and Practices in Science and Technology*. Herndon: International Institute of Islamic Thought, 1994.

Mahathir, Mohammad, *Malaysia. The Way Forward*. Kuala Lumpur: Malaysian Business Council, 1991.

Mamah Dedeh, *Menuju Keluarga Sakinah* [Towards a Harmonious Family]. Jakarta: Penerbit PT Gramedia Pustaka Utama, 2009.

Mandaville, Peter, *Transnational Muslim Politics. Reimagining the Umma*. New York: Routledge, 2001.

Md Akhir, Md Nasrudin, Siti Rohaini Kassim, Nor Nazihah Abd Ghani and Nurulaida Ramli, 'Halal Executive as a Measure for Standardization: The Role of Higher Learning Institutions', in Takayuki Yoshimura and Satoshi Ktsunuma (eds), *International Seminar on Islam and Multiculturalism: Islam in Global Perspective*. Tokyo: Organization for Islamic Area Studies (Waseda University), 2015: 11–12.

Miller, Monica R., *Religion and Hip Hop*. London and New York: Routledge, 2013.

Mir-Hosseini, Ziba, 'Muslim Women's Quest for Equality: Between Islamic Law and Feminism', *Critical Inquiry* 32 (2006) 4: 629–45.

Mir-Hosseini, Ziba, Kari Vogt, Lena Larsen and Christian Moe, 'Introduction. Muslim Family Law and the Question of Equality', in Ziba Mir-Hosseini, Kari Vogt, Lena Larsen and Christian Moe (eds), *Gender and Equality in Muslim Family Law. Justice and Ethics in Islamic Legal Tradition*. London: I.B. Tauris, 2013: 1–6.

Musawah, 'Who we are: Planning committee', 2009. Available at: www.musawah.org/who_we_are.asp (accessed 9 January 2009).

Musawah, 'Home', 2015a. Available at: www.musawah.org (accessed 25 February 2015).

Musawah, 'Musawah International Advisory Group', 2015b. Available at: www.musawah.org/about-musawah/international-advisory-group (accessed 25 February 2015).

Musawah, 'Portrait', 2015c. Available at: www.musawah.org/about-musawah (accessed 25 February 2015).

Musawah, 'Knowledge building project', 2015d. Available at: www.musawah.org/what-we-do/qiwamah-and-wilayah#sthash.fiW9b7Cv.dpuf (accessed 5 February 2015).

Muppies, 'Annual report', 2014. Available at: http://muppies.org/2014AnnualReport.asp (accessed 20 May 2015).

Muppies, 'Application guide', 2015. Available at: http://muppies.org/apply.asp (accessed 20 May 2015).

Ng, Cecilia, Maznah Mohamad and beng hui tan, *Feminism and the Women's Movement in Malaysia. An Unsung (R)evolution*. New York: Routledge, 2006.

Peletz, Michael G., 'Malaysia's Syariah Judiciary as Global Assemblage: Islamization, Corporatization, and Other transformations in Context', *Comparative Studies in Society and History* 55 (2013) 3: 603–33.

Rahayu, Mundi, 'Veiling Practice in Indonesia after the Reformation Era: Between Religious Practice and Transregional Consumer Practices'. Paper presented to the conference *Trans-L Encounters. Religious Education and Islamic Popular Culture in Asia and the Middle East*, Marburg, 26–28 May 2016.

Reuters, 'Islamic Economy Award', 2015. Available at: http://updates.thomsonreuters.com/events/ieawards/ (accessed 2 March 2015).

Richter, Malvin, 'Conceptualizing the Contestable. 'Begriffsgeschichte' and Political Concepts', in Gunter Scholtz (ed.), *Die Interdisziplinarität der Begriffsgeschichte* [Interdisciplinarity of the history of concepts]. Hamburg: Meiner, 2000, 135–44.

Roose, Kevin, 'Muslims on Wall Street, bridging two traditions', *The New York Times* (online), 14 April 2012. Available at: www.nytimes.com/2012/04/15/business/muslims-on-wall-street-bridging-two-traditions.html?_r=2&hpw=&pagewanted=all# (accessed 7 May 2015).

Rudnyckyj, Daromir, *Spiritual Economies. Islam, Globalization, and the Afterlife of Development*. Ithaca, NY: Cornell University Press, 2010.

Siddiqui, Mohammad Nejatullah, 'Islamization of Knowledge: Reflections on Priorities', *American Journal of Islamic Social Sciences* 28 (2011) 3: 15–34.

Sisters in Islam Forum (ed.), 'Islam and Feminism: Growing the Seeds', *Baraza! A Sisters in Islam Bulletin* 7 (2014). Petaling Jaya: SIS Forum (Malaysia).

Sloane-White, Patricia, 'Working in the Islamic Economy: Sharia'ization and the Malaysian Workplace', *Sojourn* 26 (2011) 2: 304–34.

Sperling, Valerie, Myra Marx Ferree and Barbara Risman, 'Constructing Global Feminism: Transnational Advocacy Networks and Russian Women's Activism', *Signs* 26 (2001) 4: 1155–86.

Stark, Jan, *Kebangkitan Islam. Islamische Entwicklungsprozesse in Malaysia 1981–1995* [Kebangkitan Islam. Islamic Development Processes in Malaysia 1981–1995]. Hamburg: Abera, 1999.

Stephan-Emmrich, Manja, '*Navigating 'Translocal Pious Lives': Tajik Students of Islam between Religious Ideals and Everyday Secular Realities'*. Lecture in the Seminar Series for the Global Culture Research Group, Department of Anthropology and Sociology, University of Amsterdam (Netherlands), 14 June 2013.

tan, beng-hui, *Sexuality, Islam and Politics in Malaysia: A Study on the Shifting Strategies of Regulation*, Singapore: National University of Singapore, 2012, electronic dissertation. Available at: www.scholarbank.nus.edu.sg/handle/10635/33243.

Tilly, Charles and Sidney Tarrow, *Contentious Politics*, Boulder: Paradigm Publishers, 2007.

Van Schendel, Willem, 'Geographies of Knowing, Geographies of Ignorance: Jumping Scale in Southeast Asia', *Society and Space* 20 (2001) 6: 647–68.

Weck, Winfried, Noorhaidi Hasan and Irfan Abubakar (eds), *Islam in the Public Sphere. The Politics of Identity and The Future of Democracy in Indonesia*. Jakarta: Center for the Study of Religion and Culture, 2011.

Welsh, Bridget, 'New Identities, New Politics: Malaysia's Muslim Professionals', *NBR Analysis* 18 (2008) 3: 35–51.

Wildan, Muhammad, 'Popular Piety in Indonesia: 'Aestheticization' and Reproduction of Islam'. Paper presented to the conference *Trans-L Encounters. Religious Education and Islamic Popular Culture in Asia and the Middle East*, Marburg, 26–28 May 2016.

Part II

Areas and pluri-locality

5 At home away from home (emotional geographies)

Drawing from the empirical case studies of Chapter 4, this chapter analyses the findings from the perspective of connectedness across borders. It shows that 'new' geographies (or areas) emerge when the focus of analysis shifts from conventional area boundaries towards boundaries defined by particular concepts, norms, and principles that are shared across geographical distances. It 'jumps' the conventional scales of areas and suggests the recognition of trans- and pluri-local areas shaped by shared concernment.

Trans- and pluri-local settings

In the beginning of the 2000s, Peter Mandaville (2001) published his critique of state-centrism in the discipline of International Relations (IR). He questioned 'whether political identity remains the exclusive reserve of a single national-territorial referent' (Mandaville 2001: 49). His arguments built on the observation of social interaction across national borders and between territories that are not defined as political units in international politics. His suggestion was to concentrate 'on the ways in which international sociopolitical life manages increasingly to escape the constraints of the territorial nation-state' and reconceptualise IR accordingly (Mandaville 2001: 49). His empirical findings were drawn from what he designated as *Transnational Muslim Politics* (title of the book). The constitution of new political identities through social interaction that disregards nation-state boundaries evoked the emergence of transnational politics. Furthermore: 'It is when the nexus of globalisation and political practice is viewed in this sense that the possibility of translocal politics begins to emerge' (Mandaville 2001: 49). Aside from the transnational, the translocal is a central notion in Mandaville's argumentation. The concept of translocality gained particular recognition in the social sciences through the work of Arjun Appadurai (1996; see below). Mandaville, while appreciating Appadurai's work, offers a more specific definition that is informed by translocality as a form of travel; it pays particular tribute to the acts of moving and transcending:

> Translocal spaces are hence constituted by those technologies and infrastructures which allow peoples and cultures to cross great distances and

DOI: 10.4324/9781315642123-7

> to transcend the boundaries of closed, territorial community. Translocality does not refer simply to a 'place', nor does it denote a collectivity of places. Rather it is an abstract (yet daily manifest) space occupied by the sum of linkages and connections *between* places (media, travel, import/export, etc.). The notion of locality is included within the term in order to suggest a situatedness, but a situatedness which is never static. Translocality can be theorised as a mode, one which pertains not to how peoples and cultures exist *in* places, but rather how they move *through* them. Translocality is hence a form of travel.
>
> (Mandaville 2001: 49f)

Around the 1990s and 2000s, migration studies (from where the concept of transnationality emerged) also demanded an adjustment of theories and concepts to empirical reality. Geographical and territorial demarcations were seen as losing their structuring power for social connectivity and interpersonal relations. Community building was increasingly observed to be occurring by other than spatially informed means. Place, space and locality, however, have not lost their importance. The locally palpable effects of global warming, for example, may hark back to developments in a geographically-distant locale. The specificity of some geographical places in relation to their meaning for other places elsewhere in the world cannot be glossed over; textile production in Bangladesh is pertinent to the supply of global fashion chains the world over. This nexus is one central aspect of the concept of 'glocalisation' (Pries 2003). I will not elaborate on glocalisation in the present study, but turn to another 'trans' term in migration studies, namely transmigration (Glick Schiller 1995).[1] In distinction to former studies of migration, transmigration scholars focus on the change of place by migrants as a constant feature of their life. Changing places, not staying at one particular destination, became identified as a permanent pattern (Pries 2003: 24). Ludger Pries (2003: 24f) points out that the frequent change of places in different national societies has become a normal part of transmigrants' survival strategies. 'These movements in a pluri-local, transnational social space are both physical-geographic movements and, even more often, emotional and social identity-related 'location changes" (Pries 2003: 25; translation C.D.). Pluri-locality hence refers to the perception of living in and belonging to different locations at the same time. The social sciences are challenged with further developing the conceptual framework for analysing these forms of pluri-local existence and belonging – not only in migration studies, but all the more in Area Studies, IR and other disciplines that research international cooperation.

Another theme that frequently comes up in the context of transnationality and transmigration is that of diaspora. Although the present study does not rely on diaspora studies for the identification of connectivities across space and time, a few thoughts deserve to be expanded. Fiona Adamson (2012: 35) argues that social sciences' 'methodological territorialism' has led to the neglect of the importance of cultural, symbolic and linguistic artefacts for the mobilisation of, for instance, international movements. 'Revolutionary socialism was inherently an international movement based on transnational mobilization by political entrepreneurs' (Adamson 2012: 39). The pattern of transnational mobilisation is then transferred to 'diaspora politics' in that Adamson sees diasporas as 'effects' – as 'outcomes of processes of political mobilization; socially constructed identity communities; and transnational imaginaries' (Adamson 2012: 35). Diaspora entrepreneurs, as she calls them, engage in 'diasporic politics' in order to 'construct or deploy identity categories that can be used to create transnational identity communities' (Adamson 2012: 34). The networks they create are different from the international movements of socialism, liberalism etc. because of their reification and reproduction of a particular *identity* category (national, ethnic, sectarian or religious) on a transnational arena – whereas the said movements are based on shared *beliefs* (Adamson 2012: 26, 34; emphasis added). In addition to the well-known types of transnational networks that have been developed by social movement theorists (e.g. Kekk and Sikkink 1998), Adamson introduces the type of 'transnational identity networks' (Adamson 2012: 32). This type of transnational identity networks, which can also be attributed as pluri-local networks, depending on the places the identity category occupies, is particularly helpful to conceptualise the emotional/faith-based geographies that form the basis of my discussion of global cooperation. Based on the empirical findings of the preceding chapters, I relate Mandaville's (2001) insights on transnational Muslim politics to Pries' (2003) idea of emotional mobility in pluri-local settings. I draw on Fiona Adamson's (2012) notion of transnational identity networks for the conceptualisation of connectivities between different locales. My approach differs from that of Mandaville and Adamson to the extent that my prime intention is not to carve out the 'political' in the performance of transnational actors nor do I focus on diasporas. Rather, I start with the idea that networking is not necessarily driven by political aspirations, but to a large extent is shaped by the concerns of actors who I would like to call 'knowledge entrepreneurs'. From there, I move to inspecting pluri-local identity networks. Finally, I ponder the meaning of trans- and pluri-local connectivity for the notion of areas. I end with the suggestion to examine areas in spatial yet non-geographically-defined translocal textures.

Knowledge entrepreneurs

The term 'knowledge entrepreneur' is not a new one. It has been used in the context of entrepreneurship in both business and industry. There, knowledge entrepreneurs are mainly conceived of as persons 'managing and synthesizing knowledge' and 'conducting conventional business in innovative ways' (Carayannis and Formica 2006: 1). 'Intellectual venture capitalists' is another phrase to designate their professional orientation (Carayannis and Formica 2006: 1). Instead of investing their entrepreneurial skills in the production of material goods and products, knowledge entrepreneurs make knowledge the basis of their industrial production. Knowledge leading to innovation is key to their performance. Obviously, the aspect of material profit-making through innovation is inherent in this line of reasoning. In distinction to the rather managerial understanding of knowledge entrepreneurs in business and industry, my comprehension of knowledge entrepreneurs points to another utilisation of innovation capacities and discards the aspect of material profit-making. Innovation in an epistemic field of production can comprise anything from bringing about entirely new ways of conceiving of knowledge (as in the Islamisation of Knowledge project) to the re-thinking of pre-existing knowledge by introducing new perspectives and/or shifting foci (as in the many reformist projects in the course of Islamic resurgence and in knowledge-building projects of women's rights' networks). The implication of an entrepreneurial dimension rests on the classical meaning of the term entrepreneur as the person who founded an enterprise, owns it and who consequently takes responsibility for its performance, being held accountable for its success or failure.[2] Entrepreneurs are convinced they know how to lead an enterprise to success. In the classical imagery, the default entrepreneur was male and prone to a paternalistic management style. Today's knowledge entrepreneurs comprise both male and female actors, Musawah activists being an example of the latter, as shown below.

The protagonists of IoK displayed a classical kind of entrepreneurial spirit by introducing ('founding') a new epistemic base for the perception of knowledge: all knowledge comes from God. They were held responsible and accountable for what they published and taught. In some cases, the mental act of founding an epistemic approach later materialised in the establishment of educational institutions such as universities – places of further knowledge production and knowledge dissemination. The increase in acceptance and adoption of particular ideas and thought – reflected in formal political backing as well as appreciation in civil society – may be regarded as a non-material profit. In the case of universities of global outreach like those introduced in Chapter 3 (Al-Azhar, Al-Madinah, Al-Mustafa), which stand out with regard to the numbers of enrolments of foreign students and export activities through branches established in other countries, one could even speak of a knowledge industry. Knowledge entrepreneurs whose 'enterprises' operate in a faith-based world risk being rejected as scholars and intellectuals. They provoke reactions from followers and critics alike, often polarising their audience to a great extent. While drawing severe criticism certainly happened to some thinkers (SN Al-Attas being an example), the presence of their intellectual legacies cannot be denied. Leaving a thought trace in people's concern for making their religious identity reconcilable with the challenges of daily life shows that the dissemination of knowledge occurred in tangible forms. It trickled down to places and spaces of factual economic activity: in the Islamic economy that operates with religious principles on management and shop floor levels, as well as in the greater landscape of services and consumer commodities.

It is apparent that a causal relationship between, for instance, Nursholish Madjid (as a knowledge entrepreneur) and today's community of headscarf designers in Indonesia is impossible to prove. Such coherence, if it exists, is not visible as is, for instance, the mass support for popular religious leaders in public spaces during speeches or sermons – events which are frequently accompanied by a particular symbolism in attire. However, popular religious leaders in Indonesia cannot perform without resorting to an authoritative repertoire of religious knowledge. We are yet again back to knowledge and its dissemination. The knowledge spread by popular religious leaders is framed in an appealing language, with terms and concepts taken from the register of acknowledged sources. Credible opinions and arguments based on such sources garner support and are well received by the wider public. Once the principle that it is necessary to give *sadaqah* (a voluntary donation, صدقة), for instance, has transformed to a general attitude of many believers, it is no major step to also think in entrepreneurial terms of economising donation mechanisms to enhance people's readiness to spend (e.g. *sadaqah* functions in prominent localities). While this is a presumed trajectory of how to get from scholarly religious knowledge to mass consumption of religious knowledge, Daromir Rudnyckij's (2010) introduces a real one based on explicit fieldwork. It is introduced in his study of the Krakatau steel factory as a case of a spiritual economy. The protagonist is the electrical engineering professor Imaduddin Abdulrahim at the renowned Bandung College of Technology, whom I referred to in Chapter 3 in the context of transnational and transregional connectedness among Muslim students. Imaduddin led the Salman mosque on the campus of the college, which acted as a magnet for Indonesian university students in the 1970s. 'Muslim students came from across the archipelago for short, intensive courses dedicated to religious study' Rudnyckyj relates (2010: 57). 'The movement spread in rhizomatic fashion across the archipelago after students who had come to the Salman mosque returned to their campuses to disseminate the religious lessons that they had been exposed to in Bandung' (Rosyad 2006: 33 quoted in Rudnyckyj 2010: 57). This is all the more remarkable because Imaduddin himself had no particular academic record in religious studies. His story is described as follows:

> Although Imaduddin had an engineering degree and had never attended an Islamic institute of higher education, his father had studied at Al-Azhar University in Cairo and provided him with instruction in Qur'anic recitation and interpretation while he was a child growing up in Langkat, North Sumatra (Rosyad 2006: 24). Widely known by the nickname 'Bang Imad,' Imaduddin became a well-educated and highly skilled engineer. [...] [Returning to Bandung after studies in the USA; C.D.], he became increasingly interested in reform movements elsewhere in the Muslim world that sought to reconcile Islam with modernity.
>
> (Rudnyckyj 2010: 57f)

Imaduddin was a friend of Malaysia's Anwar Ibrahim, who invited the former to lecture on Islam and modernisation in 1967, when he (Anwar) was still the president of ABIM. In his later works, Rudnyckyj (2010: 58) writes,

'Bang Imad sought to make explicit the connection between Islamic principles and economic practice'. The Salman mosque movement which was led by him 'was the bellweather of a broader transformation in the role of Islam in Indonesian public life' (Rudnyckyj 2010: 59). It was 'historically significant because it marked a change in the way in which Islam was viewed by middle-class Indonesians' (Rudnyckyj 2010: 59). Imaduddin's approach of fruitfully joining science and technology studies with Islam – an approach that was also successfully implemented in Malaysia – attracted the growing middle class of the country irrespective of Suahrto's suspicion towards Islamic activism in those days. Indicative of this shift is also the transformation of the Krakatau steel factory, where employees and managers of the 1950s and 1960s had no qualms consuming alcohol on site and at parties. Since the factory recruited high numbers of engineering graduates from Bandung's technology college, the growing influence of the college's mosque movement came with their entry into the ranks of employees. Imaduddin's training bestowed the students and later employees with 'the argument that there was an economic ethic inherent in Islam that could facilitate Indonesian development' (Rudnyckyj 2010: 59). The training prepared the milieu from which later human resources programmes by the name of 'Emotional and Spiritual Quotient' or ESQ for the corporate world spread first across the country and subsequently also abroad (cf. Rudnyckyj 2010: 2–24).

The fact that Imaduddin learned about recitation and interpretation from his Al-Azhar-trained father speaks of the far-reaching impact of this institution of higher learning. Likewise, the snowball effect of the training in religious studies at Salman mosque speaks of the dynamics of knowledge dissemination in the 1970s atmosphere of Islamic resurgence. Today's ESQ and similar trainings for personnel in business and industry include a component of monetary profit-making, aside from the objective of intensifying trainees' Islamic faith and making Muslim virtues commensurable with corporate demands. Moreover, in such training, knowledge from various sources (including conventional guidebooks for business success and the like) is merged and combined to arrive at an Islamic business ethic. There is no genuinely new knowledge created or a new epistemic approach offered. The knowledge spread in the training is applied knowledge; in this sense it is different from the knowledge elaborated in the project IoK. ESQ is a training meant to internalise applications of knowledge rather than an epistemic project. The trainers in ESQ and similar programmes do not match the understanding of knowledge entrepreneurs mentioned above. Rather, they are the ones who make the knowledge that has been generated by others applicable to the situation in everyday life in general and in the competition of a globalised market in particular. They make it compatible with consumer and corporate demands and reach out to broader masses. But they gained their knowledge from scholars and institutions that may be classified as knowledge entrepreneurs and sites of 'industrialised' knowledge production.

The development described was furthermore brought about by transnational connectivities. Anthony Bubalo and Greg Fealy hint at external influences on religious learning in a study of the rise of Islamism in Indonesia:

> [T]he transmission of Islamism to Indonesia has both pull and push factors. On the one hand, many Indonesian Muslims actively seek knowledge from the Middle East, whether as students studying there or as consumers of publications and electronic media. On the other hand, Middle Eastern governments, charitable organisations and private donors keenly promote their interpretations of Islam within the region, funding Islamic infrastructure such as mosques, schools and colleges, sponsoring visits by preachers and the publication of books and journals, and providing scholarships for study in Arab countries. Thus, Indonesian Muslims who have a Middle Eastern orientation have abundant opportunities to further their interest.
>
> (Bubalo and Fealy 2005: 49)

Similarly, religious schools in Malaysia were funded by Middle Eastern governments, underlining the ties between Southeast Asia and the Middle East (Nasr 2001: 85). Putting the situation into a broader perspective, what came with the wave of Islamic resurgence in its various guises – via individual knowledge entrepreneurs, collective actors and different types of religious leaders emerging in the wake of religious revival – was a pluralisation of knowledge that naturally entailed a pluralisation of religious authority. My conversations with scholars of religious studies in Southeast Asia during recent years add up to a picture similar to the one I could draw of scholarly communities in Europe. In political theory and the history of ideas, for instance, colleagues in the field would either affiliate themselves with one or more famous thinkers of the past, or their being influenced by a certain thinker's idea would be attributed to them. Phrases like 'He is so Kantian' (referring to German philosopher Immanuel Kant) or 'She is very Hegelian' (referring to German philosopher Friedrich Hegel) are not unusual in this context. Similarly, in Indonesia or Malaysia, I would hear 'Oh, yes, he is wonderful but too Ghazalian' (referring to Persian theologian and philosopher Muhammad Al-Ghazâlî) or 'Their approach is very Khaldunian' (referring to Egyptian historian and polymath Ibn Khaldûn). In other words, the pattern of scholarly communities identifying with particular thinkers and thought is no different in the Muslim or the non-Muslim world. A common pattern among Muslim scholars is also to refer to Western and Islamic thinkers alike and to merge their approaches (e.g. Al-Ghazâlî and Kant); among non-Muslim scholars in the Western world, this is rarely the case. Western non-Muslim approaches in the history of ideas often lack the language proficiency in Arabic or Persian that is necessary to immerse oneself in the thought of Islamic thinkers of the past. But even if scholars published their ideas in English in more recent history – as did Fazlur Rahman, Seyyed Hossein Nasr or SN Al-Attas – their reception has been rather marginal in the relevant disciplines and academic discourses in the non-Muslim West. The same can be said for Confucian or other influential non-Western scholars whose original works were for a long time rarely available in the dominant languages of global knowledge.[3]

The knowledge entrepreneurs in the realm of the Islamisation of knowledge and Islamic resurgence acquired credibility and authority among followers aside from traditional religious authorities such as *imâms* or *mullahs* or *'ulamâ'* in mosques, *madrasahs* and related institutions of religious learning. This is not to be understood as a substitution of 'traditional' by 'modern' authorities, but rather in the sense of Mandaville's (2007) 'pluralization of religious authority' through the pluralisation of religious knowledge. Mandaville's focus is directed at the politicised dimension of plural authority, but his assessment nonetheless hints at general aspects of the pluralisation phenomenon which merit attention:

> To focus on the politicization of pluralized authority, then, is to examine how it is that disparate political tendencies seek to define their agendas and prescriptions as authoritative in light of (often distant) geopolitical events. Such an approach looks at the battle for hearts and minds *within* the Muslim world, and the discursive politics through which various movements try to mobilize sympathies and politicize constituencies by articulating Muslim identity in relation to world affairs.
>
> (Mandaville 2007: 111)

The quote is interesting since the author refers, on the one hand, to distant geopolitical events as triggering occurrences for the legitimation of particular interpretations as authoritative ones; on the other hand, he links this to the articulation of a Muslim identity. More precisely, an event such as '9/11' triggered reactions of Muslims everywhere in the world because they were forced to position themselves towards what had happened. Condemnation of the attack, resorting to the holy sources to render the argument authoritative, was uttered a-plenty. Identification of Muslims with an explicit normative dissociation from violent action ensued simultaneously. Authoritative exclamations endorsing the use of violence surfaced, of course, at the same pace.

In distinction to Mandaville's temporal placement of the pluralisation of religious authority as a phenomenon of globalisation, I would date it back as far as to the late 1960s. When articulations of a particular identity are somehow linked with geopolitical events on a broader scale, then the movements of Islamic resurgence may well be considered as a reaction to overwhelmingly Western – secularly – defined concepts of modernisation (cf. Rahman 1984; Roy 1994; Esposito 1999; Eickelmann 2000; Kepel 2000). I would even suggest that the Islamic resurgence movements be conceived of in a similar manner as a social movement, as scholars have done with regard to the '1968' phenomenon and the subsequent new social movements in the Western world (environmental movements; second wave women's movements; 'no nuke' movements and the like). These movements opposed the primarily market-driven model of modernity and the support lent to it by many governments. Likewise, supporters of IoK/

Iok and activists of Islamic resurgence were indubitably motivated and mobilised by ideas of opposition towards dominant, powerful systems of learning and lifestyle. Radical forms of Islamism are akin to radical forms of political extremism in the West. 'The turn to Islamism in Malaysia', Vali Nasr writes, came during a decade when Islamism rose in prominence across the Muslim world' (Nasr 2001: 85). It is also appropriate, in the same vein, to compare the later boom of *halâl* certification with that of fair-trade certificates. To allude at the commensurability between supporters of global justice and political correctness with those of Islamic correctness is very plausible. Paying attention to *halâl* products in everyday life is as much a behavioural trend informed by knowledge about religious principles as paying attention to fair trade products is informed by knowledge about power relations in world trade. Getting back to the pluralisation of knowledge and religious authority, not only geopolitical events but also globally concurrent yet phenomenologically similar events (leftist opposition in 1968 and Muslim opposition towards un-Islamic regimes; *halâl* certification and fair trade certification) serve to pluralise what is accepted as authoritative. An example in regard of the cases discussed in the previous chapter is the transnational movement Musawah for Equality in the Muslim Family, which I classify as a collective rather than an individual knowledge entrepreneur.

Musawah is a case in point for knowledge entrepreneurship diminishing traditional and patriarchal orientated scholars' monopoly over religious knowledge. The almost uniform (although pluralised along schools of thought and multiple authoritative interpretations by numerous personages) male-dominated interpretation of the sources are questioned. Musawah activists put forward their own knowledge-building project by analysing concepts of Islamic sources in a manner that brings them 'in line with the lived realities of Muslim families today' (Musawah 2016). The approach is deliberately participatory, recognises non-traditional expertise and starts out from contexts rather than texts (Musawah 2016). Musawah 'creates new knowledge about women's rights in Islam' (Musawah 2016) and does so from within Muslim legal traditions. When Mandaville (2007: 103) sees the construction of religious authority as being conventionally manifested in three main components, namely textuality, discursive method and personification,[4] Musawah goes beyond these components by explicitly attending to contexts rather than texts and by moving away from identifying interpretative authority with individual persons (i.e. personified knowledge). Knowledge building and disseminating is an intentionally collective activity in Musawah's strategy. Hence, I see Musawah as a knowledge entrepreneur who generates genuinely new knowledge but does so in a different manner from the founder and (paternalist) owner model described above.

In sum, knowledge entrepreneurs like those introduced in the empirical accounts of the preceding chapters apply diverse methods of knowledge generation and dissemination, but they have in common the characteristic of producing approaches to religious knowledge which have the potential to become authoritative for followers of their thought. The group of the IoK/Iok protagonists introduced in Chapter 3 employed primarily textual (publications) and institutional (establishment of universities and research institutes) means to promote their epistemic take on Islamised knowledge. They were respected knowledgeable personalities who influenced the scholarly discourse to a remarkable extent (discursive method), for instance, through academic supervision and teaching. The subsequent generations of intellectuals also diffused their epistemic approaches to religious knowledge by way of establishing institutions of higher learning (e.g. Paramadina University; UIN; INSISTS). The discursive method proved particularly advantageous to some of them – Indonesian scholar Nurcholish Madjid and his public outreach being a case in point. A pattern that explicitly differs from the preference of textuality and personification is that of Muslim women's rights activists such as the members of Musawah. Utilisers of applied knowledge like Imaduddin, the trainers of Islamic business ethics or popular religious like Aa Gym (cf. Chapter 3) are not knowledge entrepreneurs in the described sense, but mediators who convey selected segments of religious knowledge to a particular, though at times huge and massive, target group. They are also influential in attracting the Muslim middle-class' attention and shaping the role of Islam in public life (Rudnyckyj 2010: 59; Nasr 2001: 87). In terms of networking, all knowledge entrepreneurs had or have transnational connections which have served to shape their identities as intellectuals, academics or scholar activists. The case of Muswah is most illustrative in this regard since the network's very origin is based on transnational cooperation. But the transnational and transregional was also instrumental for the intellectual profile building of individual scholars – Fazlur Rahman and the IoK protagonists being good examples. Learning and intellectual exchange across states and regions and also across philosophical traditions (Western and Islamic) formed the basis for their scholarly records and to some extent also their credibility as authorities in religious studies. Apart from such individual traits of knowledge entrepreneurs, activist groups in Islamic resurgence movements relied on transnational networking, too. The *tarbiyah* movement making use of translations from Arabic texts of the Muslim Brotherhood in their *dakwah* activities (cf. Chapter 3) is certainly a case in point. Likewise, Malaysian *dakwah* groups became a conduit for ideas of Middle Eastern and South Asian movements (Nasr 2001: 85). Both knowledge entrepreneurs and *dakwah* acitivsts have accelerated the pluralisation of both religious knowledge and religious authority. In the following section, I discuss the effects of the pluralisation of religious knowledge for trans- and pluri-local identity networking. I use the terms trans- and pluri-local synonymously. Translocal simply indicates that something goes beyond a certain locale; pluri-local is more precise in that it indicates that actors feel (emotionally) present or at home in several places. The important semantic pillar is the local in distinction to signifiers of bigger scales like the national.

Trans- and pluri-local networks

Ismail Fajrie Alatas relates an interesting observation of a Yemeni-Indonesian geography brought about by pilgrimage and study abroad in recent decades:

> After spending three to four years in Hadramawt, the Indonesian students would return to their homeland with a renewed proselytizing zeal. They began establishing *majelis taklim* (Islamic study groups), transmitting what they had learned to the wider public and paving the way for the revival of Ba Alawi tradition in Indonesia.
>
> (Alatas 2014)

Hadramawt (or Hadhramaut) is the Eastern region of today's Yemen, from where a huge portion of the local population (more than 20%) migrated to Southeast Asia during the 1930s (Lekon 2009: 87). In Southeast Asia, they settled as a diaspora and became an early example of the importance of financial remittances for poorer parts of the world (Lekon 2009). The Al-Attas (or Alatas) family branches in Malaysia and Indonesia belong to the descendants of early migrants from Hadramaut. The Ba Alawi (or Al-Sâda Al-Bâ'alwî السادة الباعلوي in Arabic) are conceived of as descendants of Prophet Muhammad and belong to the Sayyid families (families of high reputation because of their pedigree) in the region. The pattern Ismail Alatas describes is emblematic not only for transnational, but more precisely translocal connectivities. While the pilgrimage activities mentioned point to an Indonesian-Yemeni transnational connection, a closer look reveals that the link works on a subnational level given today's scale of nation-state unities. The Hadramaut is only a part of the territorial nation-state Yemen, and the Hadramis (citizens of Hadramaut descent in Southeast Asia and inhabitants of the region Hadramaut in Yemen) are a community connected by their identity as Hadramis rather than by an identity as Indonesians or Yemenis. The establishment of study groups after their return from learning abroad is a typical pattern. A Philippine colleague doing fieldwork in the Southern region of Mindanao (a region with several Muslim-majority districts in the Philippines), for instance, communicated the same pattern to me in view of Philippino Muslim students returning to their home towns.[5] The translocal (rather than transnational) in terms of geographical and territorial scales becomes apparent in these examples.

Social philosopher Anthony Giddens (1991; 1985) has elaborated that sedentary proximity as a prerequisite for the formation of communities is no longer as important as it was before the era of globalisation. In the global era, the singular 'here' is associated with plural 'theres' (Giddens 1991: 21; cf. Gupta and Ferguson 1992). Social relations expand across space and time, facilitated by progressive means of communication and transportation. In (human and social) geography and cultural studies, the fresh understanding of space as not primarily defined by an area on the surface of the earth but as, for instance, narrative or emotional space, became subsumed under the phrases of 'spatial' and 'cultural turn' (Bachmann-Medick 2011; Leitner et al. 2008; Jessop et al. 2008; Massey 2005; Soja 1989). In social theory, Gidden's (1981) 'time-space distanciation' and David Harvey's (1999; 1989) 'time-space compression' became prominent discursive phrases. Both related to the transformations of the meaning of time and space under conditions of globalisation, capitalism and postmodernity. While Giddens and Harvey drew the rough lines, so to speak, Arjun Appadurai (1996) reflected on the sub-theme of cultural globalisation and introduced the notions of translocality and translocal identities as apparitions of post-national politics. Again, the concept of mobility (albeit not necessarily confined to migration or transmigration) is crucial for the conceptualisation of these notions (Urry 2007). Mobility, providing new forms of subjectivity and emotion simply by the fact that work or study in different places produces memories and shapes senses, is possible in physical as well as other forms of movements (e.g. mental, spiritual). Conradson and McKay (2007) have presented a conceptualisation of such forms of subjectivity which they designate as *translocal subjectivity*. They point out three parameters that inform their concept. One is the negotiation between physical presence at one place and absence at another, where the person would rather be at a particular point in time – wishing, for instance, to attend a family celebration but not being able to physically move there (e.g. too far a geographical distance, not affordable financially, not advisable in regard of local duties that have to be fulfilled etc.) (Conradson and McKay 2007: 168). A second parameter is that of distinguishing between local and national (see above: Hadramaut as part of Yemen). The local is usually a part of a bigger national entity. The identification with one or another varies according to circumstances. I may call myself a German in a foreign country but refer to a particular region of Germany when I am among fellow Germans (cf. Conradson and McKay 2007: 169). The third parameter is informed by the 'emotional and affective states that accompany [physical] mobility' (Conradson and McKay 2007: 169). This pertains especially to the hardships that migrants face when being separated from their families for long periods of time (e.g. mothers separated from their children while nursing their employers' offspring as domestic workers in distant places). Conradson and McKay's conceptualisation of translocal subjectivities is empirically based on cases of (trans)migration for, mostly, economic reasons (e.g. the above-mentioned notion of the pluri-local).

I move beyond the migration-type mobility for economic reasons and apply the concept of translocal subjectivities to cases like the one mentioned at the beginning of this section (i.e. the back-and-forth travels to Hadramaut by Indonesians and the (re)establishment of faith communities after return. This pattern of mobility is conducted more for emotional and faith-related reasons, including the sense of belonging to a specific community, the Ba Alawi. It is hence the emotional dimension in the concept of Conradson and My Kay that is particularly important for the linking of translocal subjectivities and trans-/pluri-local identity networks with my empirical cases of the preceding chapters. In much the same way as the emotional becomes constitutive for the emplacement in a 'here' and the feeling of being close to one or more 'theres', faith-based identification with different spaces, places and people may instill a sense of belonging to several 'theres'. The moment that merits attention here is the fact that such 'theres' need not be territorial places (on the surface of the earth) but can also be spaces of intellectual and/or spiritual belonging. In the Islamic economy as discussed in Chapter 4, the pluri-local identity of the manager of a corporation displays the feeling at home in several places: in the dominant, Western or secular-defined corporate world with all its competition and profit-seeking, in the alternative corporate world of applied Islamic ethical principles, and in a somehow private spiritual world that connects him/her to God, because what is performed is done for the sake of God and in the hope of *barakah* (blessing) and *falah* (success and human well being). By implication, spatial mobility of the mind also occurs in the form of flows through different linguistic worlds. Arabic terms to denote Islamic economic concepts and non-Arabic terms to denote secular concepts of management and corporate leadership both belong to the linguistic repertoire of actors in the Islamic economy. The aspect of language is significant because the vocabulary of the Islamic economy is different from that of conventional economic dictionaries; it is not just 'another (Arabic) word for the same thing', but the bulk of the terminological repertoire in the Islamic economy is composed of concepts that are non-existent in the conventional corporate and business jargon (*falah* being one of them, since this form of success and well-being applies to life in this world as well as life in the hereafter). To pick up Pries' (2003: 24) idea of transmigration, the boss/*khalīf* in the Islamic economy constantly transmigrates or crosses the imaginary boundaries between homes – those of Islamic and of secular economic thinking. The ability to transmigrate out of one's own will is a feature that links actors identifying with the Islamic economy to likeminded actors globally (see below) – and distinguishes them from those who are unable to accomplish such a transgression because they lack the knowledge of relevant principles and language. In other words, becoming part of a pluri-local network of Islamic economic actors requires an immersion into alternative epistemic and linguistic worlds. Actors in the Islamic economy feel at home in both. It should be noted that this form of transmigration and transgressing entails more than the translation of words and phrase form one language into another (cf. Chapter 1 and below).

A type of pluri-local networking in which geographical places play a role is the transnational collaboration of Muslim women's rights activists. Chapter 4 introduced the network Musawah, which identifies as a movement pursuing equality – not equity – of men and women in the Muslim family. Musawah activists find likeminded fellow activists in other transnational movements, the group Women Living Under Muslim Laws (WLUML) being one of them. What connects these women's rights activists is their particular stance on gender equality, which is not overwhelmingly shared by fellow Muslim women in their home countries (let alone Muslim men). The short sketch of attitudinal positions among Islamic feminists in the previous chapter gives an idea of the diversity in opinion with regard to women's rights and gender equality. The diversity and heterogeneity of attitudes is even higher when one takes the spectrum of Muslim women of Islamist and Salafist orientation into account. Musawah and WLUML activists are regarded as 'liberal' Muslims and are usually numerical minorities in their home countries; the majority of fellow Muslim women would regard Musawah's understanding of equality as (too) radical (cf. Fennert 2015). The emotional geography of Musawah activists is a translocal one in the sense of the identification with a notion of equality that would not represent a national stance (cf. the second parameter of Conradson and MyKay's conceptualisation of translocal subjectivities above). A Muswah member in Malaysia may thus feel more at home among fellow activists in some places of Nigeria than among other Muslim women in Malaysia. In terms of identity, Musawah activists feel and are globally connected with Muslim women who (be it actively or ideationally) support their agenda. The movement works across borders but in specifically arranged formats rather than huge national campaigns. Musawah as well as WLUML are not mass movements, but the translocal connectedness of their members allows them to nonetheless operate on a global scale. Their work is explicitly faith-based in that Islamic principles form the basis for the distillation of knowledge that confirms and approves of justice and equality as inherent elements of Muslim legal traditions. Musawah's performance is a prototypical example of translocal subjectivities emerging through active engagement in identity networking in numerous locales (i.e. pluri-local). Their members are empowered through their translocal connectivity and, consequently, through mutual knowledge exchange they provide new interpretations of Islamic authenticity. Their networking also matches Mandaville's (2001: 6) idea of translocality as a category that is 'primarily about the ways in which people flow *through* space rather than about how they exist *in* space' (italics in original).

What is most significant for translocal connectivity is that it is small communities within the Muslim community of countries which establish such connections beyond national borders. Sometimes it is merely a few individual actors who adhere to their own, selected religious authorities and strive to 'sell' their conviction to others. But larger networks may emerge from there. In the age of digital communication, networking via great geographical distances has become extremely easy – compared to the times when the internet was non-existent. The pluri-local faith-based networks described here are identity based but ideologically independent. In this regard, they have to be distinguished from mass attracting Islamic movements such as Hizbut Tahrir or Tablighi Jamaat (cf. Gugler 2011; Noor 2010). Moreover, the smaller networks that I consider relevant for global cooperation do not fit the polarising pattern 'Islam versus the West'. They often operate in and through the West, because they live and earn their money there (see Muppies in Chapter 4). The translocal areas they occupy (emotionally and rooted in a religious identity) are not territorial areas occupied in a sedentary manner, but spaces occupied by emotional belonging. In the section that follows I try to expand the notion of translocal areas 'inhabited' by members of transnational/translocal identity networks.

Translocal areas

Political scientist R.B.J. Walker reflected on world peace and justice in the late 1980s, when the bi-polar world order was still dominant in international politics. In his book on struggles for a just world peace (Walker 1988), he observes the existence of a multitude of global connections – connections whose existence does not necessarily entail from some form of universalism. Despite the global nature of these connections, people's daily lives are embedded in a myriad of particular locations and circumstances (Walker 1988, summarised in Mandaville 2001: 21). Given these connections, Walker (1988: 102) argues, one should recognise 'that in the modern world, communities and solidarities have to be grasped as a dialectical moment, as a sense of participation both in large scale global processes and in particular circumstances'. For the present study, his emphasis on the harmonious interplay of the global and the local in connecting people merits attention. I adopt Walker's observation and transfer it to a less geopolitically, IR-informed arena (which was a focus in Walker's (1988, 1990) studies on world peace and security). Taking the Islamic economy as a case in point again, I relate the feature of global connection to the particular circumstances in which religiously informed economic performance takes place. I argue that the phenomenon of Islamic economy (or Islamised, Islamicised, spiritual economy, as it has been termed) is a prime example for actors' participation in large-scale global processes while at the same time being determined and confined by very particular local – including national – circumstances. The lens I am looking through covers Islamic entrepreneurship in Malaysia/Indonesia (see Chapter 4) and Saudi Arabia. Drawing from Kayed and Hassan's (2011) study of Islamic entrepreneurship in Saudi Arabia, I propose to perceive of the Islamic economic 'world' as a translocal area.

In sketching what distinguishes entrepreneurship in an Islamic economy from entrepreneurship in non-Islamic economies, Kayed and Hassan (2011: 4f) first stress that the Western perception of entrepreneurship as an economic activity is no different from the Islamic perception. What makes the difference though, is the ethical and moral foundations on which an Islamic approach to economic activity and entrepreneurship rests. Material gains are acceptable as long as they are accumulated with the intent to please God. 'Thus, entrepreneurship in Islam has a religious dimension alongside its economic dimension', the authors relate (Kayed and Hassan 2011: 5). In regard to the religious dimension, the hereafter is of importance. 'Where Muslim entrepreneurs meet their economic needs, serve their communities and fulfill religious duties they will attain *falah* in this worldly life and be rewarded generously in the hereafter' (Kayed and Hassan 2011: 5). The intention to please God (instead of pursuing individual profit and maximising material gain) is one of the essential characteristics of Islamic economic activity. Or, in other words, economic activity is an act of worship (*'ibâda*). Contributing to the well-being of the community (*umma*) and making *halâl* (Islamically acceptable) profits are further elements in the repertoire of Islamic business activities (Kayed and Hassan 2011: 90f). They constitute production and business throughout the Islamic economy. How the doctrinal principles of Islamic economic activity may work out in practice has been described in the previous chapter. However, their implementation is not merely dependent on either the will or desire of individual actors who willingly subscribe to Islamic ethical and moral principles in their economic activity. The way the Islamic economy in Malaysia and the spiritual economy in Indonesia work, for instance, is an outcome of several factors, including the political support by government and state. What occurred in Malaysia under Mahathir and in Indonesia after the fall of Suharto (especially under the administration of Susilo Bambang Yudhoyhono, 2004–2014) was a state-led Islamisation that encouraged entrepreneurship with a commitment to Islamic ethics (cf. Nasr 2001: 105–129). In the Muslim-majority countries of the Middle East, the situation looks different. The republics in the region by and large abstained from granting religion a significant position in their blueprints for national economic development. On the contrary, religious organisation outside the realm of ritual and piety was and is a rather suspicious activity – oppressed when political aspirations are coming along with it (the Muslim Brotherhood in Egypt being an example). In the monarchies, the entanglement of religion and state is much stronger, with some kingdoms adhering to a special confessional current in Islam (e.g. Wahabbism in Saudi Arabia or Ibadiya in Oman), and others placing the supreme jurisdiction over Islamic religious affairs in the hands of the monarch (e.g. Morocco). Islam does play a role in the monarchies' economies, albeit different from the one it plays in Southeast Asian monarchical systems like Malaysia or Brunei Darussalam. The United Arab Emirates' conferring of the *Islamic Economy Award* is but one indicator of a growing interest among state leaders to associate Islam with economic performance. Islamic enterprises akin to those in Southeast Asia are, however, hard to find in the Persian Gulf monarchies. In Saudi Arabia, the notion of Islamic entrepreneurship seems to be absent from the state's entrepreneurship dictionary (Kayed and Hassan 2011: 273). In stark contrast to, for instance, Malaysia's transformation of Islamic resurgence demands into economic standards (e.g. *halâl* certification, cf. Md Akhir et al. 2015) and proactively encouraging local Malay–Muslim entrepreneurship, Saudi Arabia's government rarely made any effort to advertise Islamic entrepreneurship as an alternative to Western recipes for economic progress:

> On the sensitive question of Islamic entrepreneurship, evidence from the field indicates that the majority of Saudis have misread the notion of entrepreneurship in its wider context and from an Islamic perspective in particular. Neither state policies and institutions nor the formal and higher education systems showed more than a scanty interest in Islamic entrepreneurship.
>
> (Kayed and Hassan 2011: 273)

Critiques of lacking formal political support and incentives for entrepreneurs to act in accordance with Islamic economic principles have been articulated by some businessmen in Saudi Arabia (Kayed and Hassan 2011: 192–233). Given the fact that Saudi Arabia's largest Islamic financial institution, Al-Rajhi Bank, multiplied its savings accounts from 10 per cent of all deposits in 1978 to 53 per cent by 2007 (Nasr 2010: 20) and that the country is one of the world's leading harbours for *sharî'a*-compliant assets (Nasr 2010: 16), it is surprising that sources of Islamic finance are scarcely available to Saudi entrepreneurs. While

Malaysia developed its Islamic finance sector hand in hand with the policy of 'looking East' for the identification of suitable national development models (Milne and Mauzy 1999: 50–79), Saudi Arabia boosted its Islamic finance sector but failed, apparently, to correspondingly link the kingdom's socio-economic development agenda with incentives to embrace Islamic economic principles in other business sectors (Kayed and Hassan 2011: 232).

The promotion of Islamic finance and an increasing recognition of religious norms in economic performance can be typified as a result of the global tide of Islamic resurgence in preceding decades. The idea of committing economic thought to religious principles connects all those who demanded just that. The sketch of the two trajectories of state economic policies towards economic development and entrepreneurship shows that actors committed to abiding by Islamic norms and principles in their economic activities do not meet the same opportunities even though they have in common their living and acting in Muslim-majority surroundings and under regimes that confess themselves to the religion of Islam. The legal framework and bureaucratic regulation of individual states and administrations determine the conditions for Islamic entrepreneurship and *sharī'a*-compliant economic activity to a considerable extent. The global is forced to adjust to the local (national). This is analogous to the conditionalities coming off other religiously inspired legal frameworks and administrative institutions such as Islamic family laws and religious bureaucracies. Musawah activists have purposely chosen to cooperate across countries because the national Islamic family codes are not the same everywhere. Their stipulations are diverse in many regards (e.g. divorce, marriage or child custody). The respective regulations affect Muslim women because they are *as Muslims* subjected to these laws; but they are affected differently according to national and sub-national legal systems. In some cases, as for example in Malaysia, it is State or *negeri* law that has jurisdiction over Muslims' personal status and family affairs. It is this perspective on 'things Islamic' which informs my argument concerning translocal areas. Those described are constituted by legal, administrative and systemic conditions, frameworks and infrastructures that either expand or constrain the opportunity for action of people identifying with a particular faith or confession in their *Weltanschauung* (worldview).

In addition to formal regulations, informal ones determine the scope of human agency in certain environments. The Muslim employees of Wall Street institutions introduced in Chapter 4 are a case in point. There is no legal constraint on praying five times a day and abstaining from the consumption of alcohol. However, in their working environment there is rarely a space available that would be explicitly designated as a prayer room (as in most modern airports); their professional code of conduct often requires them to at least join their colleagues at official functions where the consumption of alcohol is a cultural requisite of business etiquette. The observation of religious norms and principles is possible, but limited in the routine of everyday work. Against this backdrop, the founding of Muslim professional associations like the Muppies (see Chapter 4) appears logical because Muslim professionals across the globe share the same concerns. The notion of shared concerns also applies to the formal realm of norms and regulations that structure people's lives (e.g. Muslim women's rights activists engaging in networks such as Musawah or WMUML). Here, the main concern is their being subject to Muslim laws and regulations that came about by patriarchal interpretations of the Islamic legal sources.

Shared concerns felt by Muslims across nations, regions and continents pertain to rights and obligations, human agency, religious practice, religious tolerance and many more aspects of personal identity that are at least partially defined by faith. When I visited a Malaysian Muslim artist a decade after the Bosnian war of 1992–1995, I asked about some paintings that seemed to convey a particular emotional loading. The artist replied that she painted them in the mid-1990s when she was extremely upset about what happened to fellow Muslims in the Balkans and felt she had to somehow express her feeling of solidarity and shared pain. I was surprised – Bosnia being far away from Malaysia and in my mind merely subsumed under the rubric of post-cold war civil conflict in the 'former Yugoslavia'. But ever since, it appears all the more comprehensible to me that the struggle of Muslims in one place triggers a wave of solidarity, including active support, in others. Shared concerns among people based on the conviction that they have something in common or are similarly affected by something because they identify with a certain faith is an emotional adhesive that nurtures the sense of belonging and connects people across huge geographical distances. It is here that translocality as a mode of travel evolves (Mandaville 2001: 6). This often refers to people travelling mentally to places rather than physically travelling there – although, of course, physical migration is not unusual. A home away from home provides emotional comfort (cf. Mallett 2004; Jackson 1995; Massey 1994). The provision of relevant services helps to generate such emotional comfort. Sometimes such services, like the establishment of institutions of Islamic banking or Islamic tertiary education, are demand driven; in other cases, such as the provision of mass products for the average consumer (*halâl* commodities, fashion items etc.), it is rather a supply that has been generated by an assumed demand. The global Muslim middle classes are those who predominantly appreciate the supply of commodities that allow them to abide by religious norms. Cosmopolitan sites like Dubai with its image of a business hub hosting 'a microcosm of the Muslim world' (Nasr 2010: 31) represent the ultimate in this regard: expensive luxury hotels complement posh mosques with air conditioning and impeccably clean facilities. Nasr (2010: 31) quotes an Arab businessman saying 'I like this place because I can shop, eat, enjoy luxury and be a good Muslim, too'. The emotional geography laid out in places like Dubai is shaped by the feeling that prosperity and faith have much more in common than poverty, violence and faith – an association frequently transported through images of conflict-ridden Muslim-majority regions of the world. The translocal areas I refer to are primarily those that have taken shape because of shared concerns and shared feelings of belonging, affectedness, and solidarity. I will expand this thought in the following chapter in which I relate the notion of trans- or pluri-local areas to the reflection on Area Studies as an academic programme.

Conclusion

This chapter has attempted to make sense of spaces and places that are not primarily defined by geographical or territorial demarcations, but more so by spaces that are captured in emotional and mental travel through them. It discussed examples of cross-fertilisation between global developments and local (sometimes national) experiences. Concerns at the local level 'travel' and go translocal, leading to shared concerns in numerous places (pluri-locality). Translocal subjectivities emerge from shared concerns across huge geographical distances and from the feeling of being at home in more than one place at a time. Switching locales is a movement occurring emotionally rather than physically. Concurrent and overlapping processes function like networks for the shaping of identities, thereby employing categories of religion and faith as markers. The establishment of Islamic financial institutions in numerous countries of the world happened concurrently as the demand for such institutions rose in the wake of Islamic resurgence. Handling one's financial affairs with the certainty of being in accordance with the principles of one's faith provides emotional comfort. The fact that Islamic banking is possible in virtually any place and at any time points to an invisible network of likemindedness across the globe. The function of identity networks as Adamson (2012) describes them becomes visible in the supply of faith-related services and *halâl* consumer commodities which are particularly appreciated among the world's Muslim middle classes. 'Being Muslim' as an identity category, however, glosses over the plurality of identities within the Muslim world. The availability of religious knowledge from countless sources and the pluralisation of religious authority have rendered the Muslim world a highly diverse terrain of subjectivities. Digital technologies facilitating the connection between people who share particular concerns and feelings are implicated across the board. The intellectual resources that inform the introduction of authoritative meanings and interpretations are nowadays plenty, too. In the formative years of Islamic resurgence (and in a time without internet and social media), individual scholars presented new approaches to knowledge and innovative perspectives on existing knowledge. I have called them 'knowledge entrepreneurs'. They paved the way for religious leaders in various guises (popular preachers, trainers etc.) reached out to the masses and exerted considerable influence on broad segments of society.

The creation of identity communities epitomises the geographies of trans- and pluri-locality. I have introduced several forms of physical and mental mobility through different spaces. One is characterised by the factual presence of actors at different geographical places (locales), yet which makes them feel closely connected to each other. They share a particular concern and engage in networking to pursue particular goals (e.g. women's rights activists). Another form of mental mobility is the switching of intellectual repertoires, which does not require an association with different geographical spaces, but travel between alternative epistemic and linguistic 'worlds'. Actors in the Islamic economy are used to doing that; they feel 'at home' in both the secular as well as the religiously informed world of corporate concepts and ethical economic principles. A third variant of pluri-locality is indeed associated with physical mobility between places. Community-building efforts by Hadramis and students returning from their study abroad represent this kind of mobility. In distinction to Pries' notion of transmigration, the connection between local spaces in different countries is based on identities – faith-based identities.

The approach to the demarcation of areas that I would endorse involves the recognition of areas that are shaped by the emotional proximity of individuals and communities rather than territorial or geographical coherence. I would hence suggest widening the analytical perspective and including emotional geographies in the concept of area in Area Studies. The emphasis is then less on politically defined areas as we find them today (Africa, Asia, Europe, Latin America, North America, Oceania and their respective sub-regions) and more on areas defined by interpersonal connectivities. Deterritorialised, mobility-prone and transient types of areas emerge by so doing. I attempt to apply this non-conventional perspective in the following chapter.

Notes

1 The 'trans' terms have become frequent in post-Cold War scholarly debates. Transnationalism was an early one (Glick-Schiller et al. 1995; Mintz 1998; Spivak 1993), later becoming accompanied by trans-regionalism (Godehardt and Lembcke 2010), trans-culturalism (Mae 2002), and translocality (Freitag and von Oppen 2010).

2 There exists a wealth of literature on entrepreneurs and entrepreneurship which I do not elaborate on in this study. Kayed and Hassan (2011: 24–60) provide a very valuable overview including a table of the most prominent definitions of the two terms.

3 Even in contemporary compilations of world philosophy the names of Islamic thinkers are not very prominent. A random check of the contents of contemporary books on 'great philosophers in world history' or similar compilations confirmed this impression.

4 Mandaville selects these three components from conventional accounts of what constitutes religious authority. Textuality refers 'primarily to the two most common scriptural reference points in the Islamic tradition: the Qur'an (the literal word of God as revealed to the Prophet Muhammad) and the Sunnah (the collected reports of Muhammad's actions and pronouncements)'; discursive method refers to 'the norms of juridical theory and praxis as developed over thirteen centuries within the science of jurisprudence, or *fiqh*'; and personification points to personified knowledge (i.e. 'the notion of authority as vested within various categories of "legitimate" producers and transmitters of knowledge such as religious scholars (*ulama*) or the charismatic leaders of mystical brotherhoods (Sufi *sheikhs*))' (Mandaville 2007: 101).

5 Personal conversation with John Conundaw, Manila, 14 November 2011.

References

Adamson, Fiona B., 'Constructing the Diaspora. Diaspora Identity Politics and Transnational Social Movements', in Terrence Lyon and Peter Mandaville (eds), *Politics from Afar: Transnational Diasporas and Networks*. London: Hurst & Company, 2012: 25–42.

Alatas, Ismail Fajrie, 'Contemporary Indonesian Pilgrimage to Hadramawt, Yemen', Contemporary Patterns in Transregional Islam (Middle East Institute), 24 October 2014. Available at: www.mei.edu/content/map/ziarah-hadramaut-contemporary-indonesian-pilgrimage-hadramawt-yemen (accessed 23 November 2014).

Appadurai, Arjun, *Modernity at Large: Cultural Dimensions of Globalisation*. Minneapolis: University of Minnesota Press, 1996.

Bachmann-Medick, Doris, *Cultural Turns. Neuorientierungen in den Kulturwissenschaften* [Cultural Turns. New Orientations in Cultural Studies]. Reinbek: Rowohlt, 2011.

Bubalo, Anthony and Greg Fealy, 'Joining the Caravan? The Middle East, Islamism and Indonesia', *Lowy Institute Paper* 05. Sydney: Lowy Institute for International Policy, 2005.

Carayannis, Elias G. and Piero Formica, 'Intellectual Venture Capitalists: An Emerging Breed of Knowledge Entrepreneurs', *Industry and Higher Education* 20 (2006) 3: 151–56.

Conradson, David and Deirdre McKay, 'Translocal Subjectivities: Mobility, Connection, Emotion', *Mobilities* 2 (2007) 2: 167–74.

Eickelman, Dale F., 'Islam and the Languages of Modernity', *Daedalus* 129 (2000) 1: 119–35.

Esposito, John L., *The Islamic Threat: Myth or Reality?* New York: Oxford University Press, 1999.

Fennert, Dana, *Islamischer Feminismus versus Pro-Familie-Bewegung. Transnationale Organisationsformen* [Islamic Feminism versus Pro-Family Movement. Transnational Forms of Organisation]. Berlin: neopubli, 2015.

Freitag, Ulrike and Achim van Oppen, "Translocality'. An Approach to Connection and Transfer in Regional Studies. Introduction', in Ulrike Freitag and Achim van Oppen (eds), *Translocality. The Study of Globalising Processes from a Southern Perspective*. Leiden: Brill, 2010, 1–24.

Giddens, Anthony, *A Contemporary Critique of Historical Materialism*. London: Macmillan, 1981.

Giddens, Anthony, 'Time, Space and Regionalisation', in Derek Gregory and John Urry (eds), *Social Relations and Spatial Structures*. London: Macmillan Education, 1985, 265–95.

Giddens, Anthony, *Modernity and Self-Identity*. Cambridge: Polity Press, 1991.

Glick Schiller, Nina, Linda Basch and Cristina Szanton Blanc, 'From Immigrant to Transmigrant. Theorizing Transnational Migration', *Anthropological Quarterly*, 68 (1995) 1: 48–63.

Godehardt, Nadine and Oliver Lembcke, 'Regional Orders in Political Spaces. A Contribution to the Theory of Regional Orders', *GIGA Working Paper Series* 124, Hamburg. Available at: http://papers.ssrn.com/sol3/papers.cfm?abstract_id=2131094 (accessed 23 June 2016).

Gugler, Thomas K., *Mission Medina: Dawat-e Islami und Tablighi Jamaat* [Mission Medina: Dawat-e-Islami and Tablighi Jamaat]. Würzburg: Ergon, 2011.

Gupta, Akhil and James Ferguson, 'Beyond 'Culture': Space, Identity, and the Politics of Difference', *Cultural Anthropology* 7 (1992) 1: 6–23.

Harvey, David, *The Condition of Postmodernity*. Oxford: Blackwell, 1989.

Harvey, David, 'Time-space Compression and the Postmodern Condition', in Malcolm Waters (ed.), *Modernity. Critical Concepts, Volume IV, After Modernity.* London and New York: Routledge, 1999: 98–118.

Jackson, Michael D., *At Home in the World.* Durham: Duke University Press, 1992.

Jessop, Bob, Neil Brenner and Martin Jones, 'Theorizing Sociospatial Relations', *Environment and Planning D: Society and Space*, 26 (2008): 389–401.

Kayed, Rasem N. and M. Kabir Hassan, *Islamic Entrepreneurship*. London and New York: Routledge, 2011.

Keck, Margaret and Kathryn Sikkink, *Activists Beyond Borders. Advocacy Networks in International Politics*, Ithaca, NY: Cornell University Press, 1998.

Kepel, Gilles, 'Islamism Reconsidered', *Harvard International Review* 22 (2000) 2: 22–27.

Leitner, Helga, Eric Sheppard and Kristin M. Sziarto, 'The Spatialities of Contentious Politics', *Transactions of the Institute of British Geographers* 33 (2008) 2: 157–72.

Lekon, Christian, 'Economic Crisis and State-building in Hadhramaut, 1941–1949. The Impact of the Decline of Southeast Asian Remittances', in Ahmed Ibrahim Abushouk and Hassan Ahmed Ibrahim (eds), *The Hadhrami Diaspora in Southeast Asia. Identity Maintenance or Assimilation?* Leiden: Brill, 2009: 81–108.

Mae, Michiko, 'Transkulturalität und Genderforschung' [Transculturality and Gender Studies], *Zeitschrift für Germanistik* Neue Folge 12 (2002) 3: 482–87.

Mallett, Shelley, 'Understanding Home: A Critical Review of the Literature', *The Sociological Review* 52 (2004) 1: 68–89.

Mandaville, Peter, *Transnational Muslim Politics. Re-imagining the Umma*. London and New York: Routledge, 2001.

Mandaville, Peter, 'Globalization and the Politics of Religious Knowledge. Pluralizing Authority in the Muslim World', *Theory, Culture and Society* 24 (2007) 2: 101–15.

Massey, Doreen, *Space, Place, and Gender*. Minneapolis: University of Minnesota Press, 1994.

Massey, Doreen, *For Space*. London: Sage Publications, 2005.

Md Akhir, Md Nasrudin, Siti Rohaini Kassim, Nor Nazihah Abd Ghani and Nurulaida Ramli, 'Halal Executive as a Measure for Standardization: The Role of Higher Learning Institutions', Takayuki Yoshimura and Satoshi Ktsunuma (eds), *International Seminar on Islam and Multiculturalism: Islam in Global Perspective*. Tokyo: Organization for Islamic Area Studies (Waseda University), 2015: 11–12.

Milne, R.S. and Diane K. Mauzy, *Malaysian Politics under Mahathir*. London and New York: Routledge, 1999.

Mintz, Sidney W., 'The Localization of Anthropological Practice. From Area Studies to Transnationalism', *Critique of Anthropology*, 18 (1998) 2: 117–33.

Musawah, 'Knowledge Building', 2016. Available at: www.musawah.org/what-we-do/knowledge-building (accessed 19 July 2016).

Nasr, Seyyed Vali Reza, *Islamic Leviathan. Islam and the Making of State Power*. Oxford: Oxford University Press, 2001.

Nasr, Vali, *Meccanomics: The March of the New Muslim Middle Class*. Oxford: Oneworld Publications, 2010.

Noor, Farish A., 'On the Permanent Hajj: The Tablighi Jama'at in South East Asia', *South East Asia Research* 18 (2010) 4: 707–34.

Pries, Ludger, 'Transnationalismus, Migration und Inkorporation. Herausforderungen an Raum- und Sozialwissenschaften' [Transantionalism, Migration and Incorporation. Challenges for Spatial and Social Sciences]. *Geographische Revue* 2 (2003): 23–39.

Rahman, Fazlur, *Islam and Modernity: Transformation of an Intellectual Tradition*. Chicago: University of Chicago Press, 1984.

Rosyad, Rifki, *A Quest for True Islam: A Study of the Islamic Resurgence Movement among the Youth in Bandung*. Canberra: ANU Press, 2006.

Roy, Olivier, *The Failure of Political Islam*. Cambridge, MA: Harvard University Press, 1994.

Rudnyckyj, Daromir, *Spiritual Economies. Islam, Globalization, and the Afterlife of Development*. Ithaca, NY: Cornell University Press, 2010.

Soja, Edward W., *Postmodern Geographies. The Reassertion of Space in Critical Social Theory*. London: Verso, 1989.

Spivak, Gayatri Chakravorty, *Outside in the Teaching Machine*. New York: Routledge, 1993.

Urry, John, *Mobilities*. Cambridge: Polity Press, 2007.

Walker, R.B.J., *One World, Many Worlds*. Boulder, CO: Lynne Rienner, 1988.

Walker, R.B.J., 'Security, Sovereignty and the Challenge of World Politics', *Alternatives* XV (1990): 3–27. Available at: http://alt.sagepub.com/content/15/1/3.full.pdf (accessed 27 July 2016).

6 Tunnel vision in Area Studies

In due consequence of Chapter 5, this chapter criticises the tendency of inward-looking in conventional Area Studies. Pointing to the political dimension of demarcating areas for scholarly analysis, it argues that Area Studies would gain in quality if tunnel vision were put aside for the sake of acknowledging hitherto neglected geographies, including emotional ones. The chapter wraps up the findings of Part II and discusses issues of hegemonic knowledge production. It argues that the exercise of re-scaling the arrangement of conventional Area Studies requires the recognition of other than the usual area units. Doing so is also a means to expound the political *Weltanschauung* that forms the ontological fundament for the arrangement of modern Area Studies.

The chapter is organised by themes. The initial theme is a literature-based reflection on critical assessments of contemporary Area Studies, including suggestions for 'new' Area Studies. This is followed by a discussion of the geographical as one element in the conceptualisation of area in Area Studies. The problematic of the geographical is manifold. Islamic Studies and Buddhist Studies are also clustered as a type of Area Studies. In fact, most of the research on phenomena pertaining to the non-Western world is frequently subsumed under Area Studies. Geographical as well as confessional and ideological units are lumped together under this rubric, thereby disregarding the idea that Western Europe is as much an area to be investigated from an Area Studies approach as any other region in the world.[1] The issue at hand is what ontologies Area Studies are associated with and how these are addressed in the conventional study programmes of Western academia. A third theme is the critique of conventional knowledge production in Area Studies from a Postcolonial and Colonial Knowledge Studies perspective. The perception of area knowledge as colonised knowledge shines through most of the arguments brought forth in this context. Finally, I relate the three themes to one another and conclude with some remarks concerning the tunnel vision that feeds into the debate on areas and Area Studies.

Critical assessments of Area Studies

Area Studies has become a signifier for various kinds of subjects in the ontological ordering of Western academia. It is a Western-invented unit of knowledge

DOI: 10.4324/9781315642123-8

production in higher education that is first and foremost distinguished from the so-called systematic disciplines of the social sciences (i.e. knowledge-generating units relying on a body of theories and a set of methods which are assumed to be universally applicable). The different intentions behind the establishment of Area Studies in Europe and the USA notwithstanding (see Mielke and Hornidge 2016b for details), scholars of Area Studies in the West were designated to study the non-Western world, including culture, religion and ethnographies. As Vincent Houben and Boike Rehbein (2010: 149) have pointed out, at least in most of Western Europe, the origins of Area Studies can be traced back to the interest in studying the 'wild' and the 'primitive' peoples, the communities of the 'subjugated foreigners' – the societies of former European colonies. Peculiarly, the majority of scholars conducting such research became organised in the discipline of anthropology (cf. Chapter 1). In order to study the non-Western world, areas had to be identified and demarcated. This process was very much politically driven, but was also informed by academic traditions such as the currents of 'Oriental Studies' in Europe. It so happened that post-World War II Area Studies embraced subjects named Southeast Asian Studies (seeking a term without immediate association to the colonial past), Sovietology/Communist Studies (referring to the systemic polarisation of capitalism and socialism/East and West) or Middle East Studies (including the Maghreb countries of North Africa but excluding Israel). Overarching subjects of study were Islamic Studies (for a long time focusing almost exclusively the Arab world), Jewish Studies, Oriental Studies, Semitic Studies or East Asian Art History, hence subjects pertaining to particular fields of interest beyond, albeit still attached to, politically defined units. During the Cold War, Germany had institutes for the study of the East (Ostwissenschaften) – a legacy of the German partition and the separation of Europe into a capitalist and a socialist bloc. In sum, what has become associated with Area Studies over the decades is a rather fuzzy arrangement of subjects which symbolise the outcome of ongoing processes of 'othering'. Areas, in other words, are those places and cognitive spaces where 'others' (not 'us') live and act. Why else would Catholic studies not be regarded a subject of Area Studies in a country like Germany?

The observation that the areas which became established as the units and subjects of Area Studies miss out on important moments of the empirical reality of people's physical and mental mobility and connectedness is by now commonly accepted. The spatial and cultural turns (cf. Chapter 5) in the humanities and social sciences have brought about fresh perspectives and stimulated the concentration on, for instance, (trans-)migration, diaspora or transcultural studies. Along with this shift in orientation, the debate on the relationship between Area Studies and systematic disciplines became reactivated (Hanson 2009; Graham and Kantor 2007; Guyer 2004; Mintz 1998) and put the usefulness of container categories such as the state or the nation into question. The debate is ongoing and as yet, the units of Area Studies have not changed significantly.

Among 'areanists', another shift received attention. This refers to what Mielke and Hornidge (2016a) call the 'mobility turn' in the production of area-related knowledge: from so-called 'trait' geographies to process-geographies. The latter are meant to capture the 'flows and motions' of ideas, ideologies, discourses, people, goods, images, technologies and techniques (Appadurai 2000: 5) and allow for the recognition of new scales of reference (van Schendel 2002). The littoral states of the Southern Red Sea, for instance, can be investigated with a fresh eye when this region forms the area of inspection (Serels 2012) – instead of dividing it up between Africa and the Middle East. Hitherto, those working on this region have to commit themselves either to departments of Middle East or African Studies. Similar discomfort ails those working on Israel and its vicinity. A colleague of mine who studied Hebrew and Arabic works on educational and socio-economic topics in this area. He is constantly asked to submit his research proposals to either a review committee from Jewish Studies or one from Middle East Studies – and finds this separation quite disturbing.[2] More such examples could be raised, including those from my own experience in the academic funding machinery that urges researchers to subscribe to an established discipline in the social sciences although the topic of study is much more related to Area Studies. Is research on informal political institutions in Malaysia by definition Political Science? Or is it also Malaysian Studies?

The discomfort with the arrangement of disciplines and areas on the one hand, and the geographical ordering of the world in Western academia on the other, has led to several demands for a restructuring of the Area Studies architecture (Appadurai 2000; 1996) particularly in view of its reflection in scholarly associations (Prewitt 1996; Cumings 1997). The end of bi-polarisation in world politics and international relations, the existence of increasingly porous borders and boundary displacements, accompanied by a renewed pondering on the relationship between Area Studies and systematic disciplines accelerated the Area Studies debate in the West – and in other parts of the world, Southeast Asia being one of them. Demands to de-centre, diversify, and redefine Area Studies as topic-centred rather than territorially informed research have since been articulated (Mielke and Hornidge 2016a; Houben 2013; Mignolo 2012; Boatca 2012; Goh 2011; Ellings et al. 2010; Chou and Houben 2006; Mignolo and Tlostanova 2006). The capacities and interests of local scholars vary, however, with regard to such new approaches. While Southeast Asian scholars are keen to have Southeast Asia recognised as a region with an established identity – and Southeast Asian Studies as a natural scholarly incarnation of this identity (Goh 2014; 2011) – others are far less enthusiastic. Eastern European and Central Asian colleagues would not easily approve of Eastern European Studies or Central Asian Studies, respectively, as academic units in Areas Studies.[3] Unsurprisingly, this is again due to political developments in these regions after the fall of the socialist regimes and the fragmentation of the Soviet Union. In many former Soviet Union countries, nation-building trumps regionalism in importance; this also trickles down to academia and the identification of subjects for study and research.

In addition to coping with critical junctures in recent history, the legacies of the Cold War are still at work, making knowledge generation itself a still predominantly Western-flavoured endeavour. Shalini Randeria (1999) has pointed to the fact that, irrespective of the noble mission of restructuring and de-centring knowledge production in general and Area Studies in particular, the epistemic foundations in most non-Western countries are, by and large, shaped by Western perspectives. The actual implementation of an 'epistemic decolonisation' (Mignolo 2007, with reference to Quijano 1992) in knowledge production is hence more difficult than one might expect. The Islamisation of Knowledge (Chapter 2) was no doubt an attempt to achieve just this: a decolonisation of hegemonic epistemic foundations and an overcoming of hegemonic geopolitics of knowledge. Its wide disregard in Area Studies' as well as Islamic Studies' discourses of the time (exceptions confirm the rule) speaks of the difficulties to gain ground in such geopolitics. The substantial neglect had effects. The momentum that Islamisation and Islamic resurgence gained in large parts of the globe was undervalued in the social sciences and Area Studies alike. Again, as mentioned in preceding chapters, I am not arguing that the IoK project triggered the wave of Islamic resurgence that ensued throughout the Muslim world, but it is but one highly illustrative example for an epistemic counter-movement acting in the *Zeitgeist* of anti- and post-colonialism. Its wide disregard in the said discourses hints at the interpretation that Islamic Southeast Asia was not much in the focus of contemporaneous Southeast Asianists, and that for Islamic scholars, Southeast Asia was too marginal a Muslim region to be bestowed with attention.

It was factually only after 9/11 that Islam re-surfaced as a religion shaping global history. A telling example for the sweeping disrespect of the Western world towards the meaning of developments in the Muslim world for global history is Michael Gilsenan's narration of his defence of a book title which did not meet the approval of the publisher in the first place. The incidence happened shortly after the 1979 revolution in Iran, hence after an incident that triggered a tremendous reaction in the Muslim world. The author was teaching at Princeton University in the USA at that time. He intended to publish a book on religion and society in the modern Middle East. He did so eventually (in 1982), but he experienced a peculiar conversation before his study could be printed with the title he had chosen, namely *Recognizing Islam. Religion and Society in the Modern Middle East*. In the preface to a later edition, Gilsenan shares with the reader that his US publisher flatly rejected the title *'Recognizing Islam'* – on the grounds that 'no one would buy a book implying that we should recognize Islam' (as in diplomatic recognition) (Gilsenan 2008: 2). A similar story is shared by Tamim Ansary, who, working in the US in the late 1990s, was hired to publish a high-school textbook on world history. When he introduced his table of contents, he was reminded by a group of advisors with authoritative say that the role of Islam in world history was not worth touching upon more than marginally. Ansary relates:

> I noticed an interesting tug and pull between my advisors and me. We agreed on almost everything *except* – I kept wanting to give more coverage

> to Islam in world history, and they kept wanting to pull it back, scale it down, parse it out as sidebars in units devoted mainly to other topics. [...] Mine was so much the minority opinion that it was indistinguishable from error, so we ended up with a table of contents in which Islam constituted the central topic in just one out of thirty chapters.
>
> (Ansary 2010: xiv, italics in original)

After this incident, Ansary chose to write a history book which gave due coverage to Islam's role in world history (Ansary 2010). The power hierarchies in terms of what is considered knowledge worth publishing and researching, and what can be neglected, jarred both Gilsenan and Ansary to the extent that they deemed it important to share their experience with their readers. Empirical reality proved their initial sense of recognising the non-Western world – of leaving the tunnel vision – correct.

Arjun Appadurai (2000: 3) echoed the impression of global power hierarchies in determining what deserves to be picked up in research and what ought to be relegated to lower ranks when he stated that 'Area Studies are the largest institutional epistemology through which the academy in the US has apprehended much of the world in the last fifty years'. This apprehension of the world has been narrowed down through the definition of the units that constitute areas in Area Studies, leading to what I call tunnel views from which expanding the gaze is not easily accomplished. My championing of a shift from tunnel vision in Area Studies towards a stronger recognition of socio-cognitive spaces of connectedness and belonging (emotional geographies), which may constitute areas in their own right, derives from the unease with the narrow lens in and across conventional Area Studies. In the following section, I raise a few examples to convey my own apprehension of areas of 'lived reality' rather than politico-geographically defined ones. A disclaimer that merits mentioning is that by stressing the importance of lived realities for the designation of emotional geographies, the importance of territorial or maritime geographies ought not to be diminished to insignificance. The point is that both deserve attention.

Scales and geographies

In the preceding chapters, I have used the concept of 'belonging' without further specification. It is, however, appropriate to reflect a bit further on the semantic facets of the term and its conceptualisation in the literature. Belonging is a heuristic concept that is not a synonym for identity but refers to relations and processes that lead to an assumed status of identity (Anthias 2013: 7; 2002: 494; cf. Pfaff-Czarnecka 2011). Belonging stresses the dynamics of situatedness, whereas identity is treated as more static. There is no universally agreed upon understanding of the concept, but most authors approve of the distinction between personal (individual) and group-related forms of attachments. Belonging as a concept allows for the identification of processes, relations, and frames of reference that enable emplacement and positioning (Anthias 2013, 2002; Pfaff-Czarnecka 2011; Antonsich 2010; Yuval-Davis 2006). It is about feeling 'at home' in the sense of an emotional attachment; transversal emotional geographies across regions and locales thus produce an 'at home' in various places. Nira Yuval-Davis (2006), moreover, distinguishes between belonging and the politics of belonging. The latter 'comprises specific political projects aimed at constructing belonging in particular ways to particular collectives' (Yuval-Davis 2006: 197). Such collectives are 'themselves being constructed by these projects in very particular ways' (Yuval-Davis 2006: 197). The present study does not strictly separate between belonging and the politics of belonging, but rather follows a general understanding of belonging as 'feeling at home' and 'feeling attached' to various spaces, places and locations as well as social, cognitive and spiritual environments.

What is the relationship between the concept of belonging and the arrangement of areas in Area Studies? One idea comes from Victor King in his reflection on Sarawak studies versus Borneo studies. Sarawak is a state of Malaysia in the East of the country. It is located on the island of Borneo, most of whose territory belongs to neighbouring Indonesia. On the terrestrial map, Borneo is a coherent space. On the political map, it is divided into Malaysian and Indonesian parts and the Sultanate of Brunei Darussalam. King (2012: 136) asks whether Sarawak studies or Borneo studies were the more suitable approach to research the sub-region of the island which forms the East Malaysian state. 'Most of the time', he writes, 'Borneo is not treated as an island entity on its own in social science and Area Studies, but Sarawak or the regions on the Indonesia part of Borneo are examined separately' (King 2012: 136). This, he says, ignores the fact that both (i.e. Malaysian and Indonesian parts of Borneo) have 'the imprint of a distinctive geographical personality' because the island is special in several regards and its geographical borders have their legitimation (King 2012: 136). No Malaysian government since the country's independence (1957) encouraged Borneo studies because Sarawak and the second East Malaysian state Sabah (also on Borneo) receive special treatment from the Malaysian government as Muslim-minority regions. Together with Malay Muslims, the indigenous communities in Sabah and Sarawak are entitled to call themselves *bumiputra* (sons of the soil); they enjoy special rights and privileges which cannot be claimed by non-*bumiputras* (cf. Derichs 2001). From a political point of view, Borneo is an inappropriate area to be granted the status of a unit of study. Geologists or physical geographers may find this inconvenient as they cannot move easily from one place on the island to the other. But political will is paramount even if inhabitants of the Malaysian and the Indonesian parts of Borneo feel closer to each other – culturally, ethnically, historically – than to their fellow citizens of their respective nation-states (cf. King 2013). (It is a four-hour flight to get from West to East Malaysia, but merely a walk [if possible] to get from Malaysian Borneo to Indonesian Borneo.) An even more drastic, non-Southeast Asian example of fragmentation despite a shared feeling of belonging is the Kurdish nation. Not only are its members dispersed across several Middle Eastern state territories (let alone diasporic communities elsewhere), but they are denied any Kurdish statehood at all. The autonomy status of Kurdish Iraq is the closest the Kurds could get to sovereign agency, but it is an exceptional concession compared to the situation in neighbouring states. Emotional belonging collides with geopolitical interests and state power. In people's lived reality, physical mobility is hampered by formal requirements; consequently, non-physical mobility rises in relevance for substantiating the idea of community and staying connected.

The relevance of political will and support for designating areas of knowledge production is, as Victor King's case of Sarawak Studies exemplifies, not an exclusive West-vs-rest issue. Although the hegemony of Western perspectives, being globally reflected in the structuring of the institutional academic landscape, is obvious, national political considerations are nonetheless determining factors. Malaysia's Sarawak studies are a case in point. Borneo is not a welcome areal unit for research, and even less so the translocal (across national borders) connections of people on the island.

The appreciation of cross-border connectedness is also discernible on a broader regional level. Goh Bang Lan, for instance, demands respect towards lived realities that have evolved in present-day Southeast Asia because the process of regional cooperation has nurtured a regional identity. Goh's concern is to re-centre knowledge production 'back to the regions themselves' (Goh 2012: 80) so that local rather than foreign entities judge standards and values of knowledge and its generation. What is universal and objective knowledge and what is a parochial form of knowledge should not be left to the discretion of powerful Western knowledge producers (Goh 2012: 80). The problem, however, lies in the question of realisation, i.e. Randeria's 'decolonization of imagination' (Randeria 1999: 380) is at stake. Goh (2012: 81) asks explicitly:

> What are the conditions and processes that enable alternative epistemologies and imaginings without the trappings of essentialism or chauvinism? If indeed the project of knowledge production has become more polycentric would the agendas and the whole idea of scholarship from regional perspectives be accepted into dominant knowledge paradigms even if they were to overthrow their fundamental disciplinary and ideological premises?

The reason for asking these questions is the observation that the structural conditions of knowledge production in formerly colonised regions of the world have rendered the theoretical and methodological approaches of Western origin accepted ones, at least in the social sciences. It is not easy to reverse the whole process and introduce new epistemic approaches to knowledge, as the criticism of the IoK project has shown. Even if alternative approaches gain momentum, as the well-consolidated institutional landscape of Islamic education illustrates, it does not automatically mean that they become recognised globally. The constant predominance of established standards – including disciplinary standards – reflects the global power relationship in knowledge production. In many parts of the globe it steers the lens through which the world is looked at.

The persistence of standardised approaches has a diverse effect on area scholarship, as the case of Southeast Asian Studies shows. The call to diversify Southeast Asian Studies (Goh 2011), for instance, disapproves of the paucity of local studies from the region, but at the same time approves of the construction of the region as a unit of study by 'global epistemic power houses' (Mielke and Hornidge 2016). While the fact that the areas of contemporary Area Studies have been constructed by knowledge producers in one particular part of the world can be criticised, it cannot be denied that, all too often, this area map has become accepted and adopted in the regions to which they pertain. The geographical areas themselves have developed into units of shared visions, values, norms and identities. Southeast Asia, Goh argues, is such an area and should be recognised as such. In her own words:

> While indeed much in the criticism of area studies as contrived geographical and cultural conceptions is warranted, what critics often forget is that the area studies map of the Cold War has been adopted throughout much of the world. Hence, as much as a territorially-bounded concept of the region can be theoretically deconstructed, there is a *lived reality* to this constructed geography.
>
> (Goh 2012: 91; italics added)

Her point is clear and merits consideration. Critical views of the designation of Southeast Asia as a coherent area and of the translation of this view into academia by way of establishing Southeast Asian Studies are, as Goh concedes, understandable to a certain extent. However, when the inhabitants of Southeast Asia have developed a sense of belonging together through their lived realities, this should be recognised and acknowledged. I have strong sympathy with Goh's view. Still, I would prefer to look at Southeast Asia and Southeast Asian Studies through a bigger lens, which I describe below.

Regarding the genesis of Southeast Asian Studies in the West, it is agreed that the name of the subject came about because the world political situation had changed after World War II and and even more after decolonisation. As mentioned above, the terms Southeast Asia and Southeast Asian Studies detracted, to a certain extent, from the legacies of the colonial powers in the region. The countries of the region adopted the designation as a coherent entity when five of them founded the Association of Southeast Asian Nations (ASEAN) in 1967.[4] Gradually and in reaction to further world political developments, ASEAN has today a membership of ten states: Brunei Darussalam, Cambodia, Indonesia, Lao PDR, Malaysia, Myanmar, the Philippines, Singapore, Thailand and Vietnam. Except for Timor Leste, the geographical region conventionally delineated as Southeast Asia is thus organised in ASEAN. Since ASEAN's founding and in accordance with growing regional cooperation in various formats, the member states have put numerous integrative programmes in place (Acharya 2011; 1997; Wei-Yen 2007; Kahn 1998). Indubitably, this forging of a Southeast Asian identity helped to close ranks among nation-states that had formerly pursued quite different, if not competing, national trajectories and separate nation-building projects (cf. Gungwu 2005). Exchange and scholarship programmes in the educational sector, awareness-raising for shared cultural values and simple practical measures such as separate lanes at airport immigrations exclusively for citizens of ASEAN member states facilitated the framing of Southeast Asian cohesion – so much so that Malaysia's Anwar Ibrahim published a book on the potentials of an 'Asian renaissance' (Anwar 1997). There was hence an apparent political will behind the demarcation of Southeast Asia as a coherent area and a place of a shared identity in lived reality. Goh, then, is certainly right when she demands that the empirical (lived) reality should not be ignored for the sake of criticising constructed geographies in Western Area Studies. Furthermore, first Singapore and then also other Southeast Asian nation-states have established institutes for Southeast Asian Studies on their own. This can be taken as a sign of the self-concept as Southeast Asians. Still I would beg to differ and substantiate my view with observations that have already been introduced in the preceding chapters.

I have no objections to Goh's diagnosis of lived realities in Southeast Asia. To my mind, however, this view overlooks connectivities that are lived reality too, but stretch beyond the region and are based on, for instance, faith and religion. As mentioned above, territorially defined geographical areas are by no means insignificant for the study of areas. But they gloss over the geographies and connectivities whose values rest in spiritual or emotional belonging. A Malaysian manager in the Islamic economy certainly subscribes as much to notions of a Southeast Asian identity as he feels attached to peers of the same faith outside Southeast Asia (cf. Sloane-White 2017). Many Muppies and Musawah members, too, are scattered across the globe but pool their expertise in their confession-based organisations (cf. Chapter 4). The relevance of faith for the feeling of belonging cannot simply be done away with.

Another aspect that merits attention is the policies of *Realpolitik* in Southeast Asia versus the rhetoric of Southeast Asian-ness. When Malaysian religious and political authorities prohibit the exercise of Yoga and the playing of the digital game 'Pokemon Go' for the country's Muslims (cf. Al Arabiya News, 2010; Bangkok Post 2016), the importance of religious principles is obviously high on the agenda. Iran banned 'Pokemon Go' a few weeks before Malaysia, and Malaysian authorities consulted Saudi Arabian and Egyptian authorities before declaring the game harmful for the country's Muslims (Bangkok Post 2016). This underlines that orientations in policy-making are not exclusively geared towards regional (Southeast Asian) concerns. Despite all regional integrative rhetoric and effective instruments of regional identity building, the picture of lived realities is painted with many colours; the scales of connectedness vary according to theme. Sometimes they cover the region of ASEAN, sometimes they cover the areas of influential players in the Muslim world (Iran, Saudi Arabia, Egypt). At other times the scale is narrowed down to only the Sunni Islamic sphere or smaller (currents within Sunni or Shi'a). In addition to the undeniable achievements in building the ASEAN community, attachments of states and people beyond the region have developed and grown. They deserve to be recognised in the same way as intra-regional connectedness has become recognised.

What I refer to with the expression of tunnel vision in Area Studies is the phenomenon of fading out areas that jump the conventional scales of segmentation in Area Studies (e.g. pursuing Sarawak Studies rather than Borneo Studies). Missing out on, for instance, the relevance of faith-related scales of connectedness – faith-based geographies – beyond a territorially bound region is a narrow view. My strong suggestion is to include alternative scales into the portfolio of area research. It is another form of re-centring and diversifying knowledge production, which is not meant to discard the approaches hitherto followed, but to echo those who claim attention for the acknowledgement of other than the established scales and geographies.

A great deal of the demands for alternative ways of generating knowledge and conducting research has been inspired by perspectives from Postcolonial Studies. The subsequent section discusses some ideas that have sprung off from this current since they have met with considerable attention in the case of Southeast Asian Studies, too.

Areas and disciplines in postcolonial perspective

Area Studies and Postcolonial Studies meet in Dipesh Chakrabarty's (2009) dictum of 'provincializing Europe'. The plea to adjust the image of Europe in relation to its place and role in global history is most comprehensible from an areanist's point of view. Southeast Asia historian Anthony Reid (2012: 51) picks up this motive and suggests provincialising globalisation. By this he promotes the thought, similar to Goh (2012), to counter the hegemonic knowledge machinery of the West by turning to local knowledge production in the social sciences. Since Reid has worked, as Goh does, in Singapore, he is familiar with the institutional and structural arrangements that were taken over in Southeast Asia from Western (Anglo-American, as Reid calls it) models. His outlook on a change towards more local knowledge production and local institutional scholarship is as cautious as Goh's, because he, too, views Southeast Asian universities' willingness to allow for a derailing of the current knowledge regime with scepticism. In strategic terms, countering the power of hegemonic knowledge regimes means 'a gradual process of replicating the centres of knowledge production in global society at the periphery, with the long-term objective of empowering and opening up of the local(s)' (Zawawi 2012: 3). In practical terms, it requires to 'sustain a younger generation of social scientists (knowledge workers) of quality' who are well aware that 'elevating locally-based publications and journals' to standards of their own means to depart from international benchmarking systems (rankings, quotation accounts etc.) (Zawawi 2012: 3). In other words, what is needed to overcome the socio-economic imperatives in global knowledge production is confronting them with distinctive local epistemologies and a fresh appreciation of local intellectual traditions. For the future or the 'afterlife' of Area Studies, Goh (2012: 81) recommends:

> first, a recognition of the connection with, but also departure from Western disciplinary practices; and second, the retention of region and nation state as analytical categories to better grasp existential experiences as well as political agencies which may differ from normative social scientific concepts.

Both Reid and Goh's projections of breaking hegemonies are nurtured by their (experience with the) empirical surroundings in Singaporean institutions of higher learning. This shapes their views considerably and tends to wipe off the numerous examples of alternative approaches to knowledge already practiced in and beyond the region (cf. Chapters 3 and 4). Indeed, there is an already existing landscape of local knowledge production which is not part of the global ranking competition. The proliferation of Islamic educational institutions in Indonesia and Malaysia – as described in the previous chapters –together with the effective links with big universities in the Middle East provide platforms for genuine, local knowledge generation. It just happens somewhere other than the scalar mould of Southeast Asia. This mould 'jumps the scale', in van Schendel's (2002) terms, and covers interlinked regions from Southeast Asia to the Middle East. When such scales or geographies are not taken into account, the gaze at Southeast Asia as a scalar unit misses out on the transregional and translocal connections in lived reality.

Some scholars appear to entertain the attitude that 'only local knowledge is good knowledge'. King (2012) discusses this phenomenon in his reflections on the contested issue of local versus non-local knowledge. While scholars like Syed Hussein Alatas, Farid Alatas or Shamsul AB are rightly seen as those who, from early on, pointed to the dependence on Western knowledge in the developing world and who criticised the dominance of colonial knowledge, King (2012: 131) warns of tendencies to favour local scholarship in an almost exclusive manner. Essentialisations of this kind feed into claims that only local scholars can apply a proper view on local affairs. In this regard, King is highly critical of the bashing of non-local area scholarship and claims, to the contrary, that non-locals can well adopt local perspectives:

> I see no particular reason why outsiders cannot develop local understandings and I have not seen any convincing argument that has been offered as to why they cannot see social and cultural life from a local perspective (however we define this and its advantages and disadvantages); nor do I accept that local scholars are in some sense privileged or at least better equipped to provide 'a local point of view'.
>
> (King 2012: 130)

There is hence a great potential for controversy in the debate on the status of local knowledge and its production. Moreover, the differing positions on who is privileged or entitled to something remind us of claims in Islamic theology that only Muslims (ideally with a strong proficiency in Arabic) can utter informed and qualified opinions on how, for instance, the sources of religious tradition are to be interpreted. It is in the context of such issues that the theme of a pluralisation of religious authority (Mandaville 2001) surfaces. Musawah and Sisters in Islam activists in Malaysia have frequently encountered the attitude of not being entitled to speak on behalf of Islam and religious tradition. Their stance towards issues such as gender equality in Islam became delegitimised by fellow Muslims, among others, with the argument that the organisations' members do not master Arabic properly.[5] In a broader dimension of the reflection on knowledge production, contesting attitudes like those mentioned here hint at issues of positionality and authenticity. Who is in which position to decree what is authentic (Islamic, local) and what is not? I will not delve into this debate,[6] but briefly relate to positionality below and in the final chapter of this volume.

Aside from King's justified indication of narrow-minded positions towards the value of local knowledge, the critical research on colonial knowledge and its repercussions for scholarship in the region of Southeast Asia have brought about perspectives which merit attention in regard of Area Studies. Malaysian scholars of colonial knowledge Shamsul and Azmi, for instance, point to a distorted view on Islam in the region because Islamic Studies have been so much focused on sources of Middle Eastern Islam instead of local Southeast Asian ones. In their words:

> Besides Islam the Southeast Asian region is heir to Hindu and Buddhist traditions as well as to three European colonial systems of government and administration: British, Dutch and French. It is evident that Islam has not escaped the influence of the others. Indeed, in some aspects of life Islam has been considerably reformulated by them as a result of having had to embed itself in a pre-Islamic metaphysical milieu and to undergo a process of reshaping by the rational-scientific logic of the European technology of rule. It follows, therefore, that in order to understand the state of contemporary Islam, Muslims and Islamic studies in Southeast Asia must begin with materials and data from the region, rather than with some middle-Eastern and theological formulation of Islam – while at the same time not denying that Islam is a universalistic theology originating in the Arabic Middle East.
>
> (Shamsul and Azmi 2011: 113)

The set-up of conventional Area Studies – including Islamic Studies with their concentration on Middle Eastern Islam – has hampered a shift of the view from Middle Eastern to original material and data from Southeast Asia in the study of the latter region's type of Islam. If reference material and data from the region were to be worked with, however, the whole apparatus of Area Studies subjects would be affected. On the one hand, the said mutual influence of the major religions in the region would have to be captured – a task hardly possible in Islamic

Studies proper and rather a theme for Comparative Religious Studies. On the other hand, the region of the Middle East would still have to be included because the universalistic theology of Islam originated there and has not ceased to exert influence at the borders of Southeast Asian nations. Working, for example, on the history of Islamic education in Malaysia then, requires cultural knowledge of Southeast Asia, Buddhist, Hindu and Islamic knowledge as well as knowledge of the Middle East (to assess how Islamic theological universals have become reshaped by local ontologies and conventions). In practical terms, a student would have to enrol in a host of different conventional study programmes if he or she were to conduct solid work on the topic. What Shamsul and Azmi hint at is thus also an oblique critique of the ontological perception of the world as represented in present-day Area Studies.

In a similar vein, Scott Thomas refers to the pitfalls of applying socio-ontological arguments that originated in the West to analyses of situations elsewhere. With reference to religion, Thomas (2007: 63) observes:

> Most scholars of early modern Europe now recognise that the confusion over the role of religion and politics, social class, or economics in the debate over the wars of religion was based on retrospectively applying a modern concept of 'religion', a set of privately held doctrines or beliefs, to societies which had yet to make the social and cultural transition to these kind (sic) of distinction.

Thomas' statement is not new, because it tackles the prominent question of the travel and universal applicability of concepts to empirical settings that are most different from the ones in which these concepts were conceived. But his statement reminds us of the path dependencies in social sciences which lead to mis-applications and dubious apprehensions. The separation of the concept of religion from the core of analytical tools in secularised sociology or political science is one such path dependency. Religion is largely separated despite the knowledge about the role of faith-based organisations for generating, (re)building, binding and bridging political and social capital. Faith-based organisations function as social networks – spaces where people feel at home – and as social narratives for 'restoring a sense of meaning in which the actions of people are consistent with their values and their beliefs, and hence consistent with their identity' (Thomas 2007: 59). Consequently, Thomas also argues in favour of applying the concept of religion – but to phenomena that allow it to do so. This means to 'apply the concepts of religion and authenticity to some of the substantive global issues that confront all of us – international conflict and cooperation, diplomacy and peace-building, the promotion of civil society, democracy, and economic development' (Thomas 2007: 59). In sum, the application of a particular concept is an important issue to address in scientific analyses. When (if at all), why and how can and should be concepts applied is a question that permeates contemporary knowledge generation; it is also closely linked with critical stances towards conventional container categories (not only in Area Studies).

From the viewpoint of critical studies of colonial knowledge, European epistemology in colonial times was too rationalist for an appropriate assessment of religions and their roles for social capital accumulation, social order and moral frames of reference in the colonised societies. Rather than being acknowledged in their functions, religions 'became 'traditionalised', 'marginalised' or simply sidelined through the application of the technology of rule and official procedures that constitute modern bureaucracy' (Shamsul and Azmi 2011: 116). The rationalist way of assessing social reality had significant consequences for the identification of analytical units. Inhabitants of a place, for instance, were not typified according to categories of religious or linguistic affiliation. Since the majority of colonial bureaucrats did not know any of the local languages and religions, their applied stratification was based on ethnic and racial categories – hence drawing from visible features of distinction rather than other intelligible markers. Benedict Anderson (1998) has vividly described this in his tracing of how the 'Chinese' became 'Chinese' in colonial Southeast Asia. The migrants from the coastal regions of today's China identified themselves by occupation, by clan affiliation, their local places of origin, or by the languages they spoke (Hokkien, Cantonese and others). '[T]he original migrants had no idea that they were Chinese' writes Anderson (1998: 13). Nationality was not a category of identification. This changed when Europeans entered the region:

> [U]nderstanding none of these languages, with their eyes glued on physiognomies, costumes, and occupations, and their ambitions set on controlling trade in the region, [the Europeans] decided that all such people were "Chinese," and proceeded to act on the basis of this decision.
>
> (Anderson 1998: 13)

Anderson's analysis is all the more striking because post-independence research on Malaysian society has – in true path dependency – been almost entirely based on the perception of Malaysia as a multi-ethnic and multi-racial society. Race and ethnicity became *the* analytical units to analyse peace, conflict, harmony, tension, economic and social stratification as well as political affairs in Malaysia. I have ridden along this path as well (cf. Derichs 2004; 2003; 2001). The colonial legacy in knowledge production was thus brought about by the structuring of social reality along the lines of visually intelligible features and out of a lack of knowledge about other markers of distinction. The caveat that has to be made, though, is one that Goh (2012) has emphasised as well. It is the fact that social stratification in Malaysian society along racial and ethnic lines is today a generally accepted perspective– a lived reality. Rather than becoming meaningless, identification with ethnic affiliation has grown in recent decades. Religion in general and Islam as the religion of ethnic Malays forms a paramount element in this regard, and has led, for example, to officially published lists of words which ought not to be used by non-Muslims (Derichs 2016). Although the colonial construction of the ethnic stratification of Malaysian society is common knowledge, altering the analytical apparatus that works through it is a long-term task (similar to that of turning to local knowledge, as mentioned above).

A crucial point in Postcolonial Studies is that colonialism was about occupying physical geographical and *epistemological* space. The conquering of epistemological space, Shamsul and Azmi (2011: 120) argue:

> involves the conquest of indigenous thought systems, hence disempowering them of their ability to define things, and subsequently replacing them with a foreign one through a systematic application of a series of colonial 'investigative modalities'.

The term 'investigative modalities' goes back to anthropologist Bernard Cohn (1996), who analysed colonial forms of knowledge using India as his object of study. An investigative modality in Cohn's understanding:

> includes the definition of a body of information that is needed, the procedures by which appropriate knowledge is gathered, its ordering and classification, and then how it is transformed into usable forms such as published reports, statistical returns, histories, gazetteers, legal codes, and encyclopaedias.
>
> (Cohn 1996: 3)

One such modality is the above-mentioned separation of religion from the body of social and political order. The claim that in Islam state and religion are inseparable is an emblematic example for the power of investigative modalities. The analysis tools of secular political science do not analyse religious institutions because, in secular thinking, the religious apparatus is not part of the political apparatus. This concept collides with the Islamic principle of the unity of state and religion. In the course of 'traditionalising' and 'marginalising' religion (see above), the idea of a unity of state and religion in Islam has, until today, been widely perceived as retrograde and backward in the secular West.

I have raised the examples of critical studies of colonial knowledge since they serve to illuminate the tunnel vision in Area Studies. The link between the above paragraphs and the said tunnel vision may not be immediately apparent, but by linking the trajectories of epistemic 'conquerings' and path dependencies with the demarcation of areas in contemporary Area Studies, the picture gets clearer. To illustrate my point, I turn to language and religion, i.e. to their relevance for sustaining faith-based, emotional geographies. In the Islamic parts of colonial Southeast Asia, the Arabic alphabet and script were used for oral as well as written communication. Arabic letters were in use throughout Persia (today's Iran), parts of South Asia (today's Urdu speaking regions), the Middle East, and the Malay world. The Qur'ân and other important sources of Islamic tradition were consumed in Arabic (similar to the Bible in Christianity which was only conveyed in non-Latin languages to the audience of believers after Martin Luther's translation and reformation). Faith, alphabet and script thus constituted elements with binding capacity for Muslim communities across huge distances. The 'use of the same Arabic alphabet' led to 'the creation of texts in Persian, Urdu and Malay, that would unify millions of followers in those linguistic constituencies under the same faith' (Shamsul and Azmi 2011: 131). This kind of linguistic and faith-based constituency represents nothing less than a historic 'area', a geographical scale that stretches across world regions. The Muslim-majority regions in Southeast Asia were later cut off from this historic area is – not exclusively, but to a considerable extent – due to the forced shift to the Latin alphabet and the relegation of religion to a marginal status in the course of European colonisation. The disclosure of historic areas like this one mirrors what is at stake in present times; a glimpse at Islamic educational infrastructures and exchange across regions suffices (including the valuation of Arabic). If lived realities were to count in the exercise of identifying areas, constituencies under the same faith, as introduced in the preceding chapters, should certainly become acknowledged as a lived reality. This would allow for the identification of areas shaped differently from those of conventional Area Studies. The historic example expounds how strong the area delineations of modern Area Studies catered to powerful, politically defined worldviews. The contemporary example urges the opening up of Area Studies for the recognition of the plurality of areas in present times.

Postcolonial perspectives on colonial knowledge and knowledge production have brought to the surface a host of fresh views on developments in the non-Western world. They have expounded the problems of constructed worldviews, including the problem of contriving areas and inventing categories to stratify societies. Partly, these constructed entities and categories have become accepted in people's lived reality. But at the same time, Western apprehensions of social reality in the non-Western world have become debunked as incongruous. The demand for a turn to local knowledge rather than striving to live up to the imperatives of global epistemic powerhouses, the demand for a provincialisation of globalisation (Reid 2012) and the request to change local institutional arrangements in higher education accordingly, are more than plausible in view of the trodden paths of conventional social science and Area Studies research. Blaming all mismatches between scientific concepts and empirical reality on Western hegemony, however, is too simple and one-dimensional. National political conditions and regional geopolitics influence knowledge production and its translation into institutional arrangements in much the same way as global conditions do. I conclude this chapter with a summary of the inferences drawn from the three themes that have been discussed.

Conclusion

Bill Maurer once lamented that science in general and social science in particular leads scholars 'down well-worn tracks to dead ends, toward answers we already know at the outset of our research' (Maurer 2005: 95). The research activity itself becomes 'the product of foregone conclusion' (Maurer 2005: 95).

This diagnosis was meant to alert scholars and encourage research which is open to any result, be it anticipated or unforeseen, pleasant or unpleasant. I venture to interpret Maurer's complaint also as a hint at what I have called 'tunnel vision' driven by scalar fixes and all sorts of indexicalities which value or devalue knowledges and epistemic approaches. While Maurer explicates his exit from the tunnel by studying Islamic banking as an alternative money project, I refer to escaping by studying areal scales that do not comply 1: 1 with the area arrangements in conventional Area Studies. In the preceding sections of the chapter, I have discussed three themes that merit attention in a critical assessment of tunnel vision in Area Studies. One theme was devoted to the task of stock taking, i.e. scrutinising what has been already debated in the literature. In this regard, the literature reveals that the debate on Area Studies is not an utterly recent one but has accompanied all the major 'turns' in the social sciences that have become prominent in the last two or three decades (spatial turn, cultural turn, and mobility turn). The spatial and mobility turns in particular have exerted their influence on Area Studies discourses, leading to various demands for new Area Studies architectures. A remarkable milestone in this context was the integration of spaces in the concept of area that are not primarily territorial-geographically defined (trans- and pluri-local spaces, emotional geographies, see Chapter 5). In extension of this thought, areas in Area Studies might become defined according to the research interest and question at hand, rather than being swallowed by narrow ontological views (cf. Mielke and Hornidge 2016a).

The issue of geographical scales and geopolitics in Area Studies (the second theme of the present chapter) triggered a host of arguments in the discursive field. Prominent, among others, became the quest for de- and re-centring area-related knowledge production, combined with the call to (re-)turn to local knowledge and local epistemic traditions. The case of Southeast Asian Studies illustrates that this concern is well-founded. While scholars acknowledge that the notion of Southeast Asia as a coherent entity is very much a brainchild of former colonial powers, there is the equally important insight that the people in the region have adopted the idea of Southeast Asia and made it part of their lived reality. I have argued that I am very sympathetic to paying respect to lived realities. Having said that, the recognition of lived realities then requires us to look at those that stretch beyond the borders of Southeast Asia. Faith-based geographies on transregional and translocal scales, as described in Chapter 5, deserve to be granted the status of an area of lived reality, too. Even within regions, this issue of scales and delineations is pertinent, the idea of Borneo Studies or the inclusion of Israel into Middle East Studies being cases in point. These cases also remind us of how geographies and politics are nested. The concept of belonging is helpful in identifying attachments across boundaries which are all-too-often glossed over when the lens of 'codified' areas is the only one to look through.

The quest for local knowledge and local data and material to study regional phenomena has frequently informed post-colonial perspectives and critical studies of colonial knowledge (the third theme of this chapter). An issue that is not yet resolved is, however, where local knowledge begins and where it ends – or what constitutes local knowledge and who defines it? Is local knowledge confined to be produced by locals? Moreover, do we have to distinguish between local and indigenous knowledge (Evers and Gerke 2012)? In this context, opinions vary considerably (cf. King 2012). What merits to be emphasised, in my view, is the observation that colonial powers occupied not only physical but also epistemic ground. The issue of conceptual travel, of the 'if and how' of possible concept application, and the path dependency of approaches and categorisations have been prime examples of such epistemic conquering. Again, there are two sides to the story. More concretely, the fact that a 'decolonization of imagination' (Randeria 1999: 380) is not easy to implement is caused to a considerable extent by the internalisation of Western perspectives in post-colonial non-Western academia. The example of ethnic and racial features as markers of distinction in present-day Malaysia is one case of a path dependency that is almost impossible to reverse. In sum, the research on colonial knowledge is highly important for a revision of present-day Area Studies architectures. What is to be avoided is the tendency of painting black-and-white pictures, i.e. the tendency, for instance, to consider only local knowledge as good knowledge. Epistemic hegemony is not exclusively a matter of West versus rest. How then, could a re-scaling of the global terrain of knowledge production be accomplished? How can Area Studies be pushed forward, energised and modernised to match the situation in empirical reality, in lived realities? How can tunnel vision be avoided?

The push for rethinking not only the relationship between Area Studies and disciplines, but also the approaches used in Area Studies themselves points to the ever-increasing importance of a solid reflection on the situatedness of research, and on researchers' own positionality. South–South relations, for example, serve to shift the perspective and de-centre 'the West from historical and political narratives' (Freitag 2013: 2; see also Bhambra 2010). De-centring also trains scholars to depart from container categories and territorialised units, so as to more aptly map the field of inquiry. The approach is conscious of the fact that 'historians produce geographies and not vice versa', as Arjun Appadurai (2013: 66) rightly recalls. It also takes into account the significance of shifting the view from the centres to the peripheries of knowledge production, and from conventionally demarcated regions to non-demarcated regions – alternative geographies that are based on emotions, believes or other forms of 'distant proximity' (Rosenau 2003).

Respecting the contribution of the social sciences to the deepening of knowledge, Area Studies and disciplines yet take 'different points of departure' (Houben 2013: 3). Area Studies depart from 'a certain space', whereas disciplines start off from 'a particular thematic field of study' (Houben 2013: 3). Both departures might meet in a perception of Area Studies as defined by themes and research questions (see above), albeit not in the sense of piggy-backing on the theoretical and methodological apparatus of the disciplines.

Rather than approaching the object of study with pre-cast theories and methods, generating them from a concentration on socio-spatial relations and spaces constituted by human experience, belonging, emotional attachment and shared situatedness is of increasing importance. The theme of and the research interest in the Islamic economy or Muslim women's rights advocacy, as two empirical examples of this volume, can then constitute an area in a trans- and pluri-local setting. Such an approach would allow to focus 'human action and interaction and its role in communicatively constructing space' (Mielke and Hornidge 2014: 18), and divert attention from the exercise of othering and the comparison of predefined units. The problem of comparison, in this context, is not that comparative studies were per se problematic, but that in endeavours such as 'Comparative Area Studies' (Ahram 2011) the prior definition and delineation of the units of comparison closes the road for detecting the unconventional, the unconceptualised, the untheorised. Comparing areas requires the definition of units; when the identification of these units follows the trodden paths of conventional area delineations in Area Studies, not much is won. The underlying epistemic problem is that the researcher positions him- or herself towards the object of study in a way that forecloses the discovery of hitherto unknown areas. The reverse approach, which I would favour, is to indeed depart from human interaction and lived reality in order to, by doing so, *arrive at* the identification of areas – instead of starting off from areas that I have defined before commencing my research. Speaking with Mielke/ Hornidge and Houben, the task is to escape the scalar fixes of physical spaces (Mielke and Hornidge 2014) and look out for scales of forms instead of scales of units (Houben 2013). In times of globalisation, this approach seems to be more appropriate to capture what is going on 'out there', i.e. to capture the 'spatial pluralization' (Mandaville 2007: 111) and the pluralisation of 'habitats of meaning' (Houben 2013: 8) in lived realities.

In the final chapter of this volume, I combine the findings arrived at thus far with a view on the study of global cooperation. My main concern in the final chapter are the emotional and behavioural dimensions of (global) human cooperation, which are not particularly focused on actors themselves but rather on the forms of connectivity between them.

Notes

1 The same demand was raised in the USA, i.e. including it in the field of Area Studies (cf. Cumings 1997).
2 Personal conversation with Achim Rohde, Marburg, 24 November 2015.
3 Admittedly, this is anecdotal evidence drawn from various conversations with local scholars; I have not conducted a statistical double check.
4 The five initial member states were Indonesia, Malaysia, the Philippines, Singapore, and Thailand.
5 In numerous public speeches of Musawah and Sisters in Islam (SIS) activists, the employment of this and similar delegitimising tools were mentioned. My personal conversations with religious authorities or politicians who are hardly in favour

of SIS activities confirmed the oft-held opinion that the women activists of the two organisations are 'no true Muslims' and 'too much influenced by Western thinking'.

6 For contributions to this debate see Lindholm 2008; Jackson 2003; Sheppard 2002; Haraway 1988, 1991; and Bennoune 2013.

References

Acharya, Amitav, 'Ideas, Identity, and Institution-Building: From the 'ASEAN Way' to the 'Asia-Pacific Way'?', *The Pacific Review* 10 (1997) 3: 319–46.

Acharya, Amitav, *Whose Ideas Matter? Agency and Power in Asian Regionalism*, Ithaca, NY: Cornell University Press, 2011.

Ahram, Ariel I, 'The Theory and Method of Comparative Area Studies', *Qualitative Research* 11 (2011) 1: 69–90.

Al Arabiya News, 'Yoga banned for Muslims in Malaysia: official', 2 November 2010. Available at: www.alarabiya.net/articles/2008/11/22/60600.html (accessed 19 July 2016).

Anderson, Benedict, *The Spectre of Comparisons. Nationalism, Southeast Asia and the World*. London and New York: Verso, 1998.

Ansary, Tamim, *Destiny Disrupted: A History of the World through Islamic Eyes*. New York: Public Affairs, 2010.

Anthias, Floya, 'Where Do I Belong? Narrating Collective Identity and Translocational Positionality', *Ethnicities* 2 (2002) 4: 491–514.

Anthias, Floya, 'Identiy and Belonging. Conceptualisations and Political Framings', *Nordic Journal of Migration Research* 2 (2013) 2: 102–10.

Antonsich, Marco, 'Searching for Belonging – An Analytical Framework', *Geography Compass* 4 (2010) 6: 644–59.

Anwar Ibrahim, *The Asian Renaissance*. New York: Times Books International, 1997.

Appadurai, Arjun, 'Sovereignty without Territoriality: Notes for a Postnational Geography', in Patricia Yaeger (ed.), *The Geography of Identity*. Ann Arbor, MI: University of Michigan Press, 1996, 40–58.

Appadurai, Arjun, 'Grassroots Globalization and the Research Imagination', *Public Culture* 12 (2000) 1: 1–19.

Appadurai, Arjun, *The Future as Cultural Fact*. London: Verso, 2013.

Baharuddin, Shamsul Amri and Azmi Aziz, 'Colonial Knowledge and the Reshaping of Islam, the Muslim and Islamic Education in Malaysia', in Kamaruzzaman Bustamam-Ahmad, and Patrick Jory (eds), *Islamic Studies and Islamic Education in Contemporary Southeast Asia*. Kuala Lumpur: Yayasan Ilmuwan, 2011: 113–35.

Bangkok Post, 'Pokemon no go for Malaysian muslims', 6 August 2016. Available at: www.bangkokpost.com/news/asean/1054529/pokemon-no-go-for-malaysian-muslims (accessed 8 August 2016).

Bennoune, Karima, *Your Fatwa Does Not Apply to Me. Untold Stories from the Fight Against Muslim Fundamentalism*. New York and London: Norton & Company, 2013.

Bhambra, Gurminder K., 'Historical Sociology, International Relations and Connected Histories', *Cambridge Review of International Affairs* 23 (2010) 1: 127–43.

Boatca, Manuela, 'Catching Up with the (New) West. The German 'Excellence Initiative', Area Studies, and the Re-Production of Inequality', *Human Architecture: Journal of the Sociology of Self-Knowledge* 10 (2012) 1: 17–30.

Chakrabarty, Dipesh, *Provincializing Europe. Postcolonial Thought and Historical Difference*. Princeton, NJ: Princeton University Press, 2009.

Chou, Cynthia and Vincent Houben (eds), *Southeast Asian Studies. Debates and New Directions*. Leiden: International Institute for Asian Studies, 2006.

Cohn, Bernard, *Colonialism and its Form of Knowledge*. Princeton, NJ: Princeton University Press, 1996.

Cumings, Bruce, 'Boundary Displacement: Area Studies and International Studies during and after the Cold War', *Bulletin of Concerned Asian Scholars* 29 (1997) 1: 6–26. Available at: www.mtholyoke.edu/acad/intrel/cumings2.htm (accessed 29 September 2015).

Derichs, Claudia, 'Multiculturalism and its Institutional Manifestations in Malaysia', in Hartmut Behr and Siegmar Schmidt (eds), *Multikulturelle Demokratien im Vergleich*. [Multicultural Democracies in Comparison]. Wiesbaden: Westdeutscher Verlag, 2001, 268–88.

Derichs, Claudia, 'Nation-Building in Malaysia – A Sociological Approach and a Political Interpretation', in Hazim Shah, K.S. Jomo and Phua Kai Lit (eds), *New Perspectives in Malaysian Studies*. Kuala Lumpur: Malaysian Social Science Association, 2003: 226–48.

Derichs, Claudia, *Nationenbildung in Malaysia als strategisches Staatshandeln. Bemühungen um die Schaffung nationaler Identität* [Nation-Building in Malaysia as Strategic State Action. Efforts to Create a National Identity]. Hamburg: Institut für Asienkunde, 2004.

Derichs, Claudia, 'Participation, Legal Discourse and Constitutional Rights – the "Allah" Issue in Malaysia', in Noorhaidi Hasan and Fritz Schulze (eds), *Indonesian and German Views on the Islamic Legal Discourse on Gender and Civil Rights*. Wiesbaden: Harrassowitz, 2016: 121–32.

Ellings, Richard J., Robert M. Hathaway, Colin Clarke, Anand Yang, Davis E. Bobrow, Amitav Acharya and Parag Khanna, 'Roundtable. Are We Adequately Training the Next Generation of Asia Experts?', *Asia Policy*, 9 (2010): 1–43.

Evers, Hans-Dieter and Solvay Gerke, 'Globalisation of Social Science Research on Southeast Asia', in Zawawi Ibrahim (ed.), *Social Science and Knowledge in a Globalising World*. Petaling Jaya: Strategic Information and Research Development Centre, 2012: 103–16.

Freitag, Ulrike. 'Researching "Muslim Worlds". Regions and Disciplines', *ZMO Programmatic Texts* 6, 2013.

Gilsenan, Michael, *Recognizing Islam. Religion and Society in the Modern Middle East*. New York: St Martin's Press, 2008 [1982].

Goh Beng Lan (ed.), *Decentring and Diversifying Southeast Asian Studies: Perspectives from the Region*. Singapore: Institute of Southeast Asian Studies, 2011.

Goh Beng Lan, 'Southeast Asian Perspectives on Disciplines and Afterlives of Area Studies in a Global Age', in Zawawi Ibrahim (ed.), *Social Science and Knowledge in a Globalising World*. Petaling Jaya: Strategic Information and Research Development Centre, 2012: 79–102.

Goh Beng Lan, 'Moving Theory and Methods in Southeast Asian Studies', in Judith Schlehe and Mikko Houttari (eds), *Methodology and Research Practice in Southeast Asian Studies*. New York: Palgrave, 2014: 27–43.

Graham, Loren and Jean-Michel Kantor, '"Soft" Area Studies versus "Hard" Social Science. A False Opposition', *Slavic Review* 66 (2007) 1: 1–19.

Gungwu, Wang (ed.), *Nation Building: Five Southeast Asian Histories*. Singapore: Institute of Southeast Asian Studies, 2005.

Guyer, Jane I., 'Anthropology in Area Studies', *Annual Review of Anthropology* 33 (2004): 499–523.

Hanson, Stephen E., 'The Contribution of Area Studies', in Todd Landman and Neil Robinson (eds), *The SAGE Handbook of Comparative Politics*. London: Sage Publications, 2009: 159–74.

Haraway, Donna, 'Situated Knowledges: The Science Question in Feminism and the Privilege of Partial Perspective', *Feminist Studies* 14 (1988) 3: 575–99.

Haraway, Donna, *Simians, Cyborgs and Women. The Reinvention of Nature*. London: Free Association, 1991.

Houben, Vincent and Boike Rehbein, 'Regional- und Sozialwissenschaften nach dem Aufstieg des globalen Südens' [Regional and Social Sciences after the Rise of the Global South], *Asien* 116 (2010): 149–56.

Houben, Vincent, 'The New Area Studies and Southeast Asian History', *Dorisea Working Paper Issue* 4 (2013). Available at: www.dorisea.de/sites/default/files/DORISEA%20WP%204%20Houben%20The%20New%20Area%20Studies%20and%20Southeast%20Asian%20History.pdf (accessed 2 August 2016).

Jackson, Peter A., 'Mapping Poststructuralism's Borders: The Case for Poststructuralist Area Studies', *Sojourn. Journal of Social Issues in Southeast Asia* 18 (2003) 1: 42–88.

Kahn, Joel S. (ed.), *Southeast Asian Identities: Culture and the Politics of Representation in Indonesia, Malaysia, Singapore, and Thailand*. London: I.B.Tauris, 1998.

King, Victor, 'Knowledge from the Margins of Malaysia: Globalisation and Research on the Ground', in Zawawi Ibrahim (ed.), *Social Science and Knowledge in a Globalising World*. Petaling Jaya: Strategic Information and Research Development Centre, 2012: 117–63.

King, Victor, 'Culture and Identity: Some Borneo Comparisons', *Working Paper* 1, Institute of Asian Studies, University Brunei Darussalam, 2013. Available at: http://ias.ubd.edu.bn/assets/Files/WORKING.PAPER.SERIES.1.pdf (accessed 3 August 2016).

Lindholm, Charles, *Culture and Authenticity*. Hoboken, NJ: Wiley-Blackwell, 2008.

Mandaville, Peter, *Transnational Muslim Politics. Re-imagining the Umma*. London and New York: Routledge, 2001.

Mandaville, Peter, 'Globalization and the Politics of Religious Knowledge. Pluralizing Authority in the Muslim World', *Theory, Culture and Society* 24 (2007) 2: 101–15.

Maurer, Bill, *Mutual Life, Limited. Islamic Banking, Alternative Currencies, Lateral Reason*. Princeton, NJ: Princeton University Press, 2005.

Mielke, Katja and Anna-Katharina Hornidge, 'Crossroads Studies: From Spatial Containers to Interactions in Differentiated Spatialities', *Crossroads Asia Working Paper* 15 (2014). Available at: www.ssoar.info/ssoar/handle/document/39751 (accessed 12 February 2015).

Mielke, Katja and Anna-Katharina Hornidge (eds), *Knowledge Production, Area Studies and the Mobility Turn*. New York: Palgrave, 2016a.

Mielke, Katja and Anna-Katharina Hornidge, 'Introduction: Knowledge Production, Area Studies and the Mobility Turn', in Anna-Katharina Hornidge and Katja Mielke (eds), *Knowledge Production, Area Studies and the Mobility Turn*. New York: Palgrave, 2016b: 1–16.

Mignolo, Walter D., 'DELINKING: The Rhetoric of Modernity, the Logic of Coloniality and the Grammar of De-coloniality', *Cultural Studies* 21 (2007) 2–3: 449–514.

Mignolo, Walter D., *Local Histories/Global Designs. Coloniality, Subaltern Knowledges, and Border Thinking*. Princeton: Princeton University Press 2012.

Mignolo, Walter D. and Madina V. Tlostanova, 'Theorizing from the Borders. Shifting to Geo- and Body-Politics of Knowledge', *European Journal of Social Theory* 9 (2006) 2: 205–21.

Mintz, Sidney W., 'The Localization of Anthropological Practice. From Area Studies to Transnationalism', *Critique of Anthropology*, 18 (1998) 2: 117–33.

Pfaff-Czarnecka, Joanna, 'From "Identity" to "Belonging" in Social Research. Plurality, Social Boundaries, and the Politics of the Self', in Sarah Albiez, Nelly Castro, Lara Jüssen and Eva Yokhana (eds), *Ethnicity, Citizenship and Belonging. Practices, Theory and Spatial Dimensions. Etnicidad, ciudanía y partenencia. Prácticas, teoría y dimensiones especiales*. Madrid and Frankfurt: Iberoamericana and Vervuert, 2011: 199–220.

Prewitt, Kenneth, 'Presidential Items', *Items* 50 (1996) 1: 15–18 and 50 (1996) 2/3: 31–40.

Quijano, Aníbal, 'Colonialidad y modernidad/racionalidad', *Perú Indígena* 13 (1992) 29: 11–20 (reprinted as 'Coloniality and Modernity/Rationality', *Cultural Studies* 21 (2007) 2–3: 168–78).

Randeria, Shalini, 'Jenseits von Soziologie und Soziokultureller Anthropologie: Zur Ortsbestimmung der Nichtwestlichen Welt in Einer Zukünftigen Sozialtheorie' [Beyond Sociology and Socio-Cultural Anthropology: Determining the Place of the Non-Western World in a Future Social Theory], *Soziale Welt* 50 (1999) 4: 373–82.

Reid, Anthony, 'Provicialising Anglo-America' in Zawawi Ibrahim (ed.): *Social Science and Knowledge in a Globalising World*, Petaling Jaya: Strategic Information and Research Development Centre, 2012, 51–9.

Rosenau, James N., *Distant Proximities. Dynamics beyond Globalization*. Princeton, NJ: Princeton University Press, 2003.

Serels, Steven, 'Famines of War: The Red Sea Grain Market and Famine in Eastern Sudan, 1889–1891', *Northeast African Studies* 12 (2012) 1: 73–94 (special issue on Space, Mobility and Translocal Connections across the Red Sea Area).

Sheppard, Eric, 'The Spaces and Times of Globalization: Place, Scale, Networks, and Positionality', *Economic Geography* 78 (2002) 3: 307–30.

Sloane-White, Patricia, *Corporate Islam. Sharia and the Modern Workplace*. Cambridge: Cambridge University Press, 2017.

Thomas, Scott M., 'How Shall We Then Live? Re-Thinking Religion, Politics and Communities', in Berma Klein Godewijk (ed.), *Religion, International Relations, and Development Cooperation*. Wageningen: Wageningen Academic, 2007: 57–78.

van Schendel, Willem, 'Geographies of Knowing, Geographies of Ignorance. Jumping Scale in Southeast Asia', *Environment and Planning D: Society and Space* 20 (2002) 6: 647–68.

Wei-Yen, Denis Hew (ed.), *Brick by Brick: The Building of an ASEAN Economic Community*. Singapore: Institute of Southeast Asian Studies, 2007.

Yuval-Davis, Nira, 'Belonging and the Politics of Belonging', *Patterns of Prejudice* 40 (2006) 3: 197–214.

Zawawi Ibrahim, 'A Missing Scape? Discoursing Social Science and Knowledge in a Globalising World', in Zawawi Ibrahim (ed.), *Social Science and Knowledge in a Globalising World*. Petaling Jaya: Strategic Information and Research Development Centre, 2012: 1–19.

7 Connectivity and cooperation

Concluding thoughts

> Next to its global political relevance, however, religion gives meaning to life; brings people together with a shared sense of identity and belonging; shapes ideas about everyday life, values and norms, and the world at large. In the sense of creating community it has often a local reference, but also comprises relationships, social interaction and an exchange of goods and services.
>
> (Berma Klein Godewijk 2007: 346)

This chapter pulls all the strings together and relates the topic of area knowledge and its production to the notions of connectivity and global cooperation. Its main inference builds on the empirical findings of Chapters 3 to 5 and the propositions of Chapter 6. People feeling close to each other, sharing concerns and negotiating worldviews have become emotionally, spiritually or socio-cognitively connected across geographical distances; their connectivity (facilitated, for instance, by mastering a certain language or feeling affected by particular problems) is a vantage point for reflecting on cooperation across the globe. In concluding the study, the chapter suggests getting oneself into the language, codes, concepts, norms and principles of alternative epistemic settings in order to understand the behavioural dimensions of (global) human cooperation.

Cooperation on a global level

Theoretical contributions to the topic of global cooperation have been a prominent theme in political science and international relations (IR). The bulk of theories in these disciplines addresses modes of cooperation between states; cooperation among non-state actors surfaced in the course of studies on transnationalism and global governance. Within the major currents of IR, inter-state cooperation with a focus on institutions is a standard approach. Robert Keohane, Joseph Nye, Robert Axelrod and Allen Buchanan have contributed major works to this field (Buchanan and Keohane 2006; Keohane 1986; Axelrod and Keohane 1985; Keohane and Nye 1977, 1987). Power and interdependence are early key terms in institutional perspective; in later years, institutions of global governance are discussed. Constructivist approaches

DOI: 10.4324/9781315642123-9

have included non-state actors in their reflections, but are generally still orientated towards states (see Wendt 1999, 1992; Goldstein and Keohane 1993). Explicitly non-state orientated views primarily address domestic actors in states, thus departing from states as actors but still taking the state as the frame of reference and foreign policy as a medium of cooperation (cf. Moravcsik 1997; 1992).

The notion of global governance occupied a lot of attention in the wake of development policies' stronger commitment to civil society actors and the terminological and conceptual shift from government to governance. It has received strong criticism, but also earned much approval (see Weiss 2013 for an overview). Approaches deriving from the global governance current in IR look at multi-level governance or complex governance regimes. Apart from differences in the major IR approaches to cooperation, what the discipline shares is the consideration of state-society relations as a central field of analysis. Even in the theories that are categorised as liberal IR theories (Moravcsik 1997), it is states that are perceived as actors who demonstrate a certain behaviour ('state behaviour'). Inter-state relationships are not dissolved from social contexts, but are seen as relationships that are embedded in domestic, inter- and transnational social contexts (Hurrell 2007). It is state-society relations that 'have a fundamental impact on state behaviour in world politics' (Moravcsik 1997: 513) rather than social behaviour as an independent category exerting influence on world politics. I return to the term 'behaviour' below, since recent approaches to cooperation suggest that individual behavioural predispositions do, in fact, matter in the analysis of world politics. The observation is my entry point for discussing cooperation. My argument takes it further and I suggest, in the sense of Berma Klein Godewijk's quote above, to include it in analysis of the connectedness between people based on shared concernments, belongings, values and norms.

An initial setting of the stage for the reflections in this final discussion took place during various periods of fieldwork in different parts of the Muslim world (a term which I am going to clarify below).[1] Locating transnational links, trans- and pluri-local connections and a remarkable degree of trans-regional cooperation between the Middle East and Southeast Asia on various economic, political and social sites was indeed a precursor for the thoughts assembled in this present study. Globalisation proceeding at a meteoric pace, digital communication and social media facilities becoming household tools in even the remotest areas, and technically facilitated access to information of all provenience accelerated the flows of ideas, opinions, summons, invitations to debate and the like. From a political point of view, globalisation promoted the spread of transnational grassroots politics and civil society mobilisation for political concerns – be they local, global, or a merger of both (i.e. glocal). New forms of non-state politics have emerged, gradually placing 'the political' outside the container of the state and creating new structures based on personal situatedness rather than bounded forms of political *communitas*. Geographies of identities and social relations that cannot be grasped by the notion of physical-geographical spaces hinted at what can be called new socio-spatial entities or, as others have deemed appropriate, emotional geographies (Davidson, Bondi and Smith 2005).

The spatiality of emotion is probably one of the most intriguing aspects of global cooperation analysis of our time. A telling case in point, albeit not related to any of my empirical work, is the formation of the so-called 'Islamic State' (IS) or *Da'esh*. It is all too obvious that feeling emotionally affected – attracted, as it were – by the ideology, propaganda and actions of IS made numbers of youths in various countries turn to, if not physically move to, the places under control of this particular group. By the end of 2015, even the staunchest ignorant had to admit that there was more to the phenomenon of *Da'esh* than a bunch of inhuman criminals, a horde of gangsters roaming in regions of Iraq and Syria. The political role of IS not only for affairs in the Middle East but for international relations at large (Who sides with whom and why in fighting IS?), including the issue of millions of refugees and internally displaced persons caused by IS occupations, is significant. I am raising this example particularly because the aura and appeal of IS has puzzled so many observers especially in the West. It could have been different, I suspect, if experiential affectedness and emotions (i.e. relational flows) had been familiar concepts to explain human interaction on a global level. Why do we not take emotional attachment and affect into analytical account, but still find it utterly 'normal' when democrats cooperate? Is it so puzzling when non-democrats choose to do just the same? The question seems naïve because democrats and non-democrats cooperate harmoniously, too, in the global geopolitical power game. The world is not divided between democrats and non-democrats. But the question is not so much naïve as it is formulated misleadingly. That is, the problematic diagnosis behind it is that cooperation in the social sciences is analysed by utilising either political regime terms (democratic, autocratic, dictatorial etc.), terms of power relations (national interest, hegemonic interests comparative advantages, etc.), or terms of responsibility (responsibility to protect, development assistance, management of public goods, preservation of commons etc.). Geopolitically motivated cooperation is mostly reserved for state actors, whereas voluntary cooperation out of ethical and moral motivation is rather relegated to civil society actors. Economic cooperation may draw from both state and private sources, but it is in either regard predominantly associated with winning and profit-making. Cooperation based on emotional attachment, then, is hardly taken into account. The case of IS makes it clear that emotional or affective appeal is not a priori radiated by role models of humanity. On the contrary, the more gruesome the acts of violence became, the more followers from 'foreign' countries and regions seem to have been attracted by an IS ideology. A humane version of emotional attachment, in contrast to *Da'esh*, was the late Tunisian vendor Mohamed Bouazizi, whose self-immolation in December 2010 triggered the events of what came to be known as the Arab Spring.

While there are countless examples that could be listed for the role of emotions in the generation of world politically relevant events and developments,[2] the point I want to make is very humble. What I want to stress is the potential that I see in including emotional geographies into the analytical apparatus of global cooperation. Bringing this potential into effect, however, requires a critical reflection of the knowledge-producing machinery that social sciences and Area Studies find themselves enmeshed in. Moreover, it requires to bridge between the reflection of individual, everyday situations and the reflection of cooperation on much bigger scales, i.e. from the local to the global, from the individual or small group to the mass scale. How do we get from local, personal, individual or small group inclinations to global cooperation? How do the empirical examples of faith-based, emotional geographies fit these moulds? The subsequent paragraphs address these questions in three stages, each of which is related to the discussion in the preceding chapters and its application to the study of cooperation. I begin with an introduction of a notion that is called the 'behavioural dimensions of global cooperation' (Messner, Guarín and Haun 2013). In view of the mainstream literature on global cooperation, this is a rather unusual approach. It is, however, a useful template for bridging the said scales (local to global, small to big). From there, I shift the perspective to the notion of religion and its role in international politics in general, and development politics in particular. In a final step, I relate my critique of conventional arrangements of knowledge production in Area Studies and disciplines to the quest for an analysis of cooperation that is more sensitive towards alternative epistemic approaches. I conclude the chapter with a reflection of the challenges for knowledge production in contemporary academia, and the opportunities I see for addressing these challenges in assessments of interpersonal cooperation on a global level.

The cooperation hexagon and meccanomics

A meaningful approach to re-think the conditionalities of knowledge production in the field of global cooperation has been made by scholars who emphasise its behavioural dimensions. The approach is highly innovative in that it employs the findings of evolutionary biology, mathematic modelling, and laboratory experiments for the political scientific study of cooperation. Experiments with humans and closely related species form the basis for data gathering. The basic assumption for the development of a behaviourally orientated theorisation of interpersonal cooperation is that cooperation is an essential part of human nature, in as much as self-interest and selfishness are. Results from human psychology and a range of experimental settings deliver the information for the collocation of 'seven fundamental mechanisms that affect whether and how cooperation takes place' (Messner, Guarín and Haun 2013: 15). These seven identified mechanisms are reciprocity, trust, communication, reputation, fairness, enforcement and we-identity. From these attributes, the authors form what they call a 'cooperation hexagon' (Messner, Guarín and Haun 2013: 15). Six of the attributes are allocated around reciprocity, which forms the centre. The gist of the predication of the hexagon is that cooperation is 'happening around us all the time' and therefore 'any theory about human institutions that knowingly ignores this fact is simply inadequate' (Messner, Guarín and Haun 2013: 31). This finding is all the more significant in times of conflict, turmoil, war, and suspicion in global politics – given that the missing link between the results from experiments relating to small groups of persons and larger scales of human interaction (up to the level of the United Nations) can be provided.

Since the authors' intent is to contribute to theories of cooperation in international politics, they logically ask how an 'upscaling' of their findings to numerically bigger levels of human cooperation, i.e. to more complex forms of interaction, is possible: 'How, in other words, does our knowledge about human cooperation help us to understand the challenges of global governance and international cooperation?' (Messner, Guarín and Haun 2013: 22). The authors' reasoning in this regard is winning, and can also be transferred to the theme of emotional geographies and global cooperation. I will outline the thread of thought, which is segmented into three logical compositions, in a concise manner (for details see Messner, Guarín and Haun 2013: 23f). The first logical conclusion from the results of laboratory experiments and evolutionary biology is that if cooperation is a natural trait of human behaviour, will the mechanisms of cooperation allow it to work in small communities as well as larger ones? If this potential function of cooperation were accepted, the view should turn to those forums of decision-making which are relevant for the success or failure of global cooperation. What the authors bring to notice in this regard is that while these forums are high-level policy networks in the field of global governance, the number of persons factually active in decision-making are not many. It is comparatively small groups of people who represent huge entities of international politics such as nations, regimes, associations and the like. The experiments with small groups of individuals hence match the situation in global forums of decision-making (quantitatively). The third element of the logic is that the reason for the contemporary lack of cooperation in so many areas of global politics is not an impact of human's inability or unwillingness to cooperate, but more so a result of an 'underprovisioning of the basic mechanisms for cooperation' (Messner, Guarín and Haun 2013: 24). Were the behavioural dimensions of global cooperation taken into account, the theories of international relations would be profoundly affected. Although the authors do not offer a new and genuine theory of international cooperation of their own, they expose encouraging and thought-provoking directions which could be followed in the pursuit of such a new theory.

I draw from this reflection on behavioural dimensions of global cooperation and take them as a vantage point for my own suggestion of how to assess potentials for cooperation. I take the reverse direction of reasoning, i.e. in contrast to the above-mentioned line of argument (scaling up), I start from the large scale of international cooperation and trickle down to the level of small groups and individuals. In the diagnosis of the state of affairs of international cooperation in the Muslim world, I follow Vali Nasr, who has extensively studied phenomena he calls 'Islamic Leviathan' (Nasr 2001) or, in economic respect, 'Meccanomics' (Nasr 2010).

With the term Islamic Leviathan, Nasr refers to the function of the religion of Islam for the building and accumulation of state power in various nation-states, particularly in Malaysia and Pakistan. With the term Meccanomics, he refers to the ability of state actors to blend Islamic piety and capitalist market orientations, hence their success in making Islam business-friendly and religious piety a feature of consumer-orientated modernity. His focus lies on the Muslim middle class. This perspectival setting makes Nasr's findings applicable to the empirical cases discussed in the preceding chapters, most notably with respect to middle classes. In principle, Nasr provides a 'scaled up' version of the findings that I have discussed in the small-scale empirical accounts of the present study. While I have raised small group examples from a couple of countries, Nasr adopts a helicopter view and looks at what has developed on an inter-state level. Before I go on sketching the development of international Islamic state and economic power as described by Nasr, my own understanding and usage of the notion 'Muslim world' should be clarified.

The term 'Muslim world' is intentionally chosen and to be distinguished from the term 'Islamic world', which is equally frequently employed in the literature. The latter expression was initially used to refer to a geographical area – the area spanning those regions of the globe where Islam is the predominant religious tradition. Later concepts of the term accounted for the fact that globalisation processes had caused a considerable deterritorialisation of Islam (brought about, among others, by migration) which dissociated the religion from geographical boundaries (Roy 2004: 30). Muslims living in all parts of the world and thus in regions where Islam is far from being the predominant tradition have become the default situation in times of globalisation. But even when it is conceded that the Islamic world is less and less bound to territories, the adjective 'Islamic' runs the risk of suggesting that there is 'one Islam' that is universally subscribed to. This is exactly what solid scholarship should avoid. The plurality of orientations, beliefs, identities, authorities and personal relationships with religious traditions in Islam demands to be acknowledged. A notion that accommodates the factual plurality of orientations and Muslims' very personal interpretations of Islam is the notion of Muslim world. The emphasis on the people who are affected for whatever reason by 'things Islamic' diverts the attention from an all-too-static and generalising view of Islam, from glossing over plurality and specificities. Ulrike Freitag (2013) takes this thought even further and recommends using the plural term 'Muslim worlds'. Her intention is to emphasise that:

> While Islam is a religion based on the Koran, which is recognised by all of its adherents, Muslims nevertheless live in many different worlds, in terms of their understanding of what the religion means as well as in terms of their lifeworlds.
>
> (Freitag 2013: 1)

I fully subscribe to Freitag's apprehension. For the present discussion, I nonetheless use the category of Muslim world in the singular since it hints more directly at the intentional distinction from the category Islamic world.

Coming back to Meccanomics and cooperation in the Muslim world, the numbers presented by Nasr are illuminating and provide an idea of the size of Islamic proportions in global trade and consumption. At the time of his research (in the mid-2000s), Nasr found that the rising number of Muslim consumers 'comprise[d] as much as one sixth of humanity' (Nasr 2010: 15). The 'global Muslim population of a billion plus is about the same size as both India's and China's population' (Nasr 2010: 15). We may presume that the numbers have risen further. Yet they are not accommodated in conventional studies of International Relations nor in Development or Area Studies. Development Studies have noticed China and India as emerging powers (donors) and actors who challenge the OECD template of development cooperation,[3] but they have almost ignored that there is a significant Islamic development apparatus at work, too (cf. Chapter 1). Apart from this apparatus, cooperation in the sector of Islamic finance is another illuminating case for assessing the clout of the Muslim world in global affairs. Even when the website on Islamic finance (islamicfinance.com) warns that the information it provides is not warranted, its content allows for a rough estimation of the scope and scale of Islamic financial institutions and Islamic capital markets. A posting from December 2014 states that estimates of the size of the market oscillated between $1.66 trillion and $2.1 trillion; the prognosis for 2018 was a rise to $3.4 trillion (Mohammed 2014). The post states: 'Based on $1.66 trillion, Islamic Finance assets represented 1% of the global financial market of $127 trillion in assets. To put this into context, $1.66 trillion is about the size of the balance sheet assets of HSBC as of 2013' (Mohammed 2014). Top ranking asset holders are Malaysia, Saudi Arabia, the United Arab Emirates, Kuwait and Qatar. In those countries, the major banks of the world have established branches and offer Islamic financial services. Europe has centres of Islamic finance, too, London being a major one (Nasr 2010: 17). Not surprising against this backdrop, the Dow Jones hosts several Islamic market indices (Dow Jones 2016). 'Corporate Islam' (Sloane-White 2017) is thus a common feature of international finance, trade and industry.

In Nasr's view, the Muslim middle classes that have grown and expanded in this climate of a globally present Islamic economy should by no means be ignored by the West, but rather become those with whom the West does business (Nasr 2010). This recommendation aside, the number of Muslim consumers and the numerous branches of business – not only Islamic financial services but also the range of Islamic economy businesses mentioned in Chapters 4 and 5 – suggest that cooperation in the Muslim world is not a niche phenomenon. On the contrary, the cooperation of numerous actors is a central requirement in order to make it possible to cater to an ever-growing number of Muslim consumers. Apart from services, trade and industry, the sector of Islamic education is catering to particular Muslim concerns in the field of knowledge production and learning (cf. Chapters 4 and 5). The scale of potential as well as actual cooperation within the Muslim world is hence well comparable to other scales of global cooperation through networks, organisations, nations or regimes. It appears that religious principles have a share in shaping global markets, businesses, education and more. In the following paragraphs, I explore in how far religion and the commitment to a particular faith is a distinctive factor for assessing cooperation in the Muslim world as compared to global cooperation in the secular world. More precisely, I attend to religion as an element of the behavioural dimensions of interpersonal connectedness and, from there, return to the 'cooperation hexagon' of Messner, Guarín and Haun (2013). The assumptions underlying the seven mechanisms of the hexagon, I argue, speak of a particular epistemic and ontological approach to knowledge. Alternative approaches can be thought of, however, and it is these that are of interest with regard to the overarching topic of the present study: knowledge production, Area Studies and global cooperation.

Religion and international cooperation

When the Shi'ite current of the Muslim world was shocked by the execution of four Shi'ites in Saudi Arabia in January 2016, among them the prominent cleric Sheikh Nimr al-Nimr, the Indonesian government felt inclined to mediate between the two big players in Islamic world politics: Iran and Saudi Arabia. The execution heightened tensions in bilateral relations between the two regional powers. The *Jakarta Globe* reported from the ranks of experts in Indonesia's administration:

> As the world's biggest Muslim-majority country, the archipelago is in a strategic position to resolve tension in the Middle East, they [= the experts, C.D.] added. […] "Indonesia could be seen as strategic mediator because we are not in the Middle East … and both Iran and Saudi Arabia would believe that Indonesia is neutral," Hikmahanto told the Jakarta Globe, arguing that Indonesia has yet shown significant involvement addressing international issues during [president] Joko's period. As the world's biggest democratic Muslim-majority country, Indonesia has the chance to promote a more positive image of Islam, Hikmahanto said.[4]
>
> (Karensa 2016)

In the field of international relations, as this anecdote illustrates, religion is more than an element of privately held beliefs and faithful adherence to certain principles and values. Religion is not a void concept in the claim for political authority in the international system, but more an element of strategic political action in the competition for status and power. In stark contrast to the decades of Suharto's presidency in Indonesia (1965–98), the country has now adopted the role of a diplomatic actor who actively utilises the position of a neutral, but at the same time religiously committed, mediator. The self-concept of a mediator who is able to balance between two rivalling states is no longer based on Indonesia's legacy as the midwife of the Non-Aligned Movement, but on the fact that the majority of its population is Muslim. Religion per se, and in Indonesia's case the religion of Islam, has advanced to become an asset in positioning the nation-state in global geopolitics. The shift in orientation from explicitly non-aligned to explicitly Islamic in Indonesia's foreign policy is worth mentioning. It not only reflects what Nasr (2001) has called the making of state power through Islam, but also hints at the responsiveness of the Indonesian government to a population of voters who went through their own version of Islamisation in the preceding decades – and consequently demanded that religion play a stronger role in domestic and foreign policy (cf. Chapters 4 and 5).

Scaling down from the (inter-)state level to the level of the average believer and the communities constituted by shared faiths, Scott Thomas asks how our understanding of substantive global issues is going to be transformed when 'religion is brought back into our analysis of international development and international relations' (Thomas 2007: 65). His underlying assumption for pondering this question is that 'successful development, no matter how it is defined, can only occur if social and economic change corresponds with the moral basis of society' (Thomas 2007: 70). The examples from the Islamic economy, Muslim women's networks, professional associations and other examples in the preceding chapters confirm a strong link between moral and ethical principles on the one hand, and the idea of what social reality ought to look like on the other. In other words, ideas of 'the good life', even if not explicitly addressed by this term, are ultimately related to normative moral and ethical orientations. The social connections of faith communities rest on norms and values which resonate with their members' moral and ethical fundamentals, which, in return, are drawn from the interpretation of religious tradition. Conceptual and linguistic conventions shape such interpretations (e.g. in the case of the concept *musâwâa* مساواة [equality]). Klein Godewijk (2007: 346) goes as far as to declare that 'there is no rationality independent of any tradition, no view from nowhere'.

If this were so, it is not astonishing that development models based on religion have been introduced as an alternative to conventional ones. Faith-related knowledges and practices have been translated into conceptual templates, one of which is Islamic entrepreneurship; this has been suggested by Rasem Kayed and Kabir Hassan (2011) as an alternative to the Western model of development. In their study on Saudi Arabia, both authors hypothesise that Islamic entrepreneurship 'is more than a means to generate employment and maximise economic returns; it is rather a development alternative with great potential to contribute to the well-being of Saudi Arabia' (Kayed and Hassan 2011: 18). As such, i.e. as a development alternative, Islamic entrepreneurship should have implications 'for development theory and development studies in general, both in practical and abstract terms' (Kayed and Hassan 2011: 18). What is proposed then is a well-being model that is theoretically informed by entrepreneurship theory, modernisation theories, alternative theories of development, post-development theory, institutional theory, and the principle of *tauhîd* (توحيد oneness or unity of God). *Tauhîd* forms the basis for the concept of well-being (cf. Kayed and Hassan 2011: 19). Theorists of this conceptual linkage are Muhammad Baqir al-Sadr (1982), M. Umer Chapra (2000; 1993), Ziauddin Sardar (1997) and Muhammad Nejatullah Siddiqi (1972), all scholars with strong research records in the field of Islamic economics, which several of them acquired – not surprisingly – at IoK institutes in Malaysia and Pakistan.[5] I am not going to elaborate on the very development alternative that is discussed by Kayed and Hassan. The point is to accentuate the translation and combination of knowledges and practices that are displayed in the authors' approach or, the attempt at combining different ecologies of knowledge in Boaventura de Souza Santos' (2016) sense. In short, what the development alternative of Kayed and Hassan represents is a translation from one ecology of knowledge (of Western-origin) to another (Islamic) by using concepts (such as well-being) that are expressed through other than the conventional definitions (i.e. by employing the semantics of *tauhîd*). These concepts are articulated through a very different set of epistemic basics (i.e. those deriving from IoK traditions of conceptualising Islamic economics). What follows from this is that concepts need not always be expressed through a one-and-only definition (cf. Klein Godewijk 2012: 344). They can be expressed through different definitions according to the specific environment.

There are geographies of identities and social relations where a *tauhîd*-based explanation of the concept of well-being may be much closer to people's lived reality and moral orientations than one that is based on secular concepts. Translating a religious principle into the conceptual language of well-being and development is then an exercise of accepting empirical and experiential facts before pressing the idea of development through the grid of secular terminologies. The epistemic approach is different from conventional approaches in that it is ontologically grounded in the reference to religious sources as knowledge sources and the belief in a non-human ordering power. But it is most probably closer to faith communities' empirical reality, than if norms and structures of global society are solely defined with principles and concepts that people feel rather detached from. Musawah's struggle for equality, to pick up an example from the previous chapters, reflects exactly this when the movement articulates the combination of Islamic principles, international human rights standards and lived realities of men and women as its objective.

'In the sense of creating community', Klein Godewijk writes, religion 'has often a local reference, but also comprises relationships, social interaction and an exchange of goods and services' (Klein Godewijk 2007: 346). It is this dimension of religion which is fairly neglected in the development discourse:

> Through religion people respond to what happens both in their local life and beyond their borders. It has to be critically explored whether development policy discourse in this line would better resonate the understandings of cultural and religious identity in everyday life and in the different faith traditions.
>
> (Klein Godewijk 2007: 346)

The same is true for, I argue, the discourse on global cooperation. We thus need to ask questions about the nature and location of faith and religion within what we understand as world politics in general and global cooperation in particular.

By this I mean that theories of global cooperation have tended to assume that religion is something fairly irrelevant for particular forms of decision-making – for or against cooperation – by actors in particular spaces. But in a time of translocality, faith-based visions of the why and how of cooperation emerge from socio-spatial communities – communities who social scientists and areanists alike are reluctant to identify as geographies of lived reality (cf. Chapter 6). I speculate that the remarkable negligence in attending to such geographies is ultimately bound to the widespread non-familiarity with both the languages and the concepts that are relevant in alternative epistemic settings. Knowledge production in conventional Western-centred institutions of learning is not geared towards understanding 'other' approaches to knowledge. To explain the concept of well-being (or the 'good life') with the principle of *tauhîd* is hence next to impossible in an institutional setting where knowledge has never been thought of as something dependent on specific worldviews, ontologies, and linguistic codes. Or alternatively: in institutions where the knowledge that is generated is taken as universal, there is no motivation for appreciating any others. This brings us back to the example of the cooperation hexagon.

Epistemic approaches and behavioural dimensions

The limited imagination in the disciplines – methodologically and theoretically – and Area Studies – in terms of their identification and arrangement of units – discourages the appreciation of approaches located outside the conventional apparatus of knowledge production. The arguments brought in to nurture the idea of the above-mentioned cooperation hexagon reflect this. All six plus one (the central) mechanisms rest on the fundamental conviction that cooperative behaviour is a natural human predisposition. This conviction is 'proved' by results from natural sciences and mathematics, i.e. results stemming from the 'hard' sciences and those that are known to convince with numbers and laws of nature. We may ask, however, if this is the only way to arrive at the attributes of the hexagon. Tapping from, for instance, local epistemic approaches such as religiously grounded knowledge, the categories of trust, communication, reputation, fairness, enforcement, we-identity, and reciprocity (Messner, Guarín and Haun 2013: 15) may all be easily traced back to principles in Islamic sources. The terms would supposedly be different, but denote very similar traits of human behaviour which come about – and this is the decisive difference in reasoning – because God has bestowed humankind with a bent for cooperation. This interpretation of humans' cooperative abilities is an alternative vantage point of theorising human behaviour, an alternative mode of theorising.

Irrespective of which mode one finds personally more convincing, the fact that merits consideration is that particular epistemic contexts feed into certain argumentative grids. Taking the epistemic tradition one was socialised with for granted, the trust in its universality forecloses an examination of the ontological fundamentals that underlie one's reasoning. Why should I question them at all? So far, so good. What is problematic, though, is that when in times of strong biases in global knowledge production one particular epistemic approach assumes a hegemonic status, and is expected to be applied universally. Technical-scientific knowledge of modernity has assumed such status, elevating the term science (maths and natural sciences) in status and relegating local knowledge to a form of wisdom rather than serious science (Castro-Gómez 2007: 436–44). Gurminder Bhambra has discussed this in detail in her work on connected sociologies and global social thought. She calls it an 'epistemic disavowal' when the circumstances that have led to a certain situation are not taken notice of or even become ignored (Bhambra 2016). An example she raises is the idea of a 'world society' that was introduced by German sociologist Ulrich Beck (2002; 2000). This world society, Bhambra rightly criticises, 'is one in which the historically inherited inequalities arising from the legacies of European colonialism and slavery play no part' (Bhambra 2016: 1). Her evidence is that '[a]ny theory that seeks to address the question of 'how we live in the world' cannot treat as irrelevant the historical construction of that world' (Bhambra 2016: 2). Bhambra's standpoint is clearly informed by a postcolonial perspective on historical sociology, but it is a view which is equally relevant for studies of contemporary phenomena. In analogy to her reasoning and similar to Scott Thomas mentioned above, I would argue that any theory that seeks to address how we live in the world needs to resonate with the moral and ethical orientations of the communities or audiences that are meant to be the empirical subject of reference. Expecting results from the 'hard' sciences to be universally convincing is similar to proposing a world society and expecting the idea to be universally convincing: The relation between particular human experiences and the rationalities people have been socialised with are of minor significance. In this perception of knowledge, local circumstances that may generate scepticism about the plausibility of the underlying argument are not taken into account. But this, then, is no less than disdain for the fact that knowledge represents, in Aníbal Quijano's words, 'a relation between people for the purpose of something, not a relation between an individual and something' (Quijano 2007 [1992]: 173). If knowledge were understood as an inter-subjective relationship, it prompts to exchange experiences and venture into different rationalities, and by so doing, leaving the zone of one sole logic.

The matter becomes more complex when different approaches are recognised, because they have to be negotiated. I raise an example from my own experience in diverse 'ecologies of knowledge' (de Souza Santos 2016). When I attended a 'training session' for adolescent Indonesian *pesantren* students that was designed to convey the compatibility of the notion of universal human rights and human rights in Islam in early 2016, two ecologies of knowledge met. It was absolutely agreed upon by students and trainers that the notion of human rights is traceable in the religious sources of Islamic tradition – even though it is not referred to as 'human rights' but introduced by the notion of 'objectives of *sharî'a*' (مقاصد ألشريعة *maqâsid al-sharî'a*). Doubts about the adoption of human rights as something a person is entitled to claim, however, remained. During the Q&A sessions, several students sought advice from the main trainer (a scholar of Religious Studies) on how to go about in negotiating rights versus obligations. When it is my obligation as a wife to obey my husband, for instance, how do I go about it when he beats me and violates my rights as a human being? The trainer, feeling at home in both the discursive worlds of secular human rights and Islamic *sharî'a*, tried to guide the students in thinking of reconciliatory solutions, which worked out well. But in other cases, reconciliatory reasoning is often absent because actors are trained to follow one sole logic and that is all they can see. Having been around for some time in the circles of international development cooperation, I experienced that human rights experts from the West had next to no knowledge about concepts such as *tauhîd* or *maqâsid al-sharî'a*, and were thus already rejected and met with suspicion in local contexts when they uttered the very term human rights (which smacks of being a 'Western' term in pious communities and is therefore hardly appreciated). That means, many of those working in development cooperation are *not* at home in both worlds and are unable to convey the idea of reconciliatory thinking in a credible manner.

It is this kind of imbalance which I try to address with the demand to open up towards other epistemic approaches and immerse oneself in learning about other rationalities. Learning about and engaging with alternative ecologies of knowledge and knowledge production does not mean subscribing to the normative orientations of other rationalities or buying into their respective ontological underpinnings. It tries to recognise that there are different knowledges out there and that local knowledge is often much closer to communities' experiential environment and lived reality than other sources of knowledge. In practical terms, this requires the de-centreing of knowledge production and abstaining from 'mono-civilizational accounts of standard definitions' (Bhambra 2016: 2). It means to acknowledge, for instance, that the tide of Islamic resurgence has brought with it alternative approaches to knowledge – alternative ecologies of knowledge such as Islamised versions – and that the socio-cognitive spaces inhabited by communities and individuals who subscribe to them represent lived realities. In the formulation of Santiago Castro-Gómez, what is at stake is the acceptance of a 'coexistence of diverse legitimate ways of producing knowledge' in 'a world where epistemological plurality can be recognized and valued' (Castro-Gómez 2007: 428).

In an academic world that is increasingly driven by pressures to fulfil ranking criteria, deliver policy-relevant information, quantify its results and submit the generation of knowledge to the economy of research outputs, it seems quite illogical to take notice of other rationalities. Examining a subject matter with readily available methodological tools and theories seems more rewarding. I would nonetheless suggest escaping the limited imagination and the ontological frameworks of one's 'familiar' knowledge and looking out for the unfamiliar; sometimes something is invisible using one pair of glasses but clearly visible when using another. It is a longer way to go and a departure from trusted paths, but in the long run it may pay off because the effort to understand lived realities from their ontological fundamentals enables us to realise the relationality and contingency of knowledge production and knowledge dissemination on our globe.

I am far from discarding the dominant Western theories of global cooperation, including innovative approaches to the topic such as the research on its behavioural dimensions. They represent a particular rationality and valorisation of scientific efforts. In that regard, they are plausible and convincing to me as embodiments of a specific tradition of knowledge production. What I do not find convincing, however, is the gormlessness with which their universal validity is assumed. To me, it would make much more sense to start from what has been discussed in the present study as lived realities and emotional or 'new' geographies. It would mean inspecting what generates a feeling of belonging and consequently facilitates interpersonal cooperation – a connectedness that stretches across socio-cognitive spaces and areas which do not conform to the conventional ones in Area Studies. Looking at faith-based geographies (the empirical subject of study in the preceding chapters), there is evidence of actors' cooperation happening out of different rationalities and being related to diverse worldviews. In the concluding section of the chapter, I summarise what I consider fruitful for the study of global cooperation from a perspective that appreciates the plurality of knowledge and grants analytical value to 'new' geographies of identities and social relations.

Knowledge production, Area Studies and global cooperation

The conventional institutional set-up of Area Studies has lost track of the global developments and shifts in socio-spatial scales. Trans- and pluri-local settings, socio-cognitive spaces and 'new' geographies based on emotional connectedness and shared concernment rather than geographical proximity are cases in point. Pluri-local settings and emotional geographies have yet to become translated into institutional structures in academia. The preceding chapters have illustrated, by focusing on the case of faith-based connectivities, how new geographies evolve. I have assumed in this discussion that the comparatively little scholarly attention that has been given to the Islamisation of knowledge as well as the overarching movement of Islamic resurgence is due to dominant structural frameworks in Area Studies and systematic disciplines. Economic developments in the Muslim world, as, among others, Vali Nasr has analysed, have largely been glossed over in scholarly works. In sociological and political regard, social movement studies have hardly taken account of Islamic resurgence movements and political scientists have concentrated more on the geopolitical and security dimensions of 'political Islam' than on emerging geographies on the grassroots levels of the Muslim world. Few have, like Peter Mandaville, made alternative forms of politics that evolve from the pluralisation of religious knowledge a subject of discussion in the discipline of International Relations. Islamic Studies have addressed the huge topic of Islam and modernity and thematised the increase of radical currents in Islamist, Salafist and other ultra-conservative movements. Islamic consumerism, business, trade, and services have, in comparison, received less attention. Islamic education, although impressive and massive in its impact on learning and knowledge dissemination in the Muslim world, has rarely been examined from the perspective of global machineries of contemporary knowledge production. Islamic development cooperation has not occupied a considerable terrain in development studies – a fact that is all the more astonishing when compared to the attention directed at China and India as emerging actors in international development cooperation. The everyday life of individual and collective actors in the Muslim world, the rise of faith-conscious consumerism in Muslim communities and the vast increase of *sharī'a*-compliant services, commodities and businesses have received consideration in cultural studies, but have not yet taken firm root in the theoretical discourses of political science and IR. Nor have they inspired a re-thinking of how to look at the world – and consequently, how to translate this conceptually, analytically, and methodologically – in Western social sciences. The entrenched approaches are still dominant and a certain reluctance to engage with alternative knowledges and rationalities is conspicuous. The demand to decentre the study of areas and consequently include local knowledge into global knowledge production is one outcome of the felt unease with the way the world is conventionally explained. Opening up perspectives that underscore the importance of recognising knowledges in the plural is still a task ahead.

The present study has directed attention towards the developments in the Muslim world since the 1970s. It has intentionally addressed the themes of religious knowledge and religious education, tracing, using case studies from Southeast Asia, trans-local, trans-national and trans-regional interpersonal and institutional connections. It has discussed the politics of Islamic education and Islamic resurgence, and introduced examples of diffusions of Islamic knowledge into society at large. The study's narrative reveals that:

(a) the geographies that have emerged from faith-based transversal connections challenge the arrangement of units in conventional Area Studies;
(b) the lived realities in an extraordinarily pluralised Muslim world challenge the conventional assessments of what 'Islamic' is meant to denote; and
(c) the role of religion in politics and everyday lives of people is ultimately linked with ideas of the 'good life', with moral and ethical orientations, and understanding of 'how we live in the world'.

Taking the empirical reality of cross-regional, pluri-local and similar types of connectivities on various scales into account means to recognise new geographies, ecologies of knowledge, and alternative epistemic approaches. From the perspective of Postcolonial Studies, an epistemic decolonisation would be one channel to do so. From the perspective of studying intersubjective cooperation on a global level, a channel would be to learn about what connects people with each other, what concerns them and what makes them feel at home in all sorts of places and spaces. This is, for sure, a behavioural dimension of global cooperation – but one that is rooted not in an ontological framework of adherence to 'hard' sciences and quantifiable data. Rather than relying on this type of rationality, the assessment of cooperation would seek to loosen the reins of disciplinary boundaries and entrenched approaches to study cooperation. It would strive to understand local and alternative knowledges, epistemologies, and rationalities by starting from people's lived reality. This is a demanding approach, because International Relations and other disciplines do not encourage it and each discipline has its own way of looking at how the world works. But if Area Studies and disciplines opened up to alternative approaches and ontologies to explain human behaviour, cooperation might become a topos that can be assessed by more than one rationality. Cooperation, then, is maybe not solely a matter of global political importance, but one that has global conditions for it to occur as something that resonates with the moral and ethical orientations of actors that are meant to be the empirical subject of reference – and, last but not least, resonates with their knowledges.

It is quite apparent that studying cooperation from this vantage point is hardly possible for individual scholars alone. In practical terms, de-centring research and opening up to other knowledges and approaches requires getting oneself into the languages, codes, concepts, norms and principles of alternative epistemic settings in order to *understand* interpersonal connectivities – to understand, for instance, the behavioural dimensions of (global) human cooperation. Collective efforts that enable scholars to synergistically collaborate and valorise their respective expertise is a way to coming close to mutual understanding in the field of global knowledge production. This, too, is no doubt a form of global cooperation. Abstaining from it is then, at least in my view, an intentional 'underprovisioning of the basic mechanisms for cooperation' (Messner, Guarín and Haun 2013: 24) by our institutions of learning.

A final remark should be made concerning the issue of positionality. Choosing to work on phenomena in the Muslim world – or Muslim worlds in Ulrike Freitag's sense – as a person who did not grow up in a Muslim-majority environment and who does not identify herself as a Muslim is met with scepticism by many. Moreover, I am not a local in the regions of my fieldwork, nor do I live or work there on a permanent basis. Most of my time of studying is spent outside Muslim-majority regions. Still, I consider it permissible to do the work I do, since I harbour no intention to analyse phenomena in the Muslim world with an attitude of evaluating them on the basis of my own normative orientations. I cherish my own normative convictions, but they do not lead me to judge other rationalities. I try to understand and I am ready to exchange normative arguments when the situation requires me to do so, but not in a scholarly reflection like the present study. I criticise the way in which knowledge is produced in those fields of learning in which I feel most at home – just because I notice so many mismatches with what I see and sense when moving beyond the disciplinary and areal boundaries of my academic 'home'. The more I am puzzled by such mismatches, the more I depend on other's knowledge to understand why people adhere to some rationalities but not others. Language has a crucial role in this exercise of understanding. In this respect, I position myself clearly and refrain from venturing into research areas that are beyond my linguistic capacity.

Notes

1 In my case, this comprises mostly of communities and individuals in Muslim-majority countries of the Middle East (including Iran) and Southeast Asia. Representatives of Muslim minorities in Australia, Germany, the Philippines and the UK have been sporadic and irregular conversation partners or interlocutors for research projects other than the present study.

2 The affective attraction of places, Tahrir Square in Egypt or Gezi Park in Istanbul, for mobilising people is another case in point, but I do not have the space to elaborate here. A team in the research cluster 'Affective Societies' at Freie Universität Berlin studies such particular functions of affects. Available at: www.sfb-affective-societies.de/en/index.html (accessed 12 July 2016).

3 The number of studies covering this topic has grown tremendously and 'standard references' are hardly identifiable since interpretations of the rise of China and India as development actors are highly controversial. I therefore refrain from citing any particular studies as references.

4 Joko is the short version of Joko Widodo, the President of Indonesia since 2014. Hikmahanto is an international relations expert from the University of Indonesia.

5 Muhammad Baqir Al-Sadr was an Iraqi Shi'ite scholar who was executed in 1980 under Saddam Hussein; Umer Chapra is linked to the International Institute of Islamic Thought (an IoK institution) in Lahore, Pakistan; Ziauddin Al-Sardar is a prominent author and journalist, e.g. editor of the journal *Critical Muslim*; Muhammad Nejatullah Siddiqi was, among others, a Distinguished Professor at the International Islamic University in Kuala Lumpur.

References

Al-Sadr, Muhammad Baqir, *Iqtisâdunâ* [Our Economics]. Beirut: Dir al-Ta'aruf, 1982.

Axelrod, Robert and Robert O. Keohane, 'Achieving Cooperation under Anarchy: Strategies and Institutions', *World Politics* 38 (1985) 1: 226–54.

Bhambra, Gurminder K., 'Undoing the Epistemic Disavowal of the Haitian Revolution: A Contribution to Global Social Thought', *Journal of Intercultural Studies* 37 (2016) 1: 1–16.

Beck, Ulrich, 'The Cosmopolitan Perspective: Sociology of the Second Age of Modernity', *The British Journal of Sociology* 51 (2000) 1: 79–105.

Beck, Ulrich, 'The Cosmopolitan Society and Its Enemies', *Theory Culture Society* 19 (2002) 1–2: 17–44.

Buchanan, Allen and Robert O. Keohane, 'The Legitimacy of Global Governance Institutions', *Ethics & International Affairs* 20 (2006) 4: 405–37.

Castro-Gómez, Santiago, 'The Missing Chapter of Empire. Postmodern Reorganization of Coloniality and Post-Fordist Capitalism', *Cultural Studies* 21 (2007) 2–3: 428–48.

Chapra, M. Umer, *Islam and Economic Development: A Strategy for Development with Justice and Stability*. Islamabad: International Institute of Islamic Thought and Islamic Research Institute, 1993.

Chapra, M. Umer, 'Is it Necessary to have Islamic Economics?' *Journal of Socio-Economics* 29 (2000) 1: 21–37.

Davidson, Joyce, Mick Smith and Liz Bondi (eds), *Emotional Geographies*. Farnham, UK and Burlington: Ashgate, 2005.

de Sousa Santos, Boaventura, *Epistemologies of the South: Justice against Epistemicide*. London and New York: Routledge, 2016.

Dow Jones, 'Dow Jones Indices 2016'. Available at: www.djindexes.com/islamicmarket/?go=literature (accessed 13 August 2016).

Freitag, Ulrike, 'Researching 'Muslim Worlds'. Regions and Disciplines', *ZMO programmatic texts* 6, 2013.

Goldstein, Judith and Robert O. Keohane, 'Ideas and Foreign Policy: An Analytical Framework', in Judith Goldstein (ed.), *Ideas and Foreign Policy: Beliefs, Institutions, and Political Change*. Ithaca, NY: Cornell University Press, 1993: 3–30.

Hurrell, Andrew, 'Complex Governance Beyond the State', in Andrew Hurrell, *On Global Order: Power, Values, and the Constitution of International Society*. Oxford: Oxford University Press, 2007: 95–119.

Mohammed, Naveed, 'The size of the Islamic finance market', *IslamicFinance.com*, 27 December 2014. Available at: www.islamicfinance.com/2014/12/size-islamic-finance-market-vs-conventional-finance/ (accessed 13 August 2016).

Karensa, Edo, 'Iran-Saudi Mediation a Test for Joko's Diplomatic Team Experts', *Jakarta Globe*, 7 January 2016. Available at: http://jakartaglobe.beritasatu.com/news/iran-saudi-mediation-test-jokos-diplomatic-team-experts/ (accessed 12 January 2016).

Kayed, Rasem N. and M. Kabir Hassan, *Islamic Entrepreneurship*. London and New York: Routledge, 2011.

Keohane, Robert O., 'Reciprocity in International Relations, *International Organization* 40 (1986) 1: 1–27.

Keohane, Robert O. and Joseph S. Nye, *Power and Interdependence: World Politics in Transition*. Boston: Little, Brown, 1977.

Keohane, Robert O. and Joseph S. Nye, 'Power and Interdependence Revisited', *International Organization* 41 (1987) 4: 725–53.

Klein Godewijk, Berma (ed.), *Religion, International Relations, and Development Cooperation*. Wageningen: Wageningen Academic, 2007.

Messner, Dirk, Alejandro Guarín and Daniel Haun, 'The Behavioural Dimensions of Global Cooperation', *Global Cooperation Research Papers* 1. Duisburg: Centre for Global Cooperation Research, 2013.

Moravcsik, Andrew, *Liberalism and International Relations Theory*, Paper No. 92–6. Cambridge, MA: Harvard University, Center for International Affairs, 1992.

Moravcsik, Andrew, 'Taking Preferences Seriously: A Liberal Theory of International Politics', *International Organization* 51 (1997) 4: 513–53.

Nasr, Seyyed Vali Reza, *Islamic Leviathan. Islam and the Making of State Power*. Oxford: Oxford University Press, 2001.

Nasr, Vali, *Meccanomics: The March of the New Muslim Middle Class*. Oxford: Oneworld Publications, 2010.

Quijano, Aníbal, 'Coloniality and Modernity/Rationality', *Cultural Studies* 21 (2007) 2–3: 168–78 (reprint of 'Colonialidad y modernidad/racionalidad', *Perú Indígena* 13 (1992) 29: 11–20).

Roy, Olivier, *Globalized Islam. The Search for a New Ummah*. New York: Columbia University Press, 2004.

Sardar, Ziauddin, 'Beyond Development: An Islamic Perspective', *European Journal of Development Research* 8 (1997) 2: 36–55.

Siddiqi, Muhammad Nejatullah, *The Economic Enterprise in Islam*. Lahore: Islamic Publication, 1972.

Sloane-White, Patricia, *Corporate Islam. Sharia and the Modern Workplace*. Cambridge, UK: Cambridge University Press, 2017.

Thomas, Scott M., 'How Shall We Then Live? Re-Thinking Religion, Politics and Communities', in Berma Klein Godewijk (ed.), *Religion, International Relations, and Development Cooperation.* Wageningen: Wageningen Academic, 2007: 57–78.

Weiss, Thomas G., *Global Governance. What? Why? Whither?* Cambridge: Polity Press, 2013.

Wendt, Alexander, 'Anarchy is What States Make of It: The Social Construction of Power Politics', *International Organization* 46 (1992) 2: 391–425.

Wendt, Alexander, *Social Theory of International Politics.* Cambridge: Cambridge University Press, 1999.

Index

References to Notes will contain the letter 'n' followed by the Note number. 'IR' stands for 'International Relations'.

Abaza, Mona 35, 48–9, 60n10, 89n3, 102
'Abduh, Muhammad 36
Abdulrahim, Imaduddin 131, 132
ABIM (Islamic Youth Movement) 38, 67, 78, 104, 131
Abubakar, Irfan 70
Aceh, Indonesia 87
activism, Islamic 22, 50, 132; missionary 72; Musawah 139–40; Muslim Brotherhood 78; organised 103; political 64; repression of 20, 55; student activism 63, 64, 73, 74, 77; *see also dakwah* movement
Adamson, Fiona 128–9, 145
advocacy, assessment 96–101
aestheticisation of religion 98–101
Al-Afghânî, Jamâl ad-Dîn 21, 36, 52
aid organisations, Islamic 23
AKP (Justice and Development Party), Turkey 20, 76
Al Tawhid. Its Implication for Thought and Life (Al-Faruqi) 42
Alatas, Ismail F. 83, 87, 99, 136–7
Alatas, Syed Farid 34, 35, 41, 49, 50, 55, 56, 59n1, 60n10
Alatas, Syed Hussein 34, 35, 59n1, 160
Al-Azhar Islamic university, Egypt 60n8, 69, 71, 78, 79
Algeria 54
Al-Mustafa university, Iran 78, 79
Amin, Kamaruddin 90n6
The Anatomy of Dependence (Doi Takeo) 18
Anderson, Benedict 163
Annual Convention of the International Studies Association (ISA), 2015 25n11
Ansary, Tamim 153–4
anthropology 14
Anwar Ibrahim 67, 131
Appadurai, Arjun 12, 127, 137, 154
Arab lexicon, knowledge of 108
Arab Spring 175
Arabic language 3
Area Studies 4, 7, 150–72; Comparative Area Studies 10, 168; concept 8, 146; critical assessments 150–4; and disciplines 8–16, 159–65; establishment 151; geopolitically influenced 12; and global cooperation 186–8; and Islamic Studies 150, 151, 153, 161; new, demand for 12, 150, 166; postcolonial perspective 159–65; scales and geographies 154–9; Southeast Asian 9; terminology 1; theory-distant approach 13; tunnel vision in 12, 150, 154, 159, 164, 166, 167
Asad, Muhammad 66
ASEAN (Association of Southeast Asian Nations) 54, 157, 158, 159
Asian and Arabic science 5
Asian IR theory 15
'Asian miracle' 104
Association of Muslim Scholars of Indonesia (ICMI) 54

Association of Southeast Asian Nations (ASEAN) 54, 157, 158, 159
Al-Attas, Syed Muhammad Naguib 33, 35, 36, 41, 44–6, 47, 49–51, 57, 66, 77, 80, 102, 133; *Islam and Secularism* 37
Azra, Azyumardi 51, 71, 86, 88

Bakar, Osman 51, 80, 90n20
Balchin, Cassandra 113
Balkans 144
Al-Bannâ, Hasan 36
banking, Islamic 100
Benedict, Ruth 9
Bhambra, Gurminder 184
biographies 35
bipolarity/bipolarisation 7, 18, 21; *see also* Cold War
Borneo 155
Buddhist Studies 150

Calabrese, John 11–12, 25n9
capitalism, Islamic 88
captive mind 34
centre–periphery dichotomy 11, 13, 15, 17, 56, 66
Chakrabarty, Dipesh 159
charitable organisations, Islamic 23
China 5, 6, 11; international relations (IR) 18, 19
Christianity 23, 72, 164
Cold War 7, 13, 19, 41, 151, 152, 157; Cold War Area Studies 9; end of 12, 18, 144, 146n1
colonial knowledge 163
Comaroff, Jean and John 10
commercialisation 99–100
commodification of religion 98–101
Communism 41
community-building 146
Comparative Area Studies 10, 168
Comparative Religious Studies 162
component development theory 22
conceptual history 96
connectivity and cooperation 12, 22, 24–5, 173–91; Area Studies and global cooperation 186–8; cooperation hexagon and 'Meccanomics' 176–80; cooperation on a global level 173–6; epistemic approaches and behavioural dimensions 183–6; religion and international cooperation 180–3
Connell, Raewyn 11
constructivism 15, 173–4
consumerism, Islamic 76
Contemporary Islamic Economic Thought (Haneef) 56
context 15; context-dependence 6; contextual embeddedness 3
Conundaw, John 146n5
Convention on the Elimination of All Forms of Discrimination against Women (CEDAW) 116
cooperation: and connectivity 12, 22, 24–5, 173–91; global *see* global cooperation; international, and religion 180–3; between Muslim Southeast Asians and Middle Easterners 12
cooperation hexagon and 'Meccanomics' 176–80
cultural globalisation 137
cultural Islam 50, 70, 72, 76, 102, 103; corporate culture 107; Islamic resurgence 64, 65

Da'esh (Islamic State) 21, 66, 175
dakwah movement 63, 66, 73–7, 88, 100, 103, 136
Darul Arqam 74, 90n15
data collection and analysis 12
DDII (Indonesian Council for Islamic Propagation) 75, 78
decentralisation 86
definition problem 1–4
development aid 22
Development Assistance Committee (DAC) 22
development policy 22, 182
development studies 23, 55, 118, 179, 181, 187
development theory 22, 34, 181
developmentalism 22
diaspora politics 129
diffusion: into economy 87–8; policy making, 'Islamised' (female perspectives) 84–7; *see also* spill-over and diffusion
disciplines, and Area Studies 8–16; criticism 152; inter-disciplinary

collaboration 12, 13; intra-disciplinary competition 12; postcolonial perspective 159–65; social science disciplines 12–13; transdisciplinary collaboration 12, 13
divine order 45–6
division of labour 14
duality 42
Dubai 144

ecologies of knowledge 184
Economic and Social Council (ECOSOC) 23
economy, Islamic: assessment 96–101; diffusion into 87–8; Egyptian 6; and *shari'ised* workplaces 106–13
education: Islamic system/Islamisation 38, 47, 66–73; *pondok* school tradition 68; primary to tertiary 68–73; religious schools 133
Egypt 6–7, 19; Al-Azhar Islamic university 60n8, 69, 71, 78, 79; Muslim Brotherhood 20–1, 36, 54, 76, 78
emotional geographies vii, viii 25, 101, 127–49; knowledge entrepreneurs 129–36; trans- and pluri-local networks 136–40; trans- and pluri-local settings 127–9; translocal areas 140–5
Entangled Modernities (Conrad and Randeria) 10
entrepreneurship 141, 141–3, 146n2, 181; *see also* knowledge entrepreneurs
epistemic approaches and behavioural dimensions 183–6
epistemology 49, 56; European 163; institutional 154; Islamic 102
ethnic segmentation 13
everyday life, Islamisation in: assessment of religion, economy and advocacy 96–101; commercialisation 99–100; domestic political contexts 103–4; empirical studies 96–124; going beyond domestic politics 104–6; Islamic economy and *shari'aised* workplaces 106–13
expert knowledge 4

family 2–3, 14, 75–6; Islamic Family Law 110, 114, 121n24
Al-Faruqi, Isma'il Raji 33, 35–8, 42–4, 46, 47, 56, 57, 59n6, 66, 67, 69, 80, 102
Fazlur Rahman Collection, ISTAC 35, 41
feminism 3; female perspectives on 'Islamised' policy making 84–7; transnational Islamic, and gender justice 113–17
Fetullah Gülen schools 72, 78, 80
finance, Islamic 143, 179
forced prostitution 16
Frank, André Gunder 55
Fukushima nuclear power plant disaster (Japan, 2011) 16
fundamentalism, Islamic 58

gender equality 3, 113–17; *see also* women's rights
genocide, official admission of 16, 25n14
Al-Ghazâlî, Muhammad 133
Giddens, Anthony 137
Gilsenan, Michael 153, 154
global cooperation 1, 3, 16–25; and Area Studies 186–8; connectivity and cooperation 173–6
global governance concept 174
globalisation 120n7, 134
glocalisation 128
God, unity of 42–4
Goh, Beng Lan 13, 14, 17, 156, 157, 158, 160, 163
Green Party 52

Hadiz, Vedi 20–1, 78
Hadramawt (also spelled Hadramaut) (Yemen region) 137
hajj season 109
halâl food 98, 99, 100
halaqah (Islamic study groups) 75, 76
Haneef, Mohamad Aslam 56–7, 109
ul-Haq, Zia 54
Hassan, M. Kabir 141, 142, 146n2, 181, 182
Hassan, Riffat 85, 114–15
hegemony of Western knowledge 5
Hidayat, Komaruddin 38, 46, 47, 50, 72, 80

hijab (headscarf) 110, 130–1
history: conceptual 96; global 5; of science 5, 11; of social science 10; writing of 16, 25n
Hizbut Tahrir 140
HMI (Muslim Students Organisation), Indonesia 64, 75, 81
Holocaust 25n15
Hornidge, Anna-Katharina 4, 8, 12, 15, 151–2, 168
Houben, Vincent 151, 168
humane Islam 114
humanism 44–5

IAIN (State Institutes of Islamic Religion) 70–1, 86
Ibadiya 142
Ibrahim, Anwar *see* Anwar Ibrahim
Ibrahim, Zawawi 10, 11, 55, 56
Ideals and Realities of Islam (Nasr) 80
identity networks 145
IISO (International Islamic Federation of Student Organizations) 81
IIUM (International Islamic University Malaysia) 35, 36, 43, 67, 69
Ikhwân al-Muslimîn *see* Muslim Brotherhood
Indonesia 17, 20, 56; compared to Malaysia 65, 70; Islamisation 33, 70–3; Jemaah Tarbiyah movement 65, 73, 75–7, 104; Jemaah Tarbiyah movement, Indonesia 136; massacre (1965) 13–14; Ministry of Tourism 87; Muslim Students Organisation (HMI) 64, 75, 81; Muslim World League 75, 78; National Awakening Party (PKB) 73; New Order regime 20, 50, 63, 64, 67, 71, 76, 103; Paramadina University, Jakarta 51, 72, 82, 90n8; PKI (Communist Party) 103; Prosperous Justice Party (PKS) 65, 73, 84; State Islamic University (UIN) 51, 70, 71, 86
Indonesian Council for Islamic Propagation (DDII) 75, 78
Indonesian Council of Ulama' (MUI) 84
Inglehart, Ronald 52
innovation 129–30
INSISTS (Institute for the Study of Islamic Thought and Civilisation) 80, 81, 90n18
Institute of Islamic Thought and Civilization (ISTAC) 38, 43, 50, 51, 80, 81; Fazlur Rahman Collection 35, 41; founding of 59n2, 67
intellectus (intellect) 44
International Advisory Group, London 113
International Institute of Advanced Islamic Studies (IAIS) 51
International Institute of Islamic Thought (IIIT) 36, 37, 42, 43
International Islamic Federation of Student Organizations (IIFSO) 81
International Islamic Relief Organization 23
International Islamic University College in the State of Selangor 69
International Islamic University Malaysia (IIUM) 35, 36, 43, 67, 69
International Monetary Fund (IMF) 22, 24
international relations (IR) 7, 8–9; as branch of political science 25n5; China 18, 19; demand for a global IR 15; and global cooperation 16–25; liberal theories 174; mainstream theory 98; and social science 18; state-centrism in 127; Western 21
intra-disciplinary competition 12
The Intuition of Existence (Al-Attas) 39–40
IoK *see* Islamisation of Knowledge (IoK) project
Iqbâl, Muhammad 36, 41
IR *see* international relations (IR)
Iran 18, 158; Al-Mustafa university 78, 79; establishment of Islamic Republic 53; revolution (1979) 20, 52, 82
Islam and Secularism (Al-Attas) 37, 38–41
Islamic Civilisation 74
Islamic College (IC) 82
Islamic Cultural Center (ICC) 82
Islamic Family Law 110, 114, 121n24
'Islamic Leviathan' 178 *see* 'Meccanomics'
Islamic Party of Malaysia (PAS) 67, 74, 104

Islamic Relief (British-based NGO) 23
Islamic Salvation Front (FIS), Algeria 54
Islamic State (IS) 21, 66, 175
Islamic Studies 11, 43, 56, 69, 74, 88, 105, 186; and Area Studies 150, 151, 153, 161; Shi'ite 82
Islamic University of Madina (Al-Madina), Saudi Arabia 78, 79, 82
Islamisation 21, 25, 46, 63, 88; in everyday life *see* everyday life, Islamisation in; Islamicised policy-making, female perspectives 84–7; Islamisation of Science 33, 38; state-endorsed 68; topography 117; of workplaces 110; *see also* Islam/Islamism; Islamists
Islamisation of Knowledge (IoK) project 33–62, 70, 72, 88, 115, 117, 118, 121n19, 182; criticism/critical publications 59, 60n10; emotional geographies 130, 135–6; empirical studies 100, 104, 105; evaluations of 48–51; Islamisation of Knowledge with a capital 'K' 36–8; Malaysia 33, 50, 51, 55, 58; as project of its time 52–9; repercussions 50, 101–6
Islam/Islamism: activism, Islamic *see* activism, Islamic; call to 63; capitalism 88; changes in 64; 'civilizational Islam' 51; cultural 50, 64, 65, 70, 72, 76, 102, 103, 107; deterritorialisation 178; developmental work 23–4; economy *see* economy, Islamic; fundamentalism 58; political 50, 58, 64, 72, 74, 76, 111, 186; resurgence 20, 52, 63–5, 89; rhetoric 19–20; and secularism 38–41; Wahhabism 19, 21, 53
Islamists 41, 58, 113; vs. Muslims 22
Islamization of Knowledge: General Principles and Work Plan (Al-Faruqi) 37
ISTAC *see* Institute of Islamic Thought and Civilization (ISTAC)

Jamaah Islah Malaysia 74
Jamâ'at Al-Islâmi (JI) 36
Jamaat Tabligh 74, 77
Japan: cultural essentialism 18; and Indonesia 17; language 2–3; nuclear power research 16, 17; uniqueness 18; wartime study of (Benedict) 9
Jawi (Arabic script for Malay language) 68
Jemaah Tarbiyah movement, Indonesia 65, 73, 75–7, 104, 136
Justice and Development Party (AKP), Turkey 20, 76

Kayed, Rasem 141, 142, 146n2, 181, 182
Kemalism 36
Khaldûn, Ibn 49, 50, 133
khalifa 49, 60n12, 108–9
Khondker, Habibul Haque 10
Kim, Yung Sik 5–6, 7, 11
King, Victor 155, 160, 161
kinship 3, 14
Klein Godewijk, Berma 97, 173, 174, 182
knowledge 2, 4–7; of Arab lexicon 108; and being 44–5; colonial 163; dissemination and publication 16–17; ecologies of 184; elitist theories 48; global history 5; globalisation of 120n7; as hierarchical 45; and innovation 129–30; knowledge-generating institutions, appropriation of 17–18; theoretical 11; traditional 11; Western 38, 39, 48, 98, 156, 160
knowledge entrepreneurs 129–36, 145; *see also* entrepreneurship
knowledge production 16–25; global 159–60; and national interest 16, 17, 18, 19; polycentric nature 34; as power-related process 16; terminology 1, 3
Korean War (1950–53) 15
Koselleck, Reinhart 96
Kuala Lumpur 90n14, 109
KUIS (Kolej University Islam Antarabangsa Islam) 69

labour movement 52
labour union activism 16
language: Arabic 3; Japanese 2–3; Malay 68; Qur'anic 24
Latin alphabet 165
laws and verdicts 83–4

legal-rational authority (Weber) 49
liberalism 15
Liow, Joseph Chinyong 50, 64, 72
LIPIA college, Jakarta 82
local, the 15

Ma'arif, Syafi'i 47, 48, 59n7
Machmudi, Yon 65, 72–3, 75, 76, 77
Madjid (Majid), Nurcholish 38, 46, 47, 50, 66, 70, 72, 77, 80, 81, 82, 130–1
Mahathir Mohamad *see* Mohamad, Mahathir
Malaysia 73–5; compared to Indonesia 65, 70; Constitution 84; Department for the Advancement of Islam 68; Islamisation 66–70; Islamisation of Knowledge (IoK) project 33, 50, 51, 55, 58; Malaysians of Chinese descent 69; Muslim Student Society (PMI) 75; National University of Malaysia (UKM) 80; New Economic Policy (NEP) 103; political Islam 111–12; religious schools 133; Sarawak region 155; and Southeast Asian post-colonialism 17; United Malays' National Organization (UMNO) 65, 67, 74, 89n2, 104; University and University Colleges Act 1974 (UUCA) 73–4
Malaysia adalah Sebuah Negara Islam (Malaysia is an Islamic Nation), booklet 67
Mandaville, Peter 21, 53, 58, 127–8, 129, 134, 140, 146n4, 186
manufactured national identity 18
Masud, Muhammad Khalid 40–1
Maudûdî, Abu al-Â'lâ 36
McGill University, Canada 43, 80
Mecca, pilgrimages to 76–7, 83, 106, 108
'Meccanomics' 87, 88, 176–80
MENA region (Middle East and North Africa) 23, 101
metaphysics 161; Islamisation of knowledge 39, 40, 42, 44, 45, 46, 49, 50, 58
Middle East Asia Project 25n9
Middle East Asian turn 11–12
Mielke, Katja 12, 151–2, 168
migration studies 128
Mir-Hosseini, Ziba 115
Mitchell, Timothy 6, 7, 9, 10
mobility turn 151–2
modernisation 10, 14, 65, 67, 131, 134, 181
Mohamad, Mahathir 54, 67, 103–4, 142
Mohamad, Maznah 18
mosque movement, Salman 132
Muhammad, Prophet 146n4
Muhammad bin Saud University, Saudi Arabia 82
MUI (Indonesian Council of Ulama') 84
mulk 49
Multiple Modernities 10
Muppies (Muslim Urban Professionals) 112, 113
Musawah (knowledge-building project) 113–17, 135, 136, 144, 162, 168n5, 182; activism 139–40
Muslim Brotherhood 20–1, 54, 76, 78, 82, 136, 142; founding of 36
Muslim Student Society (PMI), Malaysia 75
Muslim Students Organisation (HMI), Indonesia 64, 75, 81
Muslim World League, Indonesia 75, 78
Muslims: activism *see* activism, Islamic; in Indonesia 56; vs. Islamists 22; Muslim communities 21–2; Shi'ite Muslims 53, 74, 82, 91n22, 180; as subjects or objects of history 38; Sunni Muslims 53, 82, 158; *see also* Islamisation; Islamisation of Knowledge (IoK) project; Islam/Islamism
myth 34

Nahdlatul Ulama 50
NAM (Non-Aligned Movement) 20, 180
Nasr, Seyyed Hossein 33, 36, 38, 43, 44–6, 47, 50–1, 57, 59n6, 66, 70, 102, 133; *Ideals and Realities of Islam* 80
Nasr, Vali 20, 87, 88, 91n25, 135, 177, 178, 179, 181, 186
Nasser, Gamal Abdel 19
National Awakening Party (PKB), Indonesia 73
national interest 16, 17, 18, 19

National Mandate Party (PAN), Indonesia 73
National University of Malaysia (UKM) 80
nationalism, Arab 19
nation-building 152, 158; Islamisation of Knowledge (IoK) project 54, 55, 57
nation-states 7, 13, 16, 53, 89, 114, 127, 137, 155, 157–8, 160, 180
necessity, law of 111
Needham, Joseph 5, 11
Neo-Confucian thought 25n4
networks: academic 51; activist 67; advocacy 104, 116; faith-based 140; global 79; Indonesian 88; policy 177; size 140; trans- and pluri-local networks 136–40; transnational identity 129, 140, 145; women's rights 115, 116, 117, 121n21, 130, 144, 181
networks, trans- and plur-local 136–40
New Economic Policy (NEP), Malaysia 103
'new Muslim project' 21–22
New Order regime, Indonesia 20, 50, 63, 64, 67, 71, 76, 103
new social movements 52
NGOs (non-governmental organisations), Islamic 23, 24
Non-Aligned Movement (NAM) 20, 180
'non-European,' defined 9–10
NoorShah M.S. 10, 11, 55, 56
normativeness 42, 43

OECD *see* Organisation for Economic Cooperation and Development (OECD)
Office of War Information, US 9
OIC (Organisation of Islamic Cooperation) 67
Okinawa, Japan 2
Organisation for Economic Cooperation and Development (OECD) 22, 23, 24, 26n19, 179
Organisation of Islamic Conference 20, 50
Organisation of Islamic Cooperation (OIC) 50, 67
Oriental Studies 151
'other,' the 151

Pakistan 18, 47; 'strategic depth' doctrine 20
Palestine Liberation Organization (PLO) 54
PAN (National Mandate Party), Indonesia 73
Pan-Arabism 19
Paramadina University, Jakarta 51, 72, 82, 90n8
Party for Democratic Struggle (PDI-P), Indonesia 73
PAS (Islamic Party of Malaysia) 67, 74, 104
patrimonialism 49
PDI-P (Party for Democratic Struggle), Indonesia 73
Persian Gulf monarchies 142
Personal Status Code 110
pesantren (religious educational institution, Indonesia) 70, 72, 77
Petersen, Marie Juul 23, 24
philanthropic organisations, Islamic 23
pilgrimages 87, 99, 109, 136, 137; to Mecca 76–7, 83, 106, 108
PKB (National Awakening Party), Indonesia 73
PKI (Communist Party), Indonesia 103
PKS (Prosperous Justice Party), Indonesia 65, 73, 84
pluri-locality 128, 129
PMI (Muslim Student Society), Malaysia 75
political Islam 64, 72, 186; *dakwah* movement 63, 66, 73–7, 76, 88, 100, 103, 136; Islamisation of Knowledge (IoK) project 50, 58; in Malaysia 111–12
political science 14
pondok school tradition 68
populism, Arab 19
postcolonial perspective, areas and disciplines in 159–65
Postcolonial Studies 159, 164, 187
post-materialist values 52
PPP (United Development Party), Indonesia 73

Pries, Ludger 128, 139
property concept 6–7
Prosperous Justice Party (PKS), Indonesia 65, 73, 84

'*qadi*' justice 7
Qaradâwî, Yusuf 66
Qatar 179
Qom (Iran) 82, 89, 119
Qur'an 48, 49, 50, 56, 57, 87, 109, 116, 146n4; interpretation 60n11; language/ terminology 24, 108; and Sunna 56, 106, 107, 110, 117; verses 71
Qutb, Sayyid 36

radioactive contamination 16
Rahman, Fazlur 21, 33, 35, 38, 41, 43, 44, 46–8, 51, 59n7, 60n10, 66, 70, 72, 80, 102, 133, 136
Ramadan 110
Randeria, Shalini 10, 153
realism 15
Realpolitik 9, 53, 158
reflexivity 15, 19
Rehbein, Boike 151
Reid, Anthony 159, 160
religion: assessment 96–101; commodification commercialisation and aestheticisation of 98–101; and international cooperation 180–3
religious pluralism 82, 84
resurgence, Islamic 20, 52, 63–5, 89, 100, 104, 134, 145; cultural Islam 64, 65
revivalism 36
Rudnyckyj, Daromir 99–100, 107, 131–2
Ryukyu islands, Japan 2

sacred science 44, 45
al-Sadr, Muhammad Baqir 181
sadaqah (voluntary donation) 131
Sakurai, Keiko 78, 79
salafism 66
Sarawak, Malaysia 155
Sardar, Ziauddin 59n6, 181
Saudi Arabia 18, 19, 20–1, 53, 64; entrepreneurship 142, 143; Islamic University of Madina (Al-Madina) 78, 79, 82; Muhammad bin Saud University 82
Schäbler, Birgit 8, 9–10
scholarship 2
science: history 5, 11; Islamisation of Science 33, 38; natural sciences 34; political science 14; sacred 44, 45; social science *see* social science; traditional 45; Western science 6, 14, 33, 34
scientific revolution 5, 6
secularism 40–1; secularisation process 44–5; *see also Islam and Secularism* (Al-Attas)
self-determination 9
semantics 2, 3
Shamsul, Amri Baharuddin 68, 160, 161
sharî'aisation of workplaces 106–13
Shi'ite Muslims 53, 74, 82, 91n22, 180
Siddiqi, Mohammad Nejatullah 36, 37, 181
Sisters in Islam (SIS) 85, 115, 162, 168n5
Six Day War 1967, 19, 53
Sloane-White, Patricia 100, 110, 121n19
social movements: Islamic 52, 64; new 14, 52, 60n14, 152
social science 3, 4, 6, 9, 12, 18, 34; history in Europe 10; methodological territorialism of 128; theories 14
socialism, Arab 19
sociology 14
Southeast Asia 13, 15; Islamic learning 69–70, 82, 88; Middle Eastern students in 120–1n18
Southeast Asian identity 157–8
Southeast Asian Studies 9, 11, 157
Southern Theory (Connell) 11
spill-over effects and diffusions 63–95; *dakwah* movement 63, 66, 73–7, 88, 100, 103, 136; diffusion into policymaking and economic practice 82–8; Islamic resurgence 63–5; Islamisation in education 66–73; laws and verdicts 83–4; primary to tertiary education 68–73; transregional connections 77–82
spiritual economies 99–100
State Institutes of Islamic Religion (IAIN) 70–1, 86

State Islamic University (UIN), Indonesia 51, 70, 71, 86
state-centrism 127
Stenberg, Leif 59n6
student activism 63, 64, 73, 74, 77; ABIM (Islamic Youth Movement) 38, 67, 78, 104, 131
Sufism 83
Suharto, Haji Muhammad (Indonesian President) 54, 63, 65, 71, 74, 86, 180; fall of 20, 50, 64, 65, 73, 76, 103, 142
Sukarno, Indonesian President 17
Sultan Omar Ali Saifuddien Centre for Islamic Studies, Brunei 51
Sunna (reports and teachings of the Prophet) 56, 106, 107, 110, 117
Sunni Muslims 53, 82, 158
synonyms 1, 2

Tablighi Jamaat 140
tafsîr (form of Qur'anic interpretation) 60n11
tamkin (self-discipline) 116, 121n26
Tarbiah movement *see* Jemaah Tarbiyah movement, Indonesia
tauhîd/tawhid (unity of God) 42–4
ta'wîl (form of Qur'anic interpretation) 60n11
textuality 135, 136, 146n4
theories: Asian IR theory 15; building of 18; component development theory 22; development 22, 34, 181; diffusion of theory, in Southeast Asia 22; international relations (IR) 98, 174; revised 22; social science 14; from the South 1; theoretical knowledge 11; theory-distant approach of Area Studies 13
Theory from the South (Comaroff) 10
Third World 20, 22, 58
Thomas, Scott 7, 13, 162, 181
Thomson Reuters Corporation 108, 111
time-space distanciation 137
Timor-Leste 157
traditional knowledge 11
translation 2, 3
translocality 127, 128, 136, 140, 144
transnational identity networks 129, 140, 145
Transnational Muslim Politics (Mandaville) 127
transnationalism 146n1
transregional connections 77–82
transregional development assistance, Islamic 22
tunnel vision, in Area Studies 12, 150, 154, 159, 164, 166, 167
Turkey 47; Justice and Development Party (AKP) 20, 76

UKM (National University of Malaysia) 80
UMNO (United Malays' National Organization) 65, 67, 74, 89n2, 104
unipolarity 18
United Arab Emirates 120n16, 142, 179
United Development Party (PPP), Indonesia 73
United Malays' National Organization (UMNO) 65, 67, 74, 89n2, 104
University and University Colleges Act, 1974 (UUCA), Malaysia 73–4

Van Asshe, Kristof 4, 8, 15
Van Schendel, Willem 12, 120n6, 160

Wadud, Amina 115
Wahhabism 19, 21, 53, 78, 82, 142
Wahid, Abdurrahman 47, 70, 73, 80
Walker, R. B. J. 140–1
Wall Street institutions, Muslim employees 143
Wan Daud, Wan Mohd Nor 51, 80, 90n19, 102
war crimes 16
Weiss, Meredith L. 74
Welsh, Bridget 111
Western hegemony 41, 165; political 47
Western knowledge 98, 156, 160; Islamisation of Knowledge (IoK) project 38, 39, 48
Western perspective 4, 19, 21; science 6, 14, 33, 34

'Why Not' question 5
Widodo, Joko 189n4
Wildan, Muhammad 64, 89n1, 99
Women Living Under Muslim Laws (WLUML) 139, 140, 144
women's rights 85, 86, 87, 96, 135, 168; activism 113, 136, 139, 144, 146; conventions/UN backed bodies 121n27, 130; initiatives/ movements 89, 101, 113, 115; networks 115, 116, 117, 121n21, 130, 144, 181; *see also* gender equality; Sisters in Islam (SIS)
workplaces, *sharī'aisation* of 106–13
World Bank 22, 24
World Conference on Muslim Education, Mecca (1977) 37
world regions 8

Yemen, pilgramages to Hadramaut 99
Yom Kippur War, 1973 75
Yudhoyono, Susilo Bambang 83, 142
Yusuf, Imtiyaz 43

Zaid, Nasr Hâmid Abû 66
Zainah, Anwar 74